A JOURNEY INTO
CHINA'S ANTIQUITY

A JOURNEY INTO CHINA'S ANTIQUITY

National Museum of Chinese History

Volume Three

Sui Dynasty

Tang Dynasty

Five Dynasties and Ten Kingdoms Period

Northern and Southern Song Dynasties

MORNING GLORY PUBLISHERS

Editor-in-Chief: **Yu Weichao**

Managing Editor: **Xiao Shiling**

Conceived by: **Yan Zhongyi**

Editor: **Zheng Wenlei**

Chinese text by: **Zhu Ruigen, Kong Xiangxing, Hu Xiaojian, Lei Shenglin,**

Zheng Enhuai, Huang Yansheng, Wang Guanzhuo

Translators: **Gong Lizeng, Yang Aiwen, Xu Keji, Wang Xingzheng**

Photographers: **Yan Zhongyi, Sun Kerang**

Assistant Photographers: **Shao Yulan, Liu Li, Dong Qing**

Maps by: **Zhang Guanying, Zhang Jie, Duan Yong, Huang Yucheng**

Designer: **Zheng Hong**

A JOURNEY INTO
CHINA'S ANTIQUITY

Volume Three

Compiled by:

NATIONAL MUSEUM OF CHINESE HISTORY

Published by:

MORNING GLORY PUBLISHERS

35 Chegongzhuang Xilu Beijing 100044 China

Distributed by:

CHINA INTERNATIONAL BOOK TRADING CORPORATION

35 Chegongzhuang Xilu Beijing 100044 China

(P.O.Box 399, Beijing, China)

First Edition   First Printing 1997

ISBN 7-5054-0507-1/J·0246

84-E-792D 38600

Printed in the People's Republic of China

Contents

Sui Dynasty

(581—618)

After establishing itself in the north, which had already been unified by the Northern Zhou, the Sui Dynasty soon reunified the whole country, ending a long period of political division. Although it lasted only 37 years, from 581 to 618, this short-lived regime contributed much to carrying on and developing the country's political and economic institutions.

Politically, it enacted reforms in its official, military and imperial examination systems and consolidated autocratic centralized power. Economically, it continued the equal land system that had begun during the Northern Wei period, which enabled agricultural production to develop substantially. Commerce and the handicrafts also developed, accompanied by an unprecedented growth in the country's population. The building of the Grand Canal promoted economic and cultural exchange between north and south and had a far-reaching impact on Chinese history. Unification of the country fostered closer relations between the interior and the ethnic minorities living along the border and strengthened ties between Taiwan and the mainland.

Along with the development of the country's economy and the increase in its social wealth, exploitation of the masses by the ruling class also became increasingly severe. This was especially true during the reign of the second Sui emperor, Yangdi. By this time, the ruling clique had become exceedingly corrupt and wasteful. Internally, they undertook expensive construction projects and indulged in extravagant inspection and sightseeing tours of the country. Externally, they waged incessant wars, which bled the people white and drastically reduced the country's population. It was not long before a peasant uprising toppled the regime.

Unification of North and South

From the period of the Three Kingdoms, through the two Jin dynasties, and into the Northern and Southern Dynasties, the country was basically in a state of political fragmentation, except for a short spell of unity under the Western Jin. The development of the economy and culture in both north and south, and integration of different ethnic groups during this time, made unity both an inevitable historic trend and an urgent wish of all the nationalities in the country. In 581 Yang Jian, a relative of the imperial family of the Northern Zhou, usurped power and established the Sui Dynasty. In 589 he conquered Chen, the last of the Southern Dynasties, and unified the country. He then carried out a series of reforms on the country's political and economic systems. At the central level he established a government consisting of three councils and six ministries. In local administration, he changed the three-level prefecture-district-county system, begun in the Han Dynasty, into a two-level system of prefectures and counties only. All local officials were appointed by the central government, a measure that consolidated central power.

1. Portrait of Emperor Wendi of Sui
Yang Jian (541–604), Emperor Wendi, founder of the Sui Dynasty, was a native of Huayin, Hongnong County (east of present-day Huayin County, in Shaanxi Province). During the Northern Zhou period, he inherited his father's title of Duke of Sui and his daughter became the empress of the Zhou emperor Xuandi. In May 580 Emperor Xuandi died and his son succeeded to the throne as Emperor Jingdi. Yang Jian was made the so-called left prime minister and commander-in-chief of the armed forces, and was given the title Prince of Sui. He thus held all real power in the imperial court. In 581 he usurped the throne and declared himself emperor, establishing the Sui Dynasty and changing the reign title to Kaihuang. In 587 he conquered the Later Liang and in 589 the Later Chen, the last two Southern Dynasties, ending the division between north and south and reuniting the country. During his reign, he reformed the official system, setting up three councils and six ministries and a two-tiered administrative structure of prefectures and counties. To strengthen centralized state power, he decreed that the appointment and dismissal of all officials of the nine highest ranks had to be made by the central government. He retained the equal land system established during the Northern Wei, raised the age of legal adulthood from 18 to 21, and reduced the period of military service from one month to 20 days. Males who had not been called up for service could pay a tax in produce or commodities (called the *yong* tax) instead. Later he exempted males above the age of 50 from military service as well as payment of the *yong* tax. These measures reduced the burden on peasants. Additionally, in order to re-register households which had not been

1

Map Showing Sui's Conquest of Chen

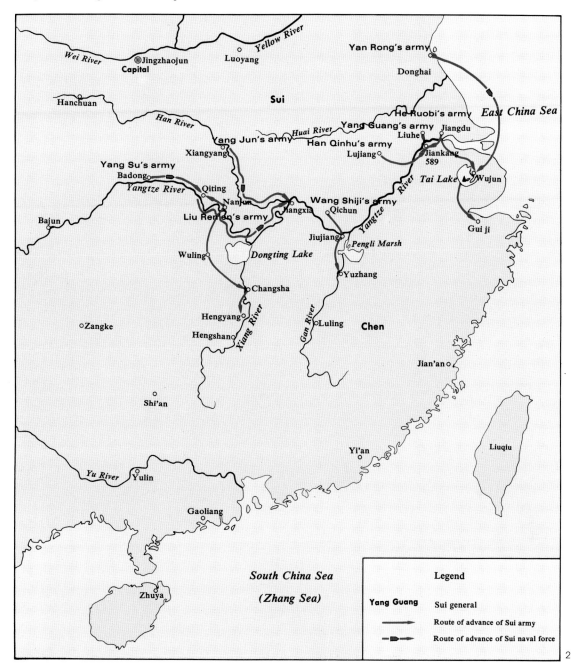

2

included in the nation's household registry, his government enacted appropriate laws, under which the prefectures and counties were required to demarcate households according to patterns set by the imperial court and to re-enter the omitted households in the nation's registry. It also exempted salt and wines from business taxes. As a result, the number of people under government jurisdiction increased, the power of local despots was reduced, and state revenues were guaranteed. In 604, in the fourth year of the reign titled Renshou, Wendi was murdered by Crown Prince Yang Guang.

2. Map showing Sui's conquest of Chen
Yang Jian, Emperor Wendi of Sui, began preparations for the conquest of Chen in 582, the year after he usurped the throne of Northern Zhou. In 588, he sent an army of half a million men to invade Chen. It advanced in eight columns by land and water under the joint commands of Yang Guang, the Prince of Jin; Yang Jun, the Prince of Qin; and Yang Su, the Duke of Qinghe. Meanwhile, the ruler and ministers of Chen indulged in wine, poetry and other forms of pleasure, believing themselves to be safe and secure south of the great Yangtze River that served as a natural barrier. Early in 589, the Sui

general Han Qinghu, leading a contingent of 500 men, crossed the river from Lujiang (present-day Hefei, Anhui Province) to Caishi under cover of darkness and surprised and overwhelmed the troops of the Chen garrison, who were still drunk from their revelry of the night before. Another Sui general, He Ruobi, crossed the river from Guangling, also meeting with little resistance, and the two forces quickly joined up at Jiankang (present-day Nanjing). Shubao, the ruler of Chen, and his two favorite concubines hid themselves in a dried well, but were discovered and taken prisoner. Chen was conquered and the country unified.

3. Celadon warrior figurines

Funerary objects of Sui, height 63.3 cm and 59 cm respectively; unearthed at Wuhan, Hubei Province, in 1953. Both warriors are clad in shining armor from head to foot with only their faces exposed. The armor, including the helmet, is covered with plates resembling fish scales. It has a basin-like collar and extends below the knees. On the breast and back of one of the warriors are round protective plates held in place by strings passing over the shoulder. The hands of the warriors rest on a rectangular shield with round golden nails along the edge and a row of small flowers in the center. So-called shining armor like that worn by these two warriors was invented during the Three Kingdoms period. It was very precious at the time and could only be worn by generals. A special feature of such armor is the two oval protective metal plates resembling mirrors on the left and right sides of both the front and the back. On the battlefield these plates reflected the sunlight, hence the source of its name. The use of such armor became increasingly popular towards the end of the Northern Dynasties. A kind of two-piece armor was also used during the Sui, but by the Tang it had been replaced by the shining armor as the chief protective clothing in battle.

3-1

3-2 ▷

4. Painted clay statuette of armored horse and rider Funerary object of Sui, 27.1 cm tall, 20.5 cm long; unearthed from the tomb of Luo Da at Guojiatan, Xi'an, Shaanxi Province, in 1982. The rider wears a helmet with a pointed top, a coat of shining armor with two breastplates, a cape covering the arms, a battle skirt and long boots reaching to the knees. The horse, too, is clad in armor. It is the image of a heavily armored cavalryman in those days. According to written records, fairly complete armor for horses had appeared during the last years of the Eastern Han Dynasty and was widely used during the Northern and Southern Dynasties. It owed its origin largely to ethnic minorities who were accustomed to fighting on horseback. Armored soldiers riding armored steeds were known as heavily armored cavalry. They were the main force in the nation's military during the Sui Dynasty. Yangdi, the second Sui emperor, used 40 contingents of such cavalry when he invaded Korea.

5. Pottery figures of warriors Sui funerary objects, 34 cm tall; unearthed from the tomb of Li Jingxun in Xi'an, Shaanxi Province, in 1957. Both warriors wear helmets that protect the ears and neck. They are clad in shining armor with two round breastplates on the left and right, a belt around the waist and black flowers on the shoulders. On the lower part of their bodies are trousers and black boots. The right arm of each warrior hangs down, the hand half-clenched in a fist with a hole in the center as if clutching a weapon. The left arms are folded in front of the chest and rest on a rectangular shield. There is a slight ridge on the back of the shields and a black animal mask painted in the center of each. The heads and bodies of the warriors were molded separately and pieced together. The whole piece was whitewashed first; then certain parts were painted in bright red or black. Although the Sui Dynasty did not last long, it fought many wars and evidently paid great attention to the making of protective equipment such as helmets and armor.

4

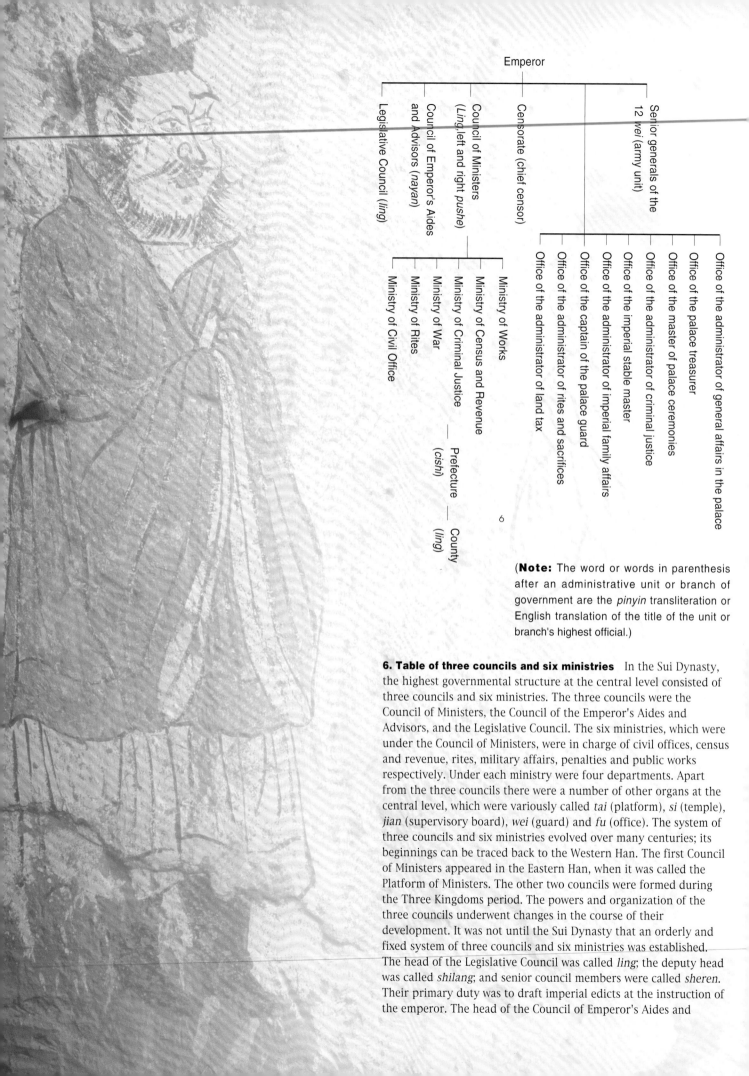

Emperor

- Senior generals of the 12 *wei* (army unit)
  - Office of the administrator of general affairs in the palace
  - Office of the palace treasurer
  - Office of the master of palace ceremonies
  - Office of the administrator of criminal justice
  - Office of the imperial stable master
  - Office of the administrator of imperial family affairs
  - Office of the captain of the palace guard
  - Office of the administrator of rites and sacrifices
  - Office of the administrator of land tax
- Censorate (chief censor)
- Council of Ministers (*Ling*, left and right *pushe*)
  - Ministry of Works
  - Ministry of Census and Revenue
  - Ministry of Criminal Justice ——— Prefecture ——— County
    - (*cishi*)　(*ling*)
  - Ministry of War
  - Ministry of Rites
  - Ministry of Civil Office
- Council of Emperor's Aides and Advisors (*nayan*)
- Legislative Council (*ling*)

6

(**Note:** The word or words in parenthesis after an administrative unit or branch of government are the *pinyin* transliteration or English translation of the title of the unit or branch's highest official.)

6. Table of three councils and six ministries In the Sui Dynasty, the highest governmental structure at the central level consisted of three councils and six ministries. The three councils were the Council of Ministers, the Council of the Emperor's Aides and Advisors, and the Legislative Council. The six ministries, which were under the Council of Ministers, were in charge of civil offices, census and revenue, rites, military affairs, penalties and public works respectively. Under each ministry were four departments. Apart from the three councils there were a number of other organs at the central level, which were variously called *tai* (platform), *si* (temple), *jian* (supervisory board), *wei* (guard) and *fu* (office). The system of three councils and six ministries evolved over many centuries; its beginnings can be traced back to the Western Han. The first Council of Ministers appeared in the Eastern Han, when it was called the Platform of Ministers. The other two councils were formed during the Three Kingdoms period. The powers and organization of the three councils underwent changes in the course of their development. It was not until the Sui Dynasty that an orderly and fixed system of three councils and six ministries was established. The head of the Legislative Council was called *ling*; the deputy head was called *shilang*; and senior council members were called *sheren*. Their primary duty was to draft imperial edicts at the instruction of the emperor. The head of the Council of Emperor's Aides and

Advisors was called *nayan*; the deputy head was called *shilang*; and senior members were called *jishizhong*. Their duties were to assemble and check memorials for the throne, verify the edicts drafted by the Legislative Council, and return, reject or revise the edicts if they considered them inappropriate.

The Legislative Council and Council of Emperor's Aides and Advisors had their offices in the palace. Their members had the right to advise and criticize so as to correct mistakes made by the emperor. The Council of Ministers was located outside the palace. The chief minister was also called *ling*, but in practice no one was ever appointed to the post; all duties were discharged by two deputies called the left and right *pushe*, who headed the six ministries. The head of each ministry was called *shangshu;* the deputy head, *shilang*. The Council of Ministers and the ministries and departments under it had the power to direct and supervise the nine *si* (offices) and three *jian* (supervisory organs), which did the actual work at the central level.

7

7. *Wuzhu* coin and *taihuo liuzhu* coin Coins of Chen, a state of the Southern Dynasties. Left to right, they are 2.45 cm and 2.5 cm in diameter and 3.35 g and 3 g in weight respectively. Both are made of copper. The *wuzhu* coin was minted in 562, the third year of the reign titled Tianjia of Chen, and therefore was also called the Tianjia *wuzhu* coin. It has a fairly wide border on both the front and the back. The *taihuo liuzhu* coin was minted in 579. It has an inner and an outer border on both the front and the back. In the beginning it was worth ten *Tianjia wuzhu* coins, but later it was devaluated to the equivalent of just one *wuzhu* coin.

8. *Buquan* coin, *wuhang dabu* coin, *yongtong wanguo* coin Coins of Northern Zhou, 2.6 cm, 2.8 cm and 3 cm in diameter and 4.3 g, 3 g and 6.1 g in weight respectively. The *buquan* coin (top) was minted in 561. It had an inner and an outer border and was worth five *wuzhu* coins of Western Wei. The *wuhang dabu* coin (lower left) was minted in 574. It also had an inner and an outer border, and its weight varied. A piece of smaller size was 2.3 cm in diameter and weighed 2.1 g. It was worth ten *buquan* coins. The *yongtong wanguo* coin (lower right) was minted in 579. It, too, had inner and outer borders and was valued at ten *wuhang dabu* coins.

8

9. *Wuzhu* coins Currency of Sui, 2.3-2.5 cm in diameter. All *wuzhu* coins of the Sui Dynasty had wide borders. Alongside the character *wu* (five) is a vertical stroke that formed a part of the inner border. The characters on the coins were written in thick and sturdy strokes. There was some confusion in the monetary system of the early Sui. In the Guandong region, east of present-day Shaanxi Province, the *changping* coins of Northern Qi were used while in the Guanzhong region of the central Shaanxi plain the *wuhang dabu* and *yongtong wanguo* coins of Northern Zhou were still in circulation. These coins not only differed in size and weight but were of poor quality. Therefore, shortly after its founding, the Sui Dynasty began to mint new *wuzhu* coins. In 583, when the new coins were ready, the Sui emperor issued edicts to places outside the passes leading into Shaanxi. Each edict was accompanied by 100 specimens of the new coins. All coins coming in from the outside had to be examined to see if they were similar to the specimens. If so, they were allowed to enter the pass. If not, they were destroyed and the metal was confiscated as palace property. After a period of reorganization, the country's monetary system was unified. That not only promoted the development of trade but made life much easier for the people.

9

10-1

10. Clay figurine of a civil servant
Sui funerary object, 65 cm tall; unearthed from a Sui tomb at Zhoujia Dawan, Wuhan, Hubei Province, in 1956. The figure is wearing a high square hat, an upper garment with wide sleeves, a skirt that hangs down to the ground, a wide belt and shoes. Abolition of the system of selecting officials according to family status and service record had begun during the Western Wei of the Northern Dynasties, and more attention was being paid to a man's ability. Emperor Wendi of Sui abolished the system of selecting officials known as *jiupin zhongzheng*, the essence of which was to protect the hereditary rights of bureaucrats. He ordered the various prefectures to recommend three persons to the central government each year. In 598 he issued an edict to the effect that officials of the five highest ranks, general administrators and prefects were to be selected from among candidates who were morally cultivated, kindly and approachable. This shows that the imperial examination system of selecting officials was in the making. By the time of Emperor Yangdi, when examinations at the highest level were instituted, the system was formally established.

Development of the Social Economy

The series of political and economic measures implemented by Emperor Wendi (Yang Jian) had a positive effect on the strengthening and consolidation of the feudal state. National unity, social stability and a lessening of taxation and corvée contributed to a fairly rapid development of agriculture and the handicrafts. In commerce, too, there were signs of prosperity. The granaries of the Sui court were full and supplies of other products were also plentiful. To a certain extent, this reflected a flourishing rural economy. On this basis the handicraft industries continued to develop, the principal activities at the time being silk-weaving, pottery and porcelain making and shipbuilding. The chief silk-weaving areas were in present-day Hebei, Henan and Sichuan provinces, Sichuan brocade being a famous traditional fabric in those days. Celadon wares fired in Gong County, Henan, and Ci County, Hebei, were beautifully shaped, with thick sturdy bodies and transparent glaze. The technique of firing white porcelain objects had reached a relatively mature stage; they had a strong, close-knit texture and a smooth, sparkling glaze.

11. Brick with record of millet paid out of a public granary Sui relic, 32.5 cm long, 16 cm wide, 6.4 cm thick; said to have been unearthed in Luoyang, Henan Province. This brick, the upper part of which is no longer complete, bears an inscription that says, "On the 23rd day of the 11th month of the 5th year (AD 609) of the reign titled Daye, 15,000 *dan* (hectoliters) of millet were paid out of a public granary." The inscription also gives the names of the person in charge of the granary, the recorder, the granary supervisor and the witness. It was a record of payment of millet from a public granary to the local authorities. According to the *Book of Sui: Biography of Zhangsun Ping*, in the 3rd year (AD 583) of the reign titled Kaihuang, Zhangsun Ping was the minister of census and revenue. He noticed that many prefectures and counties were ravaged by floods or drought and the people did not have enough to eat. So he petitioned the emperor to require that each autumn every family donate not more than one hectoliter of millet or wheat to a local public granary. This was to be stored for use as relief supplies during lean years. The quantity to be donated depended on the means of the family. The granary was called a charity or social granary, and was managed by a social worker. In 595, the 15th year of the Kaihuang reign, the ruling class, on the pretext that charity granaries were not being managed properly, ordered that grain destined for those in the prefectures of the northwest were to be deposited in government granaries instead. In the following year they placed all charity granaries in the northwest under the management of local authorities at the county level. The inscription on the brick shown here is evidence of these changes.

Map of the Sui Canal

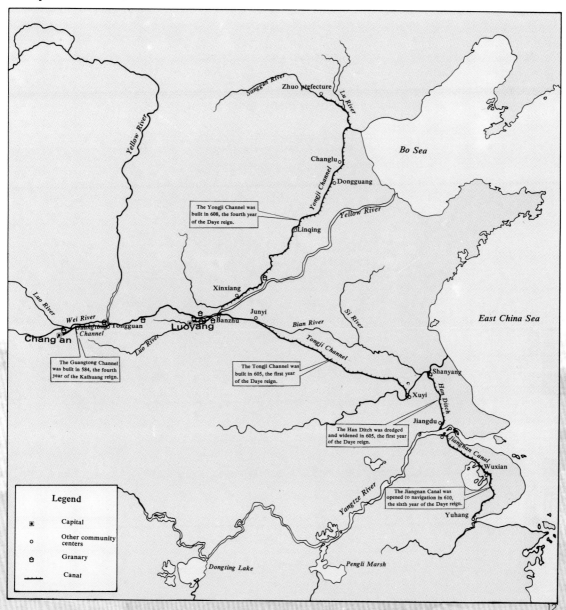

12. Map of the Sui canal The north-south Grand Canal, a giant engineering project of the Sui Dynasty, was completed in four stages. In 605, the first year of the reign titled Daye, construction began on the Tongji Channel from Luoyang to Shanyang (now Huai'an County, Jiangsu Province). This was followed by the dredging and widening of the Shanyang Ditch (the old course of the Han Ditch built by King Fuchai of Wu during the Spring and Autumn period) from Shanyang to Yangzi (southeast of present-day Yizheng, Jiangsu Province). In 608, the Yongji Channel from Luoyang north to Zuo Prefecture (now Beijing) was built. And in 610 the Jiangnan Canal from Jingkou (now Zhenjiang, Jiangsu Province) to Yuhang (now Hangzhou, Zhejiang Province) was opened to navigation. Thus, over a period of six years, a great waterway with a total length of more than 2,000 kilometers was completed. It began at Yuhang in the south, passed through Jiangdu (now Yangzhou, Jiangsu Province) and Luoyang, and extended to Zuo Prefecture in the north, linking the waters of five great river systems — the Qiantang, Yangtze, Huai, Yellow and Hai. It became a major artery of north-south transportation that strengthened economic and cultural intercourse between the northern and southern parts of the country and promoted the development of the economy.

13. Stone slab on balustrade of Anji Bridge Sui relic, 212 cm long, 84.5 cm high; unearthed at the site of Anji Bridge in Zhaoxian, Hebei Province, in 1952. The slab was found buried in mud under the bridge during repairs. On one side of the slab is a sculpture of two dragons with long horns crawling into a tunnel from opposite ends. The bridge is located 2.5 km to the south of the county town of Zhaoxian and is also called Zhaozhou Bridge. It was designed and built across the Xiao River under the direction of a craftsman called Li Chun. It has a stone arch with a wide span of 37.37 meters and a gentle slope that permits horses and carriages to pass over easily. On the left and right exterior curves of the large stone arch are pairs of smaller arches (spandrels) which can divert part of the flow during high water season, lessening the pressure on the bridge. The contrivance also economized on the use of stone and reduced the overall weight of the bridge. Over the past 1,300 years, Anji Bridge has withstood floods, quakes, the weight of heavy vehicles, and the inclemencies of wind and rain. It still spans the Xiao River — the oldest spandrel stone arch bridge in the world.

13-1

13-2

14. Celadon flask with four rings, hornless dragon handle and chicken-head spout Sui water container, 25 cm tall, mouth diameter 6.6 cm, base diameter 7 cm; unearthed from Sui tomb No. 241 at Zhoujia Dawan, Wuhan, Hubei Province, in 1956. It has a round belly, long neck, flat bottom, four rings on the shoulder, and a handle of twin hornless dragons whose mouths dip into the flask as if drinking. There are ridges resembling bamboo joints on the neck, bowstring patterns on the belly, and a spout shaped like a chicken's head. The whole flask is glazed in green. Many new types of celadon vessels appeared during the Sui Dynasty. The most obvious changes were in the shapes of flasks and jars. Flasks were of two general categories, with and without spouts. Those of the first category included flasks with chicken-head spouts, flasks with phoenix spouts and dragon handles, as well as ones with short eight-sided spouts. Flasks without spouts were more popular in the south. A basic feature of such flasks is their high bowl-like mouth. They have necks and shoulders with rings attached. A major change in the shape of jars is the appearance of bowl-shaped mouths.

14-1

14-2

15. Carved celadon jar with eight rings Sui container, 21 cm tall, body diameter 16 cm, base diameter 9.4 cm; unearthed from the tomb of Li Jingxun in Xi'an, Shaanxi Province, in 1957. It has a relatively thin body, a large mouth and a short neck. On the shoulder are eight rings, evidently for attaching of strings. The item belonged to the southern system of Sui porcelain jars. It is coated with dark blue glaze both inside and outside, on which is a pattern of fizzures. The roughcast, which is exposed on the bottom, is of a grayish yellow color. When unearthed the jar contained some walnuts.

16. Celadon box with small mouth and flat bottom Container of Sui, height 7.6 cm, mouth diameter 2.5 cm, base diameter 6.7 cm; unearthed from the tomb of Li Jingxun in Xi'an, Shaanxi Province, in 1957. It has a small mouth, shoulders that slope gently outwards, and a belly with straight sides. From the shoulders to the upper part of the belly are long narrow crevices resembling openwork. The glaze is light blue with rough broken-ice crackles; it does not cover the base nor the parts adjacent to it.

17. Seven joined celadon cups Sui water container; unearthed from the tomb of Li Jingxun in Xi'an, Shaanxi Province, in 1957. It is one of the finest examples of Sui celadon wares. The seven cups are of the same size and shape. Each has a small mouth, a bulging belly and a hollow ring base. It stands 3.5 cm high and has a mouth diameter of 2.5 cm. Below the mouth and on the belly are bowstring patterns. One of the cups stands in the center surrounded by the other six, their shoulders joined with glaze, an arrangement that is unique among ancient receptacles discovered to date. The interior of the cups is glazed all over; the exterior is glazed only down to the belly. The glaze is of a pea green color with broken-ice crackles.

18. Celadon figurines of a mouse, ox and monkey Sui funerary objects, height of mouse 15.3 cm, height of ox and monkey 16.5 cm; unearthed at Guizishan, Wuchang, Wuhan, Hubei Province, in 1955. These are images of three of the 12 animals of the Chinese zodiac. They have the heads of animals but bodies of humans, are dressed in robes and seated cross-legged. Vivid and lifelike, each holds an official tablet. The glaze is greenish yellow in color. Exquisitely made, these figurines are of high artistic value. For a long time, people believed that the theory of the 12 animals originated with Wang Yun, a minister of the Eastern Han. However, that has since been proven incorrect, for the 12 animals were mentioned in records on bamboo slips that date back to the Qin Dynasty. The earliest figurines of the zodiac animals appeared in the Sui Dynasty.

18-1

20

19. White porcelain flask with double body and dragon handles Sui water container, height 18.6 cm, mouth diameter 4.5 cm, diameter of each belly 6.3 cm; unearthed from Li Jingxun's tomb in Xi'an, Shaanxi Province, in 1957. The two bodies of the flask are joined. Above the joint is a cup-shaped mouth. Around the neck are three incised bowstring lines. The bodies are glazed up to the bowstrings and there are thin broken-ice crackles on the glaze. The roughcast is exposed at the base and on parts adjacent to it. Kaolin contains a fairly high amount of iron. When it is fired at a high temperature of 1300° centigrade, it turns

a pale blue. But when the iron content is reduced through appropriate control so that its effect on the color is removed, white porcelain can be made. The first white porcelain articles were made in China during the Northern Qi, but blue was widely present in the white. That indicated that there was still too much iron and that the firing temperature was too low—evidence that the craft had still to mature. On this porcelain flask of the Sui Dynasty, however, there is no conspicuous presence of blue in the white glaze.

20. White porcelain flask with two ears Sui water vessel, height 8.8 cm, mouth diameter 2.5 cm; unearthed from the tomb of Li Jingxun in Xi'an, Shaanxi Province, in 1957. The flask has a circular mouth and a flat body with identical designs on the two sides. The designs are shaped like inverted hearts with pearl-like ornaments along the edges. In the center of each design is an animal mask holding a honeysuckle leaf in the corners of its mouth. The flask is coated with white glaze, on which are rough broken-ice crackles. The glaze extends only to below the belly, the roughcast being exposed at the ring base.

21. White porcelain chicken-head flask with twin holds and dragon handle Sui water container, height 27.4 cm, mouth diameter 7.1 cm, base diameter 7 cm; unearthed from the tomb of Li Jingxun in Xi'an, Shaanxi Province, in 1957. Chicken-head flasks were used from the two Jin Dynasties down to the early Tang. There were marked changes in their shapes during the Sui period. The chicken head evolved from small to big, and the body from short and small to long and thin. The mouth was higher, the neck narrower, and the loop holds on the shoulder changed from bar-shaped to bridge-shaped. The chicken head of the flask shown here is more realistic than earlier examples, the handle is still modeled on the twin-dragon handle of the Southern Dynasties, and the base curves slightly outwards.

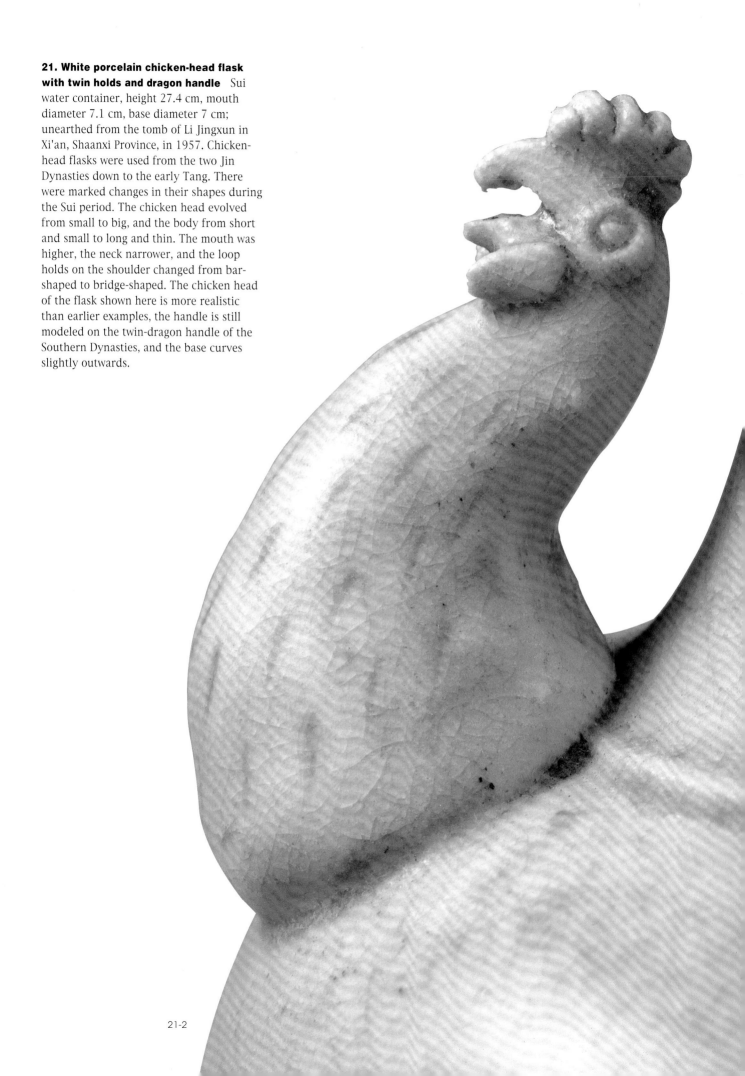

21-2

22. Glass bottle Sui water container, height 16.3 cm, mouth diameter 2.8 cm, base diameter 5.6 cm; unearthed from the tomb of Li Jingxun in Xi'an, Shaanxi Province, in 1957. Glassmaking appeared in China at a very early date. During the Western Jin period, glass was sometimes referred to as "medical jade" suggesting that it was made by smelting minerals.

Beginning in the Northern and Southern Dynasties, glassmaking became an independent craft and the first glass articles of daily use appeared. The glass bottle shown here is thick and heavy with a low transparency. It is an example of a glass vessel made for everyday use; when unearthed it contained some liquid.

23

23. Elliptical glass bottle Sui water container, 12.5 cm high; unearthed from the tomb of Li Jingxun in Xi'an, Shaanxi Province, in 1957. Viewed from above, the mouth and body of the bottle are ellipses. It was shaped by blowing. The walls are very thin and the overall shape is traditional Chinese. Chemical analyses show that it was made of alkali glass and glass with a high lead content. A bottle like this made in the Sui Dynasty shows that the technique of glassblowing in China must have been well developed more than 15 centuries ago.

24

24. Bronze mirror with animal designs, treasure of Linshan Sui relic, 18.4 cm in diameter. Carved on the back of the mirror are the four mythical animals—the green dragon, white tiger, scarlet bird and tortoise-snake—and 32 characters. During the Sui Dynasty, bronze mirrors decorated with the four mythical animals or with the 12 animals of the zodiac were regarded as talismans that could keep away evil or bring blessings. One of the stories from the collection called *Taiping Miscellany: Wang Du* tells about a Marquis of Fenyin, during the Sui Dynasty, who just before his death presented an old mirror to a man named Wang Du. He said to the man, "This mirror will keep all evil at a distance." Wang Du accepted the gift and treasured it.

25. Pottery figure of woman Sui funerary object, 33 cm tall; unearthed at Guizishan, Wuchang, Wuhan, Hubei Province, in 1956. This woman wears her hair in a round bun at the top of her head. She is dressed in a short jacket with an open V-shaped collar and narrow sleeves and a long pleated skirt that extends to the ground. Around her waist is a belt. Her right arm is stretched out while the left arm hangs down naturally. Both hands are half closed.

26. Pottery figure of maidservant Sui funerary object, 17.5 cm tall; unearthed from the tomb of Li Jingxun in Xi'an, Shaanxi Province, in 1957. This is a typical representation of a maidservant of the Sui Dynasty. Maidservants in those days usually wore their hair in a wide, flat bun.

They were dressed in short jackets with narrow sleeves and long skirts that covered part of the breasts and reached down to the ground. Their shoulders were draped in shawls. A girl was supposed to look tall, slim and pretty when dressed in this way. It is a reflection of the aesthetic values of Sui society, in which quiet delicate beauty was the fashion ideal.

25

26

27. Clay figurine of woman rider Sui funerary object, overall height 37.5 cm; unearthed at Guizishan, Wuchang, Wuhan, Hubei Province, in 1956. The rider has a Y-shaped hairdo. She is dressed in a long upper garment with round collar and narrow sleeves; wears trousers and a belt around the waist; and has shoes with pointed toes. She holds the reins in her left hand while her right hand is poised as if holding a whip. She seems to be reining in the horse, which is saddled, bridled and strapped with leather belts around the neck and hindquarters. Eight bronze bells dangle from the belt around the horse's neck, and eight ornaments resembling apricot leaves hang from the belt on each side of the horse's rear. Vivid and realistic, this is a very valuable work of art.

28. Gold necklace Sui ornament, perimeter 43 cm, weight 91.25 g; unearthed from the tomb of Li Jingxun in Xi'an, Shaanxi Province, in 1957. This necklace is made up of 28 gold beads each inlaid with ten pearls. The beads are divided into two groups, left and right, each of which is strung on a chain made of twisted strands of gold silk. The two upper ends of the chains are joined by a gold clasp with hooks. In the middle of this clasp is a circular gold ornament set with a dark blue pearl bearing an incised image of a deer. At the upper end of each group of beads is a square gold ornament inlaid with a piece of lazurite, to which a gold ring is attached. The hooks at the two ends of the clasp are passed through these rings to hold the two groups of beads in place. Suspended from the lower portions of the necklace is a piece of jewelry with a circular gold ornament at its center. This ornament is inlaid with a stone called "chicken blood" because of its color and with 24 pearls. It is flanked by two square ornaments with concave sides. Dangling from this centerpiece is a blue pearl shaped like a heart. The workmanship and decorations of this necklace are reminiscent of ancient Persian art.

29. Gold bracelets Sui ornaments, longer diameter 7 cm, shorter diameter 5.5 cm; unearthed from the tomb of Li Jingxun in Xi'an, Shaanxi Province, in 1957. Each of these twin elliptical bracelets is divided into four sections. The two ends of each section are thicker than the other parts and are inlaid with transparent, colorless half-sphere pearls on which are specks of white rust. The sections are connected by small square joints, inlaid with blue-green glass beads. The opening on each bracelet is provided with an ornamental device for fastening. At one end of this device is a petal-shaped ring inlaid with six tiny pearls; at the other end is a hook, the tip of which is also inlaid with a pearl. By means of the hook and ring, the bracelet can be fastened and unfastened at will. At the other ends of the ring and hook are movable axes the ends of which were originally encased in pearls, of which only one remains.

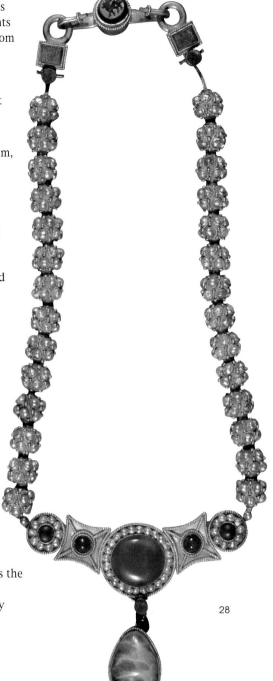

28

29

27

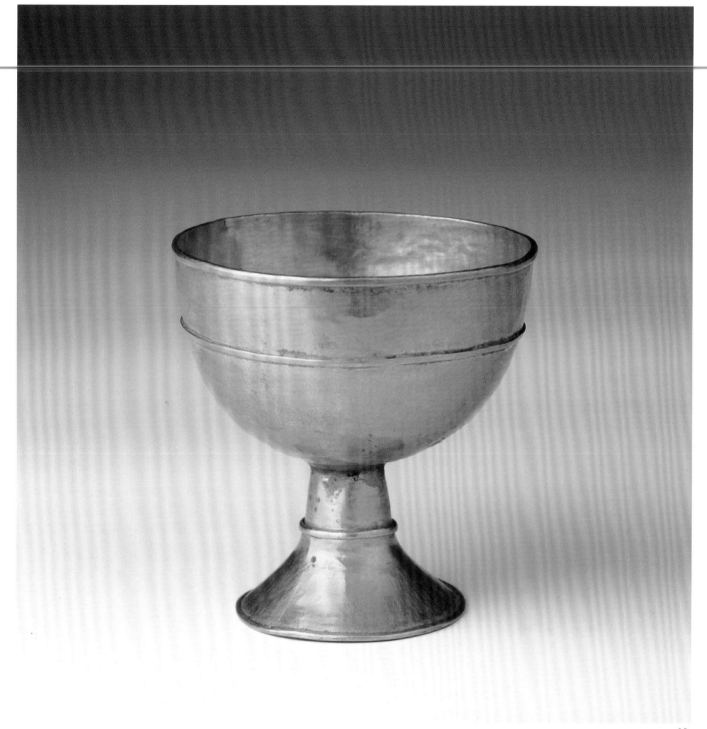

30

30. Gold cup with high stem   Sui wine cup, height 5.7 cm, mouth diameter 5.7 cm, weight 49.4 g; unearthed from the tomb of Li Jingxun in Xi'an, Shaanxi Province, in 1957. This cup has a large mouth with a rim that is turned outwards. It is encircled with a raised line called a bowstring pattern, which is actually a hoop welded upon the cup. The stem is shaped like a trumpet and hollow. There is also a raised bowstring pattern around the middle of the stem and one around the base, both of which were welded into place. The stem was also welded onto the cup, but only after a round disk was welded onto the top of the stem.

31

31. Gilded white jade cup Sui water container, height 4.1 cm, mouth diameter 5.6 cm, base diameter 2.9 cm; unearthed from the tomb of Li Jingxun in Xi'an, Shaanxi Province, in 1957. This is a cup with a straight mouth, flat lip and deep belly. It has a simulated ring base, which is actually solid with a flat bottom. The mouth is gilded both inside and out to a depth of 0.6 cm. The cup, which is made of white jade, has been well preserved. Its shape and workmanship are beautiful. They are examples of the consummate skill of the jade craftsmen of Sui.

Tang Dynasty

(618—907)

Li Yuan was a high-ranking bureaucrat of the Sui Dynasty. After capturing Chang'an in 618 he usurped the throne and established the Tang Dynasty. His son,

Emperor Taizong, succeeded to the throne in 626. He quickly restored the feudal order, consolidated the unity of the country, and took steps to revive the economy. In due course the country became very powerful. This was the period that historians call the "Zhenguan era of good government" (Zhenguan was the emperor's reign title). The period of Emperor Taizong, through that of Empress Wu Zetian and to the Kaiyuan reign of Emperor Xuanzong is known in history as the early Tang. It was an era of national unity, expanding frontiers, political stability and prosperity on the economic and cultural fronts. Relations between the various nationalities in China expanded and economic and cultural interchanges with neighboring countries in Asia and Africa were strengthened. Chang'an became the center of such interchanges, both within the country and internationally. In 755 a rebellion led by An Lushan and Shi Siming broke out, which weakened the rule of the Tang court to an extent from which it never fully recovered. In 874 the Huang Chao peasant uprising led to the total disintegration of Tang rule, and in 907 the dynasty was overthrown. Thereafter, China experienced another period of political fragmentation, known in history as the era of Five Dynasties and Ten Kingdoms.

Zenith of the Tang Dynasty

In the early days of the Tang, powerful Eastern Tujue (Turkish) tribes in the north constantly harassed the Shaanxi plains until 630 when Emperor Taizong dispatched an army that totally defeated the invaders. By the year 646, the Tang Empire had incorporated into its territory the vast lands north and south of the great Gobi Desert. Meanwhile, beginning in 640, the Tang had subdued one by one the separatist feudal regimes of Gaochang, Yutian, Qiuci, Yanpeng and Shule in the west, unifying the whole of what is now the Xinjiang Uygur Autonomous Region. At the height of its power, the empire extended to the Pacific Ocean in the east, the Aral Sea in the west, beyond Lake Baikal in the north, and to the broad regions along the South China Sea in the south. Ruling over nine million households and 52 million people, it was a great, populous and prosperous empire of many nationalities with broad lands, abundant resources and a flourishing civilization.

Establishment of the Tang Dynasty

Cashing in on the peasant uprisings against the decadent rule of the Sui, Li Yuan, a high-ranking Sui official, started an armed rebellion at Jinyang (southwest of present-day Taiyuan, Shanxi Province). Marching south, he seized Chang'an and quickly occupied the central Shaanxi plain (often referred to as Guanzhong, meaning Center of the Passes). In 618, after Sui emperor Yangdi was murdered, Li Yuan proclaimed himself emperor of a new dynasty called Tang. From 618 to 624, his armies suppressed the peasant uprisings in Hebei Province and the Yangtze and Huai valleys, and in the process gradually subdued various separatist regimes established by feudal landlords, reunifying the country. The Tang Dynasty retained the Sui system of three councils and six ministries in its administrative structure, which it took steps to improve and consolidate. In its early years, it continued to practice the equal land system and the *zu-yong-diao* system of taxation (on land, labor and households). It revived and promoted the feudal relations of production. In the armed forces, it continued the system under which soldiers were organized into units called *fu* and were registered separately from civilians in the nation's census. It initiated the imperial examination system in the selection of government officials, which broadened the social base of feudal rule.

唐太宗皇帝之真像

32

32. Portrait of the Tang emperor Taizong
Li Shimin, styled Emperor Taizong (598-649, r.626-649), was the second emperor of the Tang Dynasty. He joined his father Li Yuan's rebellion at Jinyang in 617 and fought well during the Tang wars to reunite the country. He defeated Xue Ju, warlord of Jincheng (now Lanzhou, Gansu Province), and forced his son Xue Rengao to capitulate. He repulsed the southward advance of Li Wuzhou and Song Jingang who, relying on the support of Turkish tribes, tried to invade the area east of the

Yellow River that is now Shanxi Province. He also suppressed the peasant uprisings led by Dou Jiande and others, gradually reuniting the country. After succeeding to the throne, Emperor Taizong strengthened autocratic centralized power, consolidated the country's unity, and retained the equal land system and the *zu-yong-diao* system of taxation, permitting payment of taxes in kind in lieu of corvée. He resisted the harassment of Turkish military aristocrats, encouraged closer relations between the various ethnic groups in China, and promoted economic and cultural intercourse with neighboring countries. These policies had a positive effect on the revival and development of the social economy during the early Tang. A period known in history as the "Zhenguan era of good government" appeared.

33. Painted glazed clay figurine of a civilian official Tang funerary object, 69 cm tall; unearthed from the tomb of Zheng Rentai in Liquan County, Shaanxi Province, in 1972. The figure has a quiet-looking face with a beard. He wears a headgear with a flat top and a robe whose collar, wide sleeves and lower part are adorned with brocade patterns. A sleeveless jacket is worn over the robe. On the lower part of the body are baggy trousers and on the feet are shoes with turned-up toes. The headgear and garments are gilt and painted in dazzling colors. It is a representation of how civilian officials in those days dressed when summoned to the imperial court. Zheng Rentai, the occupant of the tomb, took part in the armed rebellion launched by Li Yuan at Jinyang and in the palace coup at Xuanwu Gate, in which Li Shimin (later Emperor Taizong) murdered his elder brother, the crown prince. He served for a time as prefect of Liangzhou, held the ranks of general and *zhuguo* (a high but honorary military rank of the Tang), and was an important personage during the early Tang.

34-1

**34. Painted glazed pottery figure of a
military officer**   Tang funerary object,
71.5 cm tall; unearthed from the tomb of
Zheng Rentai in Liquan County, Shaanxi
Province, in 1972. This figure is dressed in
a magnificent suit of armor trimmed with
artistic floral patterns. It was modeled on
a member of Zheng Rentai's guard of
honor.

34-2

Table of Equal Land System

Recipient of Land	*Koufen* land (to be returned to the government after death)	*Yongye* land (not returnable)
Male aged 18-60	80 *mu*	20 *mu*
Male disabled or over 60	40 *mu*	20 *mu* if master of house
Widow	30 *mu*	
Male under 18		

One *mu* is 6.667 ares.

35

35. Equal land system   The equal land system practiced during the early Tang was a continuation of that of the Northern Dynasties, except that servants, slaves and draft oxen were no longer alloted land as in previous dynasties. The Tang system stipulated that every adult male aged 18-60 was to receive 20 *mu* of *yongye* land (land he could bequeath to his heirs) and 80 *mu* of *koufen* land (which the government would take back and redistribute upon his death). A disabled male or one over 60 received 40 *mu* of *koufen* land, while a widow received 30 *mu*. If he/she was the master of a house, he/she also received 20 *mu* of *yongye* land. When a person moved or was too poor to pay the expenses of a funeral, he was permitted to sell his *yongye* land. If he moved to some sparsely populated place where land was plentiful, or wished to sell land for use as residence, shops or mills, he could sell his *koufen* land too. During the early years of the Tang there were large tracts of land without owners in all parts of the country, so it was permissible over a period of time for peasants to own land, but the amount was far below that stipulated by law.

36. *Zu-yong-diao* taxes   This system of taxation stipulated that every adult male aged 21-60 was to pay a tax each year of two *dan* (hectoliters) of millet, which was called *zu*; and a tax of two *zhang* (about six meters) of silk and three *liang* of silk floss, or 2.5 *zhang* (about 7.5 meters) of cloth and three catties of flax, which was called *diao*. Additionally, he was required to do corvée labor for 20 days, but could pay a tax in silk instead. The tax equivalent of each day of corvée labor was three *chi* (about one meter) of silk and it was called *yong*. If a man did more than the required number of days of corvée labor, he could be exempted from the *zu* and *diao* taxes. An extra 15 days of labor would exempt him from the *diao* tax and an extra 30 days would exempt him from both. The *zu-yong-diao* taxes were exacted on the basis of the equal land system, but in practice the burden of the taxation had to be shouldered by peasants who had very little land. To them it was a heavy burden. But since corvée labor was relatively light during the early Tang and it was usually permissible to pay the *yong* tax in lieu of labor, peasants were more or less assured of sufficient time for farm work. This had a positive effect on the recovery and development of the social economy.

37. Land deed of Zhao Huaiman   Tang relic, 21.7 cm wide, 27.2 cm high; unearthed in Turpan, Xinjiang Uygur Autonomous Region, in 1959. The contents of the deed are no longer complete as it has been trimmed into the shape of the instep of a shoe. The essential message is that a man named Zhao Huaiman rented land for farming from Zhang Diren and Zhang Junfu and had to pay the landowners rent in wheat each year. Payment of the rent had to be completed within six months. Deeds unearthed in Turpan show that the land rented out to tenants included land owned by the government, by monasteries and by private individuals, and that rent was usually paid in grain, that is, it was rent paid in kind. It could be a fixed quota or it could be the sharing of the produce of the land on an equal basis between landlord and tenant. Thus, although the equal land system was practiced during the early Tang, the greater part of the available farmland still belonged to the bureaucrats and landlords, who rented it out to peasants who had little or no land.

Table of *Zu-Yong-Diao* Taxes

	Zu	2 *dan* of millet
Taxes paid each year by an adult male 21-60 years of age	Yong	60 *chi* of silk in lieu of 20 days of corvée labor
	Diao	2 *zhang* of silk and 3 *liang* of silk floss, or 2.5 *zhang* of cloth and 3 catties of flax

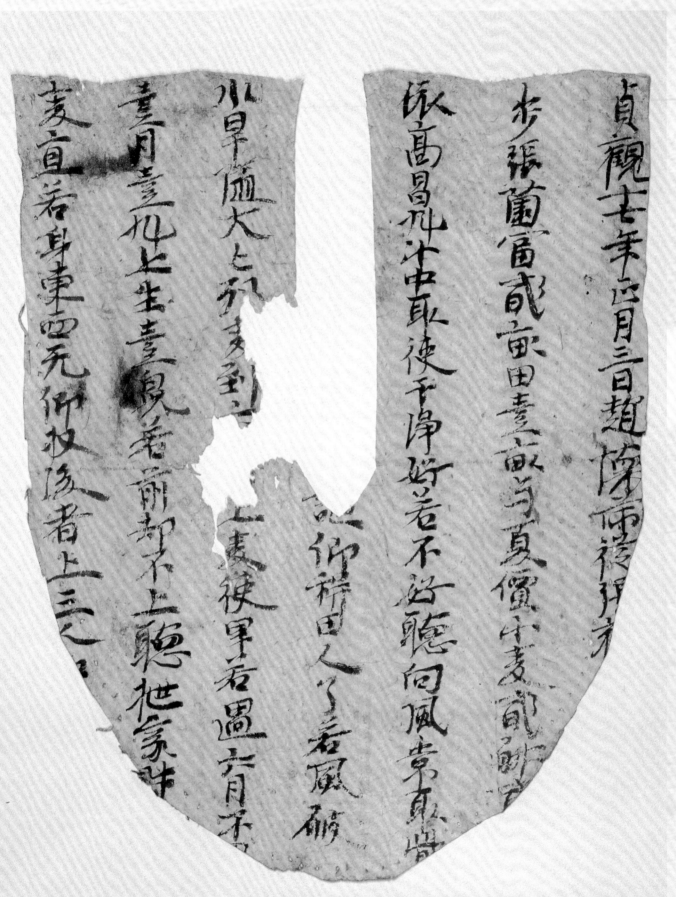

38. Portrait of Wu Zetian   Wu Zetian (624–705) was a native of Wenshui (east of present-day Wenshi, Shanxi Province). In 655, the Tang emperor Gaozong made her his empress, in which capacity she began to take part in court affairs. In 690 she usurped the Tang throne. She styled herself the Sage and Divine Empress and changed the dynastic name from Tang to Zhou (historians call it the Wu-Zhou). She was learned in literature and history and very resourceful. She initiated the practice of holding imperial examinations in the palace so that she could personally examine the candidates. She permitted both officials of the nine highest ranks and the ordinary people to make self-recommendations and in this way promoted large numbers of ordinary landlords to government posts, a measure that curtailed the power of the great aristocratic families. She resisted the harassments of the Turkish and Tubo military aristocrats, recovered Cuiye (now Tokmak in Central Asia) and other important places, re-established the four outposts at Anxi, and effectively protected the country's frontiers.

39. Rubbing from a section of the tablet of the Immortal Prince   Tang relic; the original tablet was erected at the former site of the Turned-Immortal Temple on Hou Hill, Fudian, in the town of Yanshi, Henan Province. It was 6.7 meters high and 1.55 meters wide. In 699, Wu Zetian left Luoyang, to offer sacrifices to heaven on mountains in the east. On the way she spent a night at Hou Hill and visited the Turned-Immortal Temple. To mark the event, she wrote the inscription on this tablet, which told the story of how Prince Jin, son of King Ling of the Zhou Dynasty, turned into an immortal. It was an allegory of what she believed would be her own destiny. At the top of the tablet was a line

38

39

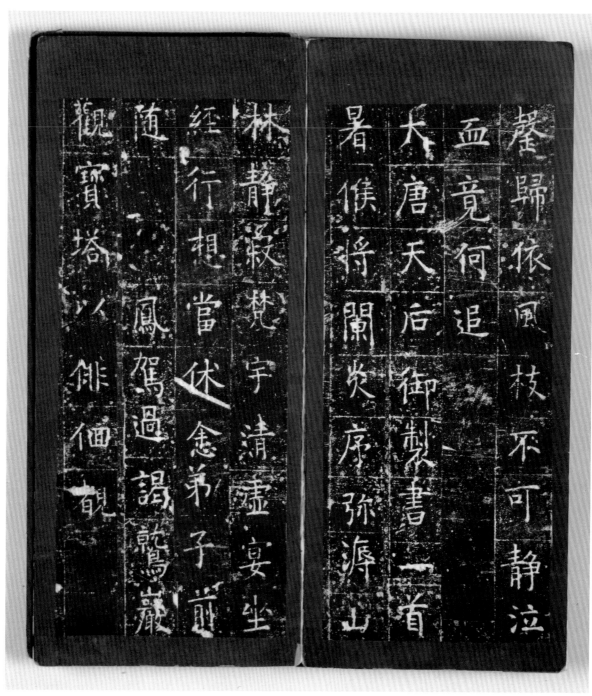

40

that read in translation, "Tablet of the Prince Who Turned Immortal," written in what might be called a flying white style, i.e. in fast strokes with white spots in each stroke. The inscription consisted of 33 lines each with 66 characters. The heading and signature and the poem "Excursion in Fairyland" on the back, including the title, are in the handwritings of the calligraphers Xue Ji and Zhong Shaojing. They are in a charming and mature style, with vigorous but orderly strokes.

40. Section of rubbing from a tablet with a poem by Wu Zetian The general meaning of the poem is that Wu Zetian, accompanying the emperor on a visit to

Shaolin Temple, noticed that a building constructed for an imperial concubine was unfinished. Saddened by the negligence, she composed the poem to express her feelings and on her return to the palace sent people to repair and complete the building.

41. Painted and gilded pottery riders
Tang funerary objects, 33-35 cm tall, 29.5-32 cm long; unearthed from the tomb of Crown Prince Yide in Qian County, Shaanxi Province, in 1971. The heads of the horses are hooded, with openings for the eyes; they are surfaced with gold. Between the two ears of each horse is a tassel. The armor pieces covering its neck,

chest and body are joined together. Behind the saddle, near the hindquarters is a hole for the insertion of an object shaped like a fan or twigs. During the Tang Dynasty, horses decked out in this way were intended only to reflect the owner's wealth and power. In general, they were used as part of a nobleman's guard of honor, not as battle steeds. The riders wear helmets and high boots, and are clad in armor with breastplates and protection for the arms. They hold the reins in their left hands while their right hands are clenched as though holding something.

Chang'an and Luoyang

Chang'an and Luoyang were the two capitals of Tang. The layouts of the two cities were basically the same, each consisting of a Palace City, an Imperial City and an Outer City. Chang'an was the western capital and the country's political, economic and cultural center. It was one of the largest cities in the world during the Middle Ages. Luoyang, the eastern capital, was a hub of transportation, through which all grain and other supplies for Chang'an transported by water had to pass.

42. Map of Chang'an city of the Tang Dynasty   Construction of this city began in 582, the second year of the Kaihuang reign of the Sui Dynasty, and was completed in the following year. It was called Daxing. The Tang emperors changed the name to Chang'an. What still remains of the old city has a perimeter of 35 kilometers with walls built of blocks of earth. It consisted of a Palace City, an Imperial City and an Outer City. The Palace and Imperial Cities were located at the center of the northern part of Chang'an. The Palace City was called Daxing Palace (Palace of Great Prosperity) during the Sui and Taiji Palace (Palace of the Supreme Ultimate) during the Tang. It was rectangular in shape. To the south it faced the Imperial City, and to the north it bordered on the forbidden imperial garden. The Tang rulers built two more

Map of Chang'an City of the Tang Dynasty

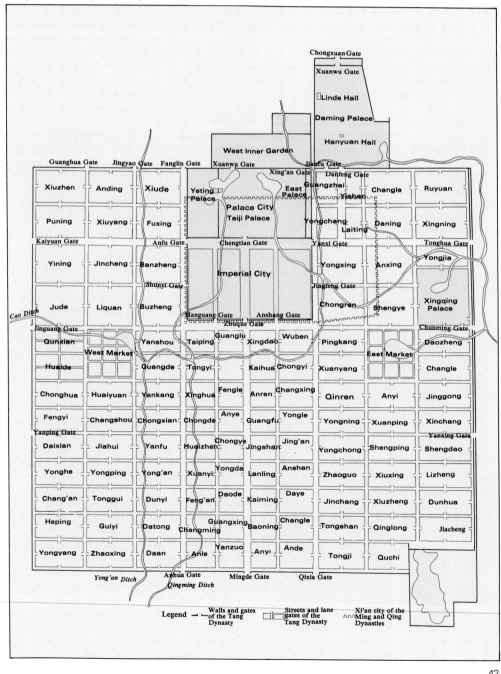

palaces, Daming (Great Light) and Xingqing (Prosperity and Celebration), northeast of Taiji Palace, at Longshou Hill and Xingqing Lane respectively. In the Outer City were 108 lanes and the East and West Markets, located to the east, west and south of the Imperial City. Surveys show that there were eleven north-south streets and ten east-west streets south of the Imperial City. The three streets that led to the three southern city gates and the three that ran clear across the city from east to west, linking the three eastern and three western city gates, were the main thoroughfares. The most impressive was the middle north-south street called Zhuque, or Scarlet Bird, which was 155 meters wide. It was joined to the main gate, called Chengtian Gate, of

44

the Palace City in the north and to Mingde Gate in the southern wall of the Outer City. Excavations have uncovered five passages each 6.5 meters wide under Mingde Gate. Neat, orderly and impressive

in appearance, Chang'an was one of the largest and most prosperous metropolises in the world during the Middle Ages.

43. Iron sluice gate in Chang'an city's sewer system   Tang relic, 72.4 cm high, 65.5 cm wide, 4 cm thick; unearthed in the Western Inner Garden of Tang Chang'an city, Xi'an, Shaanxi Province, in 1954. The gate was mounted on a riveted stone frame. Excavations made at the site show that it was located at the northernmost end of a sewer that passed under the southern wall of the garden. The part of the frame above the ground was 78 cm high. There are traces of riveting on its upper surface, suggesting that it had been covered by a stone slab. The diamond-shaped holes in the gate were for filtering out solid matter that would obstruct the flow of water.

44. Remnant of brick with legend "Government craftsman Ning Daoyang"   Tang building material, remnant length 55 cm, width 17.5 cm, thickness 9.4 cm; unearthed on the west side of the former Dragon-Head Ditch in Tang Chang'an city, Xi'an, Shaanxi Province, in 1957-59. There is a rectangular box on the surface of the brick. It has been rubbed smooth and bears five characters carved in relief that read in translation: "Government craftsman Ning Daoyang." In the Tang Dynasty there were both government and private handicrafts. The government handicrafts produced articles for use in the palace or imperial court. Two imperial offices, called Shaofu Jian and Jiangzuo Jian, were in charge of all handicrafts in the palace. The main task of the Jiangzuo Jian was construction. Its lower organ, the Zhenguan Shu, handled stonework and pottery, so the craftsman who made the brick shown here must have belonged to the Zhenquan Shu.

43

45

45. Restoration of Hanyuan Hall in Daming Palace   Daming Palace, or Palace of Great Light, was located outside Chang'an city. It stood close to the eastern section of the city's north wall, which used to be a part of the Forbidden Garden of Sui. Emperor Taizong (Li Shimin) built the palace on the slopes of Longshan Hill in 634. He called it Yong'an Palace, or Palace of Eternal Peace, but changed the name to Daming in the following year. He made it the residence of his father, Li Yuan, who had been forced to abdicate under the title of Supreme Emperor. About 30 years later, Emperor Gaozong (Li Zhi) renovated the palace and changed the name to Penglai. In 662 he moved from the old Taiji Palace in the city to this palace on the outskirts. Because Daming Palace was located to the east of Taiji Palace, it was also called the "Eastern Inner (Palace)" and Taiji the "Western Inner (Palace)." Hanyuan Hall was the first hall on the central axis of Daming Palace; it faced the palace's main entrance Danfeng Gate to the south. To the north were the Xuanzheng Hall, Zichen Hall, Penglai Hall and Hanliang Hall, the last-named facing the palace's north gate called Xuanwu. Hanyuan Hall was where the emperor presided over important events such as New Year celebrations, the grand gathering on the Winter Solstice, sumptuous banquets, reviewing of troops, inspection of prisoners of war and conferring of honorary titles. It was one of the most important halls of the Tang Dynasty. Most of the Tang emperors after Gaozong also lived in Daming Palace, which was the emperor's official residence for more than 220 years. During this time Hanyuan Hall underwent little change; it was neither destroyed nor rebuilt.

46. Square tile with floral design   Tang building material, 32.9 cm long, 32.5 cm wide, 6 cm thick; unearthed at the site of Daming Palace, Xi'an, Shaanxi Province, in 1958. At the center of the tile is a lotus design, surrounded by a pattern of grapevines and leaves. According to investigations made, square tiles like this one were used to pave the stone steps leading up to Hanyuan Hall.

46

47

48

with a row of nipples between them into an inner circle and an outer circle. In the inner circle is a lotus bloom with 12 petals. In the outer circle, which is circumscribed by another two concentric circles, are patterns of grapevines and leaves represented abstractly by round and elliptical dots. Along the four sides of the tile are double lines, also with rows of nipples between them. At each of the four corners is a floral design with curled twigs. Tiles with designs of lotus, honeysuckle, trailing plants or four-leaf squares were unearthed at the site of Linde Hall in Daming Palace, the lotus design being the most common. The steps outside

the east and west entrances of Linde Hall were all paved with lotus tiles.

48. Remnant of tile with animal mask

Building material of Tang; unearthed at site of Daming Palace in Xi'an, Shaanxi Province, in 1958. It was found at a spot to

49

47. Square tile with lotus design

Building material of Tang, 33.5 cm long on each side and 7.3 cm thick; unearthed at the site of Daming Palace in Xi'an, Shaanxi Province, in 1958. The middle part of the tile is divided by two concentric circles

the south of what used to be the palace's Chongxuan Gate, and may have been a piece of decoration on the gate tower. It was a square tile but only one corner, the upper left one, is still there and the border lines and string-of-pearls pattern on it can be discerned. The eyes and nose of the animal mask in the center of the tile have been smashed, but one can still make out the hair, brows and wide mouth with bared teeth.

49. Remnant of an animal image
Architectural member of Tang, height 14.5 cm, remnant length 21.5 cm; unearthed at the site of Daming Palace, Xi'an, Shaanxi Province, in 1958. The left half of the image is relatively intact. The brow, eye, open mouth and ear leaning backwards are still discernible. The right side of the face has been badly damaged and its features are hardly recognizable.

50. Sealing clay   Tang relics; unearthed at the site of Daming Palace, Xi'an, Shaanxi Province, in 1957. The smaller pieces are 3.4 cm long and 3.1 cm wide; the larger pieces, 9.3 cm long and 4.5 cm wide. They were made of white lime. On the back of most of the pieces are the marks of baskets. They were used to seal containers of wine and honey offered as tributes to the emperor by officials of the provinces and prefectures. The surface of each piece was rubbed smooth and bore an inscription in ink and a red seal. The inscription contained the date, the place of origin and name of the tribute, and the name and official title of the person who presented it. In those days local officials had to offer some of their native or special produce and other rarities to the emperor every year. This was what historians called "tributes from all over."

50-2

50-1

51

52

51. Plan of Xingqing Palace, stone rubbing   The original stele with the plan was made in 1080 by a man named Liu Jingyang and others on the orders of Lu Dafang, a high official of Northern Song. It was unearthed in Xi'an, Shaanxi Province, in 1934, and is now in the Xi'an Museum of Steles. Xingqing Palace was located in Xingqing Lane of Tang Chang'an city. It was originally the feudatory residence of Prince Li Longji (later Emperor Xuanzong). In 714, after the prince became emperor, Xingqing was made an auxiliary royal palace. Later, it was enlarged and became the principal palace where the emperor held court. It was 1,080 meters wide from east to west and 1,250 meters long from north to south, and was protected by walls of rammed earth on all sides. The main buildings in the palace were the Xingqing Hall, Datong Hall (Hall of Great Harmony), Nanxun Hall (Hall of Southern Fragrance), Hua'e Xianghui Lou (Tower of the Light of Flowers and Sepals) and Chenxiang Ting (Pavilion of Deep Fragrance). The palace stood between Daming Palace and Qujiang Pool, to which it was linked by small paths. Emperor Xuanzong generally administered state affairs and received foreign envoys here. During the last years of the Tang, when Zhu Quanzhong compelled Emperor Zhaozong to move his capital to Luoyang, Xingqing Palace was badly damaged.

52. Lotus eaves tiles   Tang building materials, 13 cm, 15.2 cm and 15.5 cm respectively in diameter; unearthed at the site of Xingqing Palace in Xi'an, Shaanxi Province, in 1958. These three tiles are irregularly shaped circular pieces, thick along the edges. Each is adorned with a lotus design, in the center of which is a second, smaller lotus. All eaves tiles unearthed at the sites of Xingqing and Daming Palaces had lotus designs, the only differences being in size and complexity. This may be because the lotus was the flower of Buddhism, and Buddhism was revered during the Tang Dynasty.

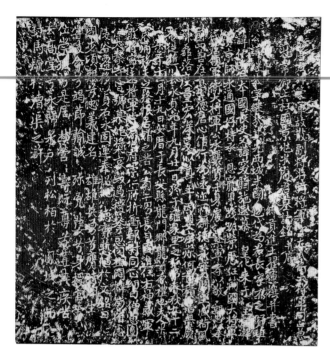

53

Xianzong's reign, Mi Jiarong, a famous singer from Maimargh, gave command performances at the Tang court. And during Emperor Xuanzong's reign, the states of Samarkand* and Kesh* dispatched special envoys to present talented girl dancers to the Tang emperor. Many musicians from southern and eastern Asia such as Biaoguo (an ancient state in the Irrawaddy valley), Funan (an ancient state that is now part of Cambodia) and Japan also came to live in Chang'an, bringing with them exotic songs and musical instruments to enrich and diversify Chinese culture.

* These ancient states are now part of Uzbekistan in the former Soviet Union.

53. Rubbing of epitaph for Mi Jifen   Tang relic; unearthed in Xi'an, Shaanxi Province, in 1957. As mentioned in the epitaph, Mi Jifen was a native of Maimargh, an ancient state of the Western Regions. He was born into a family of officials, his grandfather having served as a minister. His father, Tu Qishi, came to Chang'an during the Tang Dynasty and was given important positions, serving as a senior general in various posts. Mi Jifen himself became a member of the imperial guards and distinguished himself as a loyal soldier and filial son. He died in his home in Chang'an in 805. He had two sons, the elder of whom became an officer in the palace guards and the younger a monk in Daqin Temple.

54. Musicians on camelback, three-color figurines   Tang funerary object, height (to the top of the camel's head) 58.4 cm, height of standing figurine 25.1 cm, length from head to tail of camel 43.4 cm; unearthed from the tomb of Xianyu Tinghui in Xi'an, Shaanxi Province, in 1957. Many musicians, singers and dancers from central Asia came to Chang'an during the Tang and stayed there. Gaozu, the first Tang emperor, made Anchinu, a native of An state (now Bokhara in central Asia), one of his close aides. Cao Bao from Kebud* and his son and grandson became pipa players of high repute in Tang art circles. During Emperor

54-1

55. Rubbing of epitaph for Aluohan
Tang relic, unearthed in Luoyang, Henan Province. The text of the epitaph is blurred and can no longer be read, but according to other records Aluohan (*pinyin* transliteration) was a Persian who served as an official in the Tang government. During the Xianqing years (656-661) of Emperor Gaozong's reign, he came to China as an envoy of various tribes of Fulin, an ancient state in southwestern Asia, and later settled down in Luoyang. He died in 710 and was buried outside Luoyang's Jianchun Gate. The Tang rulers gave government posts to many foreigners who came to China. The families of some of those aliens stayed on for generations. They helped to promote the Tang government's external economic and cultural relations.

56. Persian silver coin Coin 2.9 cm in diameter minted during the reign (590–627) of Khosrow II of the Sasanian Dynasty of Persia; unearthed at the site of Tang Chang'an city, Xi'an, Shaanxi Province, in 1955. In 226, when Ardashir I of Persia overthrew the Parthian Dynasty, he minted silver coins like this one, with floral designs stamped upon both sides. On the obverse was a half-length portrait of the king, and at the center of the reverse was an image of a Zoroastrian altar and a half-length portrait of Ormazd, the supreme Zoroastrian deity, Zoroastrianism being the Persian state religion. Along the two sides were legends in Pahlavi, the Sasanian language, that read in translation, "The fire of a certain king." The Sasanian Dynasty was overthrown during the reign of Tang emperor Gaozong. A Sasanian prince, Bilusi (*pinyin* transliteration), fled to Chang'an with the remnants of his army and was granted political asylum there. After his death, his son Nilishi (*pinyin* transliteration) led several thousand troops of his remnant army back to Persia in an attempt to restore the Sasanian Dynasty. The attempt failed and he returned to Chang'an early in the 8th century and died there. This silver coin was probably brought to Chang'an by Prince Bilusi or his son.

56

57. Eastern Roman gold coin Coin of the reign (565-578) of Justin II of the Eastern Roman Empire, diameter 2.1 cm, weight 4.4 grams; unearthed at Dizhang Wan, Xianyang, Shaanxi Province, in 1953. On the obverse is a half- length portrait of the emperor and a legend that reads in translation: "Our master Justin II, father of our country." On the reverse is the portrait of a goddess wearing a helmet. The legend below the pedestal says the coin was minted in Constantinople. Another legend, virtually encircling the coin, reads : "Victory of the most venerated." The letter "E" at the end was a mark of the place where the coin was minted. In 643,King Boduoli (*pinyin* transliteration) of Fulin of the Eastern Roman Empire dispatched an envoy with presents for the Tang court. Taizong presented valuable silks to the Fulin king in return. Envoys from the Eastern Roman Empire continued to bring presents to the Tang court down to Emperor Xuanzong's time. This coin may have been brought in by one of the envoys.

57-1   57-2

58-2

58. Man of the Western Regions on camelback, pottery figure Tang funerary object, height 89.7 cm, length 26.5 cm; unearthed from the tomb of Wang Chen in Changzhi city, Shanxi Province, in 1954. The camel is proportionately tall and large. The rider is a *hu* (a general term for non-Chinese in ancient times) with deep-set eyes, bushy brows, high nose and beard. He wears a tight-fitting fur jacket with turndown collar and belt, to which a pouch is attached. He sits on a traveling bag placed crosswise on the camel's back and holds the reins in his left hand; his right hand is raised as if wielding a whip. In the Tang Dynasty, China was linked to central and western Asia and even to countries in Europe by way of the Silk Road, along which many Persian and Arabic merchants, artists and artisans made their way to Chang'an. This pottery figure is a realistic portrayal of a merchant of the Western Regions traveling along the Silk Road.

59. Map of Luoyang city in the Tang Dynasty Planned construction of Luoyang as the country's eastern capital began in 605, the first year of the Daye reign of the Sui Dynasty. It was enlarged during the Tang to include land on both banks of the Luo River. To the north it extended to the Mang Hills and to the south it faced Yique Pass, holding a strategic point in east-west communications. What still remains of the ancient city has a perimeter of roughly 27.5 km. It was an approximate square, the southern side being slightly longer. On the north, south and east sides were eight gates. The Palace City and Imperial City stood side by side in the northwestern corner. Most of the streets in the walled city have been located. There were 12 north-south streets and 6 east-west streets south of the Luo River and 4 north-south streets and 3 east-west streets north of the river. The streets leading to the city gates were the main thoroughfares and were generally wider than the others. Dingding Street, which extended from Dingding Gate in the south wall to the front entrance of the imperial city was 121 meters wide. There were three markets—North, South and West—and 107 lanes laid out with crossroads in an orderly way. New discoveries made in recent years include the Youye Gate of the Imperial City and the Hanjia Granary to the north of the East City.

60. Pit 160 of Hanjia Granary Tang relic, 52.2 cm long, 33 cm wide, 47 cm high; unearthed at the site of the Hanjia Granary, Luoyang, Henan Province, in 1971. Photo is of a section of the pit, showing the grain stored in it and the structure of the bottom. Hanjia Granary was built during the Daye years (605–618) of the Sui Dynasty and repaired and enlarged during the Tang. It stood close to the north side of the old city district of Luoyang, and measured over 700 meters from north to south and over 600 meters from east to west. The grain was stored in pits resembling jars, with a large mouth, a small dampproof bottom, and sides that bulge slightly along the middle. The bottom was rammed solid and subjected to heating. It was then covered with a mixture of burnt clay and black ashes, on which were placed one or two layers of wooden planks. Straw mats were spread over the planks, and the grain was stored on the mats. The walls of a pit were also planked and covered with mats. Sometimes a screen of reeds and stalks was placed between the wall planks and mats, and the holes in the screen were filled with husks and chaff. Discovery of the Hanjia Granary has provided valuable material for the study of the ways of storing grain and the structure of large granaries in the Sui and Tang Dynasties.

Map of Luoyang City in the Tang Dynasty

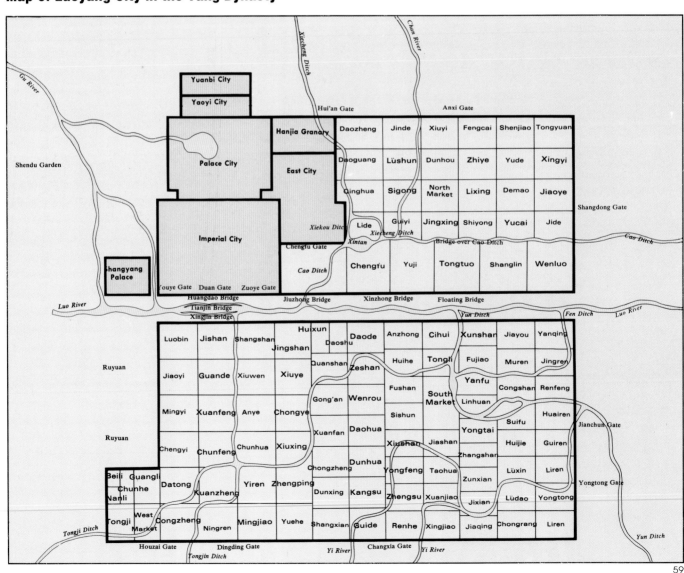

Ethnic Groups Along the Country's Frontiers

Ethnic minorities who set up regional administrations during the Tang Dynasty included the Turks, Uygurs, Tubos, Wumans (founders of Nanzhao state in the southwest) and Mohes (founders of Bohai state in the northeast). These minorities assimilated the advanced economy and culture of Tang in the course of their development and in turn influenced the Han people with their own economic and cultural creations. The joint efforts of the Han and various brother nationalities helped to promote the prosperity and power of the Tang empire.

The Turks and Uygurs

Large parts of north and northwestern China were inhabited by Turks and Uygurs during the Tang. Together with the local Han people, and through learning from each other, they were able to develop the country's border regions, which made great progress under the influence of the advanced economy and culture of the Central Plains. All these nationalities made valuable contributions to the unity and development of China.

61. Map of the Beiting and Anbei Administrative Regions of the Tang Dynasty In the winter of 629, or the third year of the Zhenguan reign of Emperor Taizong, the Tang emperor ordered Li Ji, military governor of Bingzhou, and Li Jing, minister of war, to attack the Eastern Turks. One of the Turkish leaders, Toli Khan, surrendered in the following year. Another leader, Jili Khan, fled into the Tieshan Mountains but was pursued and captured. This completed the Tang's conquest of the Eastern Turkish state. By the year 646 the Tang Dynasty was in control of all the areas north and south of the Great Gobi. It set up the Anbei Administrative Region north of the desert and the Shanyi Administrative Region south of the desert, which had control over the military governorships in those regions. In 657, Emperor Gaozong dispatched a large army to attack Shaboluo Khan of the Western Turks. The army advanced in two columns, which joined forces at the Shuang River and totally defeated the Turkish leader who was captured while in flight. The Western Turks were subdued and their territory also became part of the Tang Empire. In 702, Empress Wu Zetian set up the Beiting Administrative Region with its seat at Tingzhou (now Jimusar county in the Xinjiang Uygur Autonomous Region). Together with the Anxi Administrative Region set up earlier, it administered the vast lands north and south of the Tianshan Range.

62. Long scroll in Uygur script Tang document, 30 cm high, 261 cm wide; unearthed at Turpan in the Xinjiang Uygur Autonomous Region. The Uygurs had close relations with the Tang during the Zhenguan reign of Emperor Taizong. Not only were economic and cultural

Map of the Beiting and Anbei Administrative Regions of the Tang Dynasty

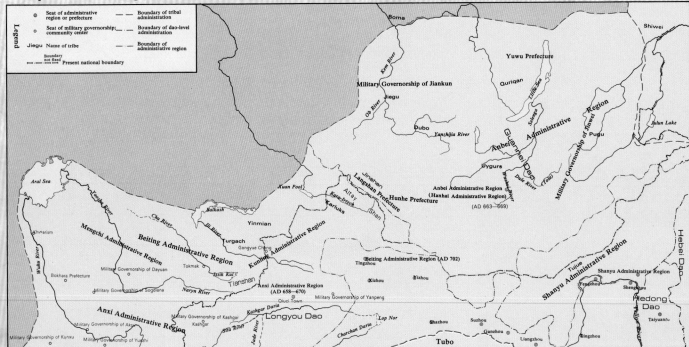

exchanges between them increasingly frequent; the Uygurs also ably assisted the Tang armies in defeating the Western Turks. By the time of the Kaiyuan reign of Emperor Xuanzong, the Uygur state had become quite powerful and the Tang emperor conferred on its chief the title of Huairen Khan. After the An-Shi rebellion, the Uygurs assisted the Tang in recovering the cities of Chang'an and Luoyang. During the Kaicheng reign of Emperor Wenzong, the Uygurs because of their internal disunity were defeated by Xiajia (a native of what is now Kirghistan) and forced to scatter. One group fled to Geluolu (south of Balkash Lake in central Asia), a second group to Anxi, an administrative region of the Tang, a third group to Hexi, or west of the Yellow River (now part of Gansu and Qinghai provinces), and a fourth group to south of what is now the Inner Mongolia Autonomous Region and northwestern

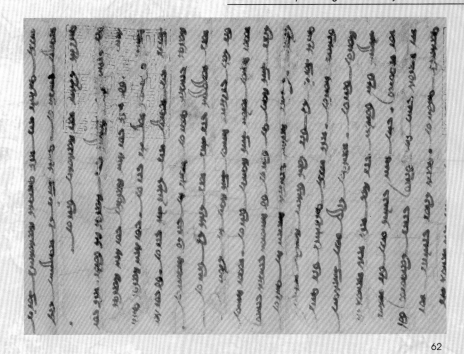

62

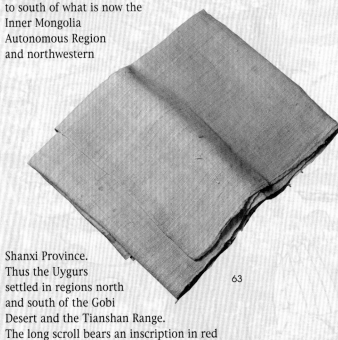

63

Shanxi Province. Thus the Uygurs settled in regions north and south of the Gobi Desert and the Tianshan Range. The long scroll bears an inscription in red ink. It mentions the Zhongshu Sheng (Legislative Council) and contains the seals of prime ministers, suggesting that the Uygurs had copied the administrative system of the Tang in setting up three councils and six ministries with the heads of the three councils as prime ministers.

63. Linen Tang material for clothing, 58.9 cm wide; unearthed at Turpan, Xinjiang Uygur Autonomous Region, in 1967. It is a piece of plain cloth with a close texture. Most of the linen fabrics unearthed at Turpan were for making clothes; some were used to pay *yong* (labor) and *diao* (household) taxes, as well as transport charges which peasants in those days had to bear.

64. Linen shoes Tang articles of daily use, 25 cm long; unearthed at Turpan, Xinjiang Uygur Autonomous Region, in 1972. The soles were made of thread twisted into yarn and twined together. The uppers were woven of thin thread, with strings attached to lace the shoes. Such shoes were not only soft and light and comfortable but looked very nice on the feet. According to documentary records, during the Kaiyuan reign of Emperor Xuanzong women considered it fashionable to wear such shoes, which moreover enabled them to move about more easily.

64

65. Cotton Tang raw material for weaving cloth; unearthed at Maral Bashi, Xinjiang Uygur Autonomous Region, in 1959. Cotton was first cultivated in the southern, southwestern and northwestern parts of China. Cotton cloth in its natural color was called *baidie* or *baixie* in ancient times. According to written records, *baidie* cloth was sold in the markets of Chang'an during Emperor Xuanzong's time. It is said that during Emperor Wenzong's reign, Xiahou Zi, a councillor, used to go to court dressed in green Guiguan clothes, which he said was thick and kept him warm. Guiguan cloth was cotton fabric made in the Guiguan region of Lingnan in southern China. The cotton balls shown here were found in a stratum that dates from the late Tang (c. 9th century) in what is now the Xinjiang Uygur Autonomous Region. A quantity of cotton seeds were unearthed at the same place, providing additional evidence that cotton was grown in Xinjiang during the Tang Dynasty.

65

66. Checked cotton cloth Tang material for making clothes, 33 cm long, 10 cm wide; unearthed at Maral Bashi, Xinjiang Uygur Autonomous Region, in 1959. This strip of cloth consists of two layers, folded and sewn together roughly at the two ends and along one side, with what appears to be a rip in its lower part. It was discovered in a stratum that dates from the late Tang (c. 9th century). A quantity of cotton seeds and fabrics with blue-and-white patterns were discovered at the same place. Weaving blue squares on a white background was apparently done with locally produced cotton on a vertical loom. This kind of loom and technique of weaving is still being used in some parts of southern Xinjiang today.

66

67. *Jiaozi* (dumplings) and other delicacies Tang foods; unearthed at Turpan, Xinjiang Uygur Autonomous Region, in 1972. Relics dating from the Tang Dynasty unearthed in the Turpan region included the remains of household registries, forms for filing lawsuits, official documents, old books such as the *Confucian Analests* and *Shennong's Manual of Materia Medica*, and various kinds of silk fabrics. These provide material evidence that the Tang government had implemented the equal land system and the *zu-diao* (land-household) system of taxation there. The techniques of farm production and of silk-weaving and -dyeing of the Central Plains and the traditional culture of the Han people had spread to the vast lands of Xinjiang. The discovery of *jiaozi* and other kinds of Han delicacies in Turpan provides yet another example of the mutual influence on life styles between Xinjiang and the interior.

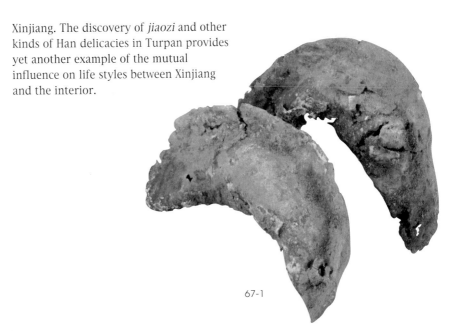

67-1

67-2

69. Pottery jar with circles painted in red   Tang funerary object, height 7 cm, mouth diameter 5.7 cm, base diameter 5.7 cm; unearthed at Turpan in the Xinjiang Uygur Autonomous Region. This pottery jar of bluish gray has a thick lip that curves outward and a bulging drumlike belly. Painted on the outside are irregular circles in red. The color of the pottery and the shape of the jar are very similar to jars generally used by the Han people. But the circles in red on the outside are an artistic feature peculiar to ethnic minorities of the Western Regions.

70. Brick with epitaph for Kangbo Miti, mother of Zhainuo Ninghun   Tang relic, 36.6 cm long, 36 cm wide, 5.9 cm thick. On the brick are four lines of Chinese characters in ink, which read from top to bottom and left to right. They say that the epitaph was written by Zhainuo Ninghun on the tomb of his mother Kangbo Miti on the 30th day of the fourth month of the first year of the reign titled Weilinde. The epitaph was found in an ancient cemetery at Astana, Turpan. It was the first epitaph to be discovered that was written in the Han language by a

68

68. Pottery bowl with painted patterns in red   Tang funerary object, height 9.5 cm, mouth diameter 15.3 cm, base diameter 8 cm; unearthed in the Xinjiang Uygur Autonomous Region. The bowl has a bluish gray background. Its sides are straight at the top, then curve inward gradually down to the ring base. Just under the mouth is a vermilion ring, and below the ring is a pattern of inverted V's and thick irregular red lines. There are white dots on the walls inside and outside, caused by impurities in the raw material which contained grains of sand.

69

70

member of an ethnic minority of the Western Regions. The script followed the Han style of writing from top to bottom, but preserved the local style of reading from left to right—a good example of the interflow of culture between the Hans and the northwestern ethnic minori-ties during the Tang Dynasty.

71. Basin with images of birds and animals, and legs like hooves
Funerary object of Tang, height 15.9 cm, mouth diameter 25.8 cm, base diameter 17.5 cm; unearthed at Turpan in the Xinjiang Uygur Autonomous Region. This is a circular basin with a

bluish gray background and a flat top. Inside are thin lines made by rotating. Parts of the outside are painted black. The smooth roughcast is coated with a layer of fine clay, on which are carved relief images of dragons, apes, tigers, horses, oxen and lions. Some of these figures are depicted seated on the ground clasping their knees; some are portrayed leaping into the air; some are strolling leisurely; and some appear to be flapping their wings. The spaces between the birds and beasts are filled with circular objects. The three legs of the basin are the front parts of three animals standing on their feet, an indication that the basin is supported by three animals. Basins like this with legs resembling animal hooves have been found at Kucha and Khotan in Xinjiang. They were usually placed at the head or feet of the dead. No more than one or two such basins were buried in one grave; apparently they were funerary objects made only for people of distinction.

71

72

72. Bronze image of warrior Tang funerary object, 4.5 cm tall; unearthed at Turpan in the Xinjiang Uygur Autonomous Region, in 1958. The warrior wears a pointed helmet and is clad in a suit of armor. His left hand is extended forward, his right hand raised, and his two feet are planted firmly as if poised for a fight. A vivid and clever portrayal, it is a reflection of the skill of craftsmen of the Xinjiang minorities.

73. *Tongbao* coin of the Kaiyuan reign Tang money, 2.3 cm in diameter; unearthed at Turpan in the Xinjiang Uygur Autonomous Region. The legend on it is in *lishu* (official script) with characters in thick, sturdy strokes. Found together with a Persian silver coin in the same tomb, it is evidence of the important role of Gaochang (ancient town near present-day Turpan) in East-West economic and cultural exchange in those days.

73

74

74. *Baoxianghua* double-wheel bronze mirror   Tang article of daily use, 10.3 cm in diameter and 1 cm thick; unearthed at Hami County in the Xinjiang Uygur Autonomous Region. On the back of the mirror are two raised circles resembling wheels. Between the two is an inscription that reads in translation: "Clean flowers, clear moon, *baoxianghua* bronze mirror." At the center of the mirror is a round knob with a hole, through which a string can be passed for hanging up the mirror. A *baoxianghua* is an artistic representation of natural flowers, chiefly the lotus. *Baoxianghua* mirrors with inscriptions were common during the Sui and early Tang. According to historic records, they were made in Yangzhou and presented as tributes to the emperor. The one shown here must have been taken from the interior of the country to minority regions in the west. It is another example of the economic and cultural interchange between the Hans and ethnic minorities.

Tubos

In ancient times the Tubos, ancestors of the Tibetan people, inhabited the Tibetan Plateau. Originally they were a branch of the Qiang tribe. During the Tang Dynasty, Tubo Tsanpo (King) Songtsan Gampo unified the Tibetan Plateau and established the Tubo Dynasty with its capital at Luosuo (present-day Lhasa). In 641 Songtsan Gampo married Princess Wencheng of the Tang royal family, and in 649 Emperor Gaozong of Tang conferred on Songtsan Gampo the titles of Fuma Duwei (an official rank) and Prince of the Western Regions. Thereafter, when a new Tsanpo succeeded to the throne, he had to receive conferment from the government of Tang. The close intercourse between the Hans and the Tibetans helped promote social and economic development on both sides.

75. Imperial sedan-chair Tang Dynasty scroll painting by Yan Liben, 38.5 cm high, 129.6 cm long. The painting depicts Tang emperor Taizong receiving Mgar Stongbtsan, a Tubo envoy, who came to Chang'an, the Tang capital, on the order of Songtsan Gampo to propose a marriage. On the right side of the painting is Emperor Taizong sitting on an imperial sedan-chair, dignified and composed. Around him are palace maids, some carrying or supporting the sedan-chair, others holding big fans and an open umbrella. On the left side of the painting is the court official of rites, wearing a round collar in red and holding a jade tablet, escorting the envoy to the emperor. The envoy (second left), wearing a brocade dress with narrow sleeves, is standing there with his hands cupped. The third person is another court official accompanying the guest. Princess Wencheng (c.625-680), after her marriage to Songtsan Gampo, introduced to the Tubos many products and techniques of the Central Plains, such as seeds, medicine, astronomy, the calendar, silkworm breeding, spinning and weaving, paper-making, building, millstone-making and brewing. The Tubos, on their part, sent medicinal herbs and horses to the country's interior.

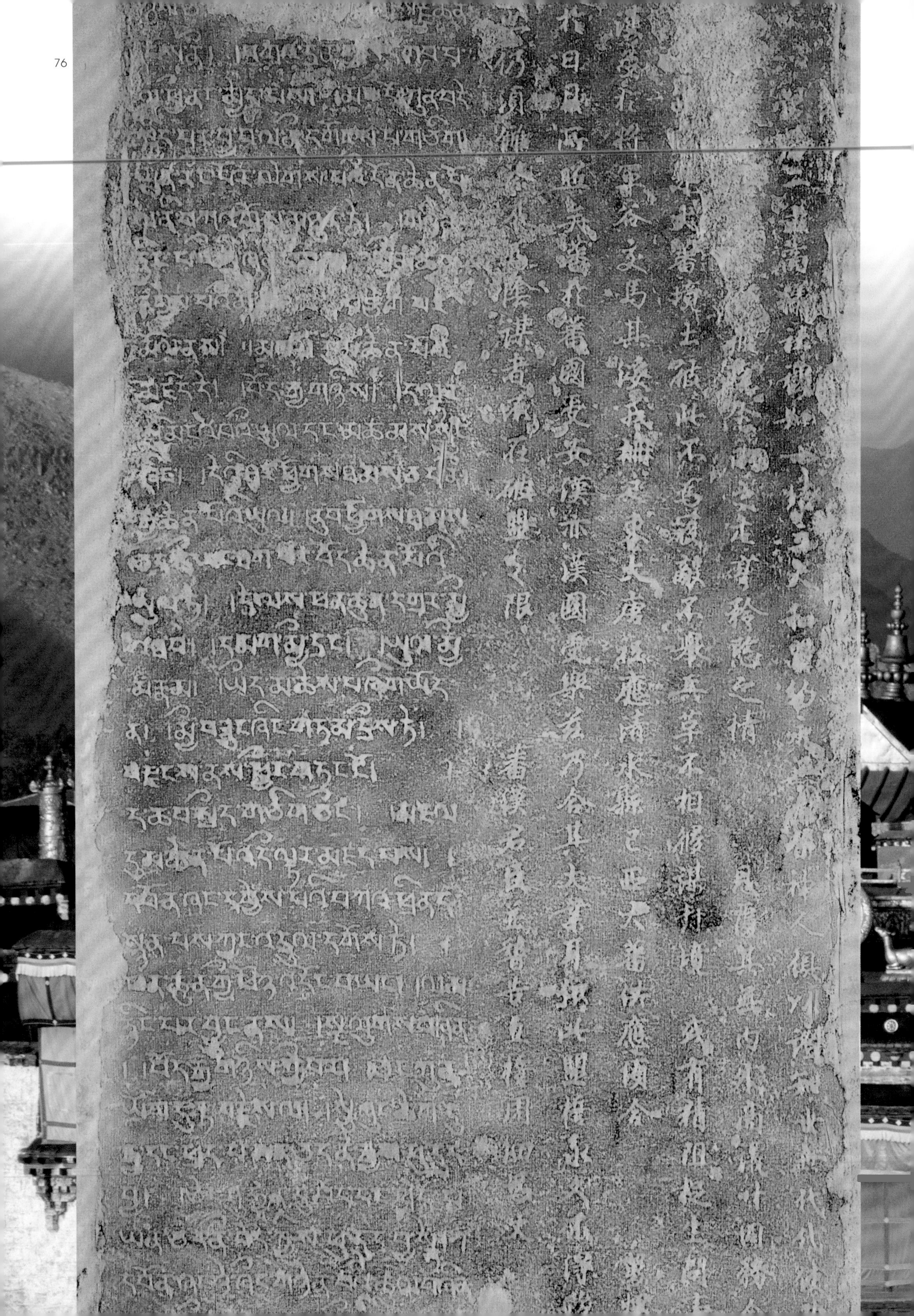

76. Rubbing from the Tang-Bo Alliance Tablet (section)   Relic of the Tang Dynasty, 4.76 meters tall and 0.95 meter wide. The original tablet stands in front of the Jokhang Monastery in Lhasa, Tibet Autonomous Region. The Tang-Bo Alliance Tablet is also called the Changqing Tablet or Uncle-Nephew Alliance Tablet. It was erected in 823 (third year of Tang emperor Muzong's reign titled Changqing) by Tubo Tsanpo Tritsug Detsan to commemorate the alliance between the Tang and Tubo formed during the first and second years of Changqing. The tablet, inscribed in Han and Tibetan scripts, records the full text of the Tang-Bo Alliance and the names and titles of officials who were present. As Tubo Tsanpo Songtsan Gampo and Tride Tsugtan married the Tang princesses Wencheng and Jincheng respectively, Tubo Tsanpo Tritsug Detsan acknowledged himself as nephew of the Tang emperor Muzong, whom he called the emperor uncle. The inscription on the tablet stresses "cooperation between the two sides as a single entity" and "the intimate feelings between uncle and nephew." It is evidence of the long-standing and close relationship between the Hans and Tibetans.

Bohai

During the Tang Dynasty, the Mohe was the chief tribe inhabiting areas along the Songhua River, lower reaches of the Heilongjiang River and upper reaches of the Tumen River in northeastern China. The Mohe comprised several dozen groups, of which the Heishui and Sumo were the most powerful. The Tang government set up an administrative office in this region and conferred on the tribal chieftain the title of governor. In 713, the first year of the Kaiyuan reign of the Tang Dynasty, Dazuorong, chief of the Sumo group, was given the titles Grand General of Zuoraowei, Prince of Bohai, and Governor of Huohanzhou. Subsequently, the area administered by the Sumo was named Bohai. The governor of Bohai was enthusiastic in assimilating the advanced production techniques and culture of the Central Plains, frequently despatching people there to study and attend imperial examinations.

77

78. Green glazed beast-head Structural part of a Tang building; height of remnant, 26.5 cm; unearthed from the ruins of Longquanfu, Upper Capital of Bohai, Ning'an County, Heilongjiang Province. The beast-head is green on the outside; it has an open mouth, a tongue sticking out, four sharp canine teeth turned outwards, two eyes wide open and two ears rolled upwards. There are two horns on the back of its head. The inside parts of the mouth and ears are yellow.

77. Remnant of a brick bearing the Chinese characters for "Upper Capital"
Building material of Tang, 14.5 cm long, 18.8 cm wide, 4.3 cm thick; unearthed from the ruins of Longquanfu, the Upper Capital of Bohai, Ning'an County, Heilongjiang Province. This is the remnant of a pottery brick, which may be of some reference value to the study of the architecture and brick-making techniques of the Upper Capital of Bohai.
Longquanfu, the Upper Capital, was one of the five capitals of Bohai; its layout closely resembled that of Chang'an of the Sui and Tang dynasties. Actually, it was designed and modeled after the layout of Chang'an city of the Tang.

78-1

79

79. Glazed ridge-end ornament

Structural part of a Tang building, remnant 8l cm long, 36 cm wide; unearthed near the site of a temple in the eastern part of the Upper Capital of Bohai, Ning'an County, Heilongjiang Province. In the Tang Dynasty, the roofs of all palatial and Buddhist halls in the Central Plains were covered with flat tiles, face upwards or downwards. The ridges were decorated with yellow and green glazed articles, and at each end of the main ridge of a building was a big glazed ornament, placed there to make the building more attractive. This folding-fan-shaped, green-glazed piece is evidently a ridge-end ornament on the roof of a hall.

80. Square brick with peony design

Building material of Tang, 39 cm square and 5 cm thick; unearthed from the ruins of Longquanfu, Upper Capital of Bohai, Ning'an County, Heilongjiang Province. In the center of the brick is a peony design with petals spread out. At each of the four corners and four sides is also a peony, with a curved branch. To the Chinese people, the peony is a symbol of riches and honor. It was held in high esteem by the Tang imperial court, which is why peony designs

appeared on so many old Tang buildings, a reflection of the fashion of the time, and even spread to faraway Bohai.

80

81-2

81. Tile bearing right-falling stroke similar to that in the character "保"

Building material of Tang, 43.1 cm long and 8.3 cm high; unearthed from the ruins of Longquanfu, Upper Capital of Bohai, Ning'an County, Heilongjiang Province. The tile shown here is hard and black. On the upper left is a right-falling stroke similar to that in the character "保" (*bao*, protection). The color and shape of the tile is very similar to a polished black semi-cylindrical tile of the Tang Dynasty. On the edges of the tile are more right-falling strokes.

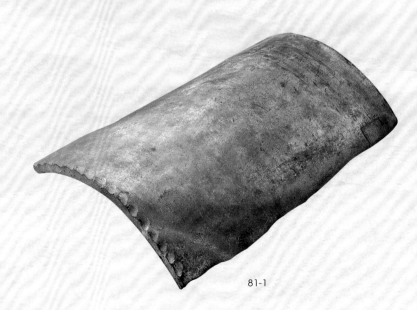

81-1

Nanzhao, or South Zhao

During the Tang Dynasty, there were many minority tribes living in areas in southwestern China, such as the Baiman (ancestors of the Bai nationality), Wuman (ancestors of the Yi, Naxi and Lisu nationalities), Heman (ancestors of the Hani nationality), and Jinchi and Yinchi (ancestors of the Dai nationality). The Wuman comprised six slave-owning groups known as the Six Zhaos, Zhao meaning "prince" or "princedom." Among the Six Zhaos, the Mengshe Zhao inhabited the southeastern part of present-day Weishan County. As this was the southernmost part of the region, Mengshe Zhao was also called Nanzhao, or South Zhao. With the support of the Tang court, Nanzhao unified the Six Zhaos. In 738 the Tang government conferred on Biluoge, the chieftain of Nanzhao, the title Prince of Yunnan. Nanzhao then moved its capital to Taihe (south of present-day Dali, Yunnan Province) and formally set up its regime. It was fairly well developed in agriculture and handicraft, maintained political, economic and cultural ties with the Tang government, and constantly sent students to study in the interior. Introduction of the advanced production techniques and culture of the Han, especially Tang painting and architectural art, into Nanzhao had a far-reaching impact on the latter.

82-1

82-2

82. Tile with characters Building material of Tang, remnant 17.3 cm long; unearthed from the ruins of Nanzhao, in Longyushan, Weishan County, Yunnan Province, in 1958. This is a pottery tile, hard and bluish gray. The two characters "寬愼" were impressed on it. They look like Han script, but actually were not. They are similar to the characters on some of the other tiles unearthed at the site of Taihe, capital of Nanzhao. Therefore, it is quite certain that they were products of the same period. Studies show that the characters are in the Bai script of Nanzhao, which resembles Han script.

83. Remnant of square floor tile Building material of Tang; unearthed from the ruins of Nanzhao, Longweishan, Weishan County, Yunnan Province, in 1958. This is a pottery square floor tile in blue. In the center of the tile is a lotus design with interlocking flowers on the four sides. The pattern and design are very similar to the tiles unearthed from Daming Palace and Xingqing Palace in Chang'an City of the Tang Dynasty. It was a floor tile used in an imperial palace.

84. Drip tile Building material of Tang, remnant length 17.3 cm, height 9.1 cm; unearthed from the ruins of Nanzhao, Longweishan, Weishan County, Yunnan Province, in 1958. This pottery tile is bluish gray, with a cloud or whorl pattern and nipples along the sides.

85. Tile-end with lotus design Building material of Tang, diameter of remnant 14 cm; unearthed from the ruins of Nanzhao, Longweishan, Weishan County, Yunnan Province, in 1958. This pottery tile-end is bluish gray. Nanzhao sent many students to study in Chengdu, Sichuan Province, and it also invited Han people to teach in Nanzhao. Large

83

85

numbers of Han peasants and craftsmen went there. Consequently, Nanzhao's cities and towns generally followed Han patterns and many of its buildings were built with the help of Han workers. The lotus design on the tile-end shown here is identical to that on tile-ends in the Central Plains, evidence of the exchange and mergence of culture and technique between the Han people and the minorities in Yunnan.

84

Economy

Social economy was on the wane during the early years of the Tang Dynasty. But the equal land and *zu-yong-diao* (land-labor-household) tax systems which the Tang government continued to implement helped to rehabilitate the peasantry and boost agricultural production. The government also eased control over commerce and the handicrafts to encourage their development. Additionally, intercourse among the various nationalities in the country and their frequent exchanges with foreign countries injected new life into Tang society. The result was a relatively long period of national unity and social stability, which ushered in an era of unprecedented prosperity for the feudal economy.

Agriculture

Improvements in farm tools and their utilization in line with local conditions were important factors in the development of agricultural production in the Tang Dynasty. Improvements in plow-making, wide use of water wheels in irrigation, and the development of water conservancy and water irrigation were clear indications of progress in farming. The expansion of cultivated land, increase of intensively-cultivated land and popularization of the three-crops-in-two-years practice helped to raise the output of land and increase grain yields, which in turn created conditions for the development of cash crops, notably the planting of mulberry, raising of silkworms and tea culture in the south.

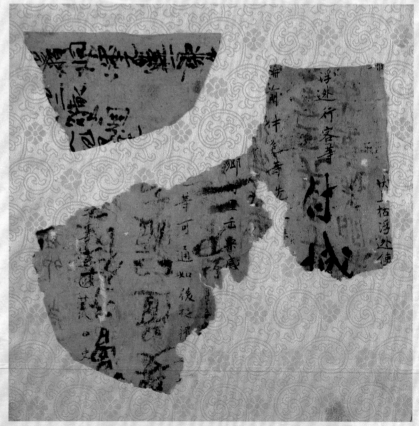

86. Census official's document Relic of Tang, remnant 20.5 cm long; unearthed in Turpan, Xinjiang Uygur Autonomous Region. The document, most of which is lost, was about peasants fleeing from home. It contained new characters initiated by Empress Wu Zetian. According to history books, between 701 and 704, or during Empress Wu's reign titled Chang'an, the empress sent an envoy on a mission to check up on runaways whose names were missing from the country's household registry. How to deal with the runaways was an important political and economic issue. Thanks to the lenient policy toward runaways during the reign of Wu Zetian, the number of registered households increased considerably. This conduced to a relatively stable society and had a positive effect on the development of agriculture.

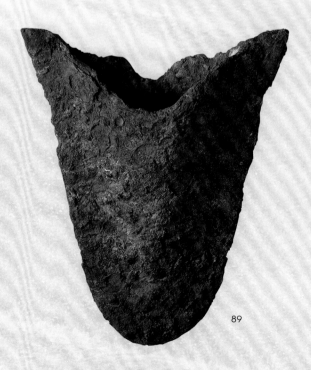

87. Iron plowshare Farm tool of Tang, 17.5 cm long and 28.5 cm wide; unearthed from a Tang tomb in Sanmenxia, Henan Province.

88. Iron sickle Farm tool of Tang, 30 cm long, 3.4 cm wide; unearthed from a Tang tomb in Sanmenxia, Henan Province.

89. Iron plowshare Farm tool of Tang, 28 cm long, 21.4 cm wide; unearthed in Tianzhen County, Shanxi Province. In the Tang Dynasty, plows varied greatly in different areas. In his book *The Classic of Plows*, Lu Guimeng of the Tang Dynasty wrote that a plow in Jiangdong was composed of 11 parts, well structured and well proportioned. It was easy to turn up the earth and regulate the depth of the penetration into the soil with such a plow. The plowshare shown here is in the shape of a triangle, with a ridge along the middle and two protruding wings. It is a sharp tool with a width greater than the length. Plowshares shaped like isosceles triangles have been unearthed in other places; some are small with a pointed tip and can be fitted with a long handle. Shares like these when fitted with wooden handles can also be used like spades.

90. Water wheel Illustration from the *Book of Agriculture* by Wang Zhen. The wheel resembles a big spinning wheel. It was placed upright in the water close to a riverbank, with many small buckets attached to the rim. Driven by the current, the wheel rotated ceaselessly day and night. The buckets when immersed in water were filled automatically, and when rotated to a higher position discharged their contents into a tube that led to fields nearby. A contrivance like this not only saved labor but enabled fields to be irrigated continuously.

91. Water wheel on high ground Illustration from the *Book of Agriculture* by Wang Zhen. This water wheel was rotated by animal or man power. An important aspect of the development of agriculture in the Tang Dynasty was the wide use of water wheels to irrigate farmland. Various types of water wheels with different driving forces were made according to the terrain. High-ground water wheels were used at places where

the bank of the river was much higher than the water level. Two wheels had to be used, one placed on the bank and the other in the water. They were linked by a rope, on which were tied the water buckets. The wheel on the bank was rotated by man or animal power, and by means of the rope it caused the wheel in the water to rotate too, drawing the buckets into the water and filling them. By the same process, the filled buckets were returned to the bank where they emptied their contents automatically.

92. Rubbing from an inscribed brick in Hanjia Granary Tang Dynasty; the original brick was unearthed from Pit No.19 at the ruins of the Hanjia Granary, Luoyang, Henan Province, in 1971. It was inscribed and placed in the pit when the grain was stored, and it recorded the variety of the grain, its origin and quantity, the date, and the location of the pit. From what has been uncovered so far by drilling, there were more than 400 pits in the Hanjia Granary. Of the extant pits,

the one with the biggest opening has a mouth 18 meters wide and the greatest depth is 12 meters. One pit still contained over 250 tons of millet. Inscribed bricks were found in most of the 14 pits that have been excavated. Discovery of these pits show that large quantities of grain were under the direct control of the Tang royal court. It also shows the development of agriculture and the convenience of water transportation at the time.

93. Pottery millstones, roller, tilt hammer and well head Funerary objects of Tang; millstone 12.1 cm high, base diameter 12.65 cm; roller diameter 10.6 cm; tilt hammer length 30.5 cm, height 13 cm; well head length 7.7 cm. All were unearthed from the tomb of Wang Chen of Changzhi, Shanxi Province, in 1954. Four categories of funerary objects of the Tang Dynasty were generally called "tomb figurines". They comprised: (a) means of transportation, (b) furniture, (c) daily necessities (including domestic animals and fowls) and (d) tomb-

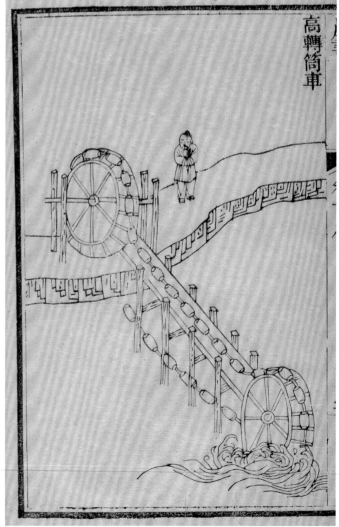

guards. The millstone, roller and tilt-hammer were related to grain processing, while the well head symbolized a well; all these were articles used in the kitchen. Burial of daily necessities as funerary objects was a custom handed down from the Han Dynasty through the Three Kingdoms, the two Jin dynasties and the Southern and Northern Dynasties. This tomb belongs to the period of Emperor Gaozong of Tang (650–683). Though small and exquisite in size, the buried objects form a complete set that shows indirectly how grain was processed in the Tang Dynasty.

92

93

Handicrafts

The development of agriculture in the Tang Dynasty provided a material basis for the development of the handicraft industry. The change of mechanism within the industry and the improvement of production techniques prepared the conditions for its further development. Government-owned handicrafts maintained a dominant position. They were large in scale, precise in their division of labor, had an abundance of raw materials and a large work force, and therefore could produce many fine artworks. Private handicrafts also prospered, though more gradually, during this time as privately owned workshops appeared in the cities. Some of the trades mentioned in historical writings were private handicrafts. These together with farming were a traditional feature of the Tang economy.

94. Celadon gourd-shaped jar
Container of the Tang Dynasty, height 17.6 cm, mouth diameter 2 cm, bottom diameter 7.4 cm; unearthed from a Tang tomb in Shaan County, Henan Province, in 1956. This gourd-shaped jar is unique in pattern and lustrously glazed. In the Tang Dynasty, celadons were produced mainly in kilns in south China, such as the Yue Kiln, Dingzhou Kiln, Wuzhou Kiln, Yuezhou Kiln,

95-1

Shouzhou Kiln and Hongzhou Kiln.
Except for the Dingzhou Kiln, the
sites of all these kilns have been
discovered, including the Tongchuan
Kiln which has not been recorded in
historical documents. In the Tang
Dynasty, the areas around present-
day Jinhua, Zhejiang Province,
belonged to the Wuzhou prefecture
where celadons were mostly
produced for the people's daily use.
They were usually of inferior quality.
The Yuezhou Kiln was located in
present-day Xiangyin County, Hunan
Province. Most of its celadon
products were glazed in bluish green.
The Hongzhou Kiln was located in
present-day Fengcheng County,
Jiangxi Province, and its main
products were bowls and cups glazed
in yellowish brown or brown. Its
celadon was rather coarse.

95. Celadon vase, Yue ware

Container of Tang, height 30.5 cm,
mouth diameter 19.3 cm; unearthed
from a Tang tomb in Yuyao County,
Zhejiang Province, in 1957. The vase
is glazed in yellow. On its belly is an
inscription of 43 characters, which

includes "fourth year of
Dazhong" and surnames.
Celadon wares made in
the Yue Kiln were the best
in the Tang Dynasty; in
the words of connoisseurs,
they were "as beautiful as
ice and snow," topping
products made in all the
other kilns.The Yue Kiln was
located in the vicinity of
present-day Shanglin Lake of
Cixi, Zhejiang Province. It
produced a great variety of
objects, with close texture and
smooth glaze. They were
bluish green and lustrous.
Their designs were mostly
incised; some were impressed or
carved. Most of the Yue Kiln
celadon wares were made
for export. Their remains
have been discovered among ancient
ruins in many countries and regions.
The inscription on this vase was
carved on the body before the vase
was glazed and fired. It is a Yue Kiln
ware with distinctive characteristics,
made over 1,100 years ago.

95-2

96-2

96. Celadon jar with two hornless-dragon ears Container of Tang, height 60.8 cm, mouth diameter 12 cm, bottom diameter 15.5 cm. The patterns of some porcelain wares of the Tang Dynasty were influenced by Persian culture, such as the phoenix-head pot and two-dragon-ears vase, which were popular in the early Tang. They possessed the characteristics of foreign vases. The jar shown here is an early Tang ware.

97. "Secret color" porcelain bowl Food vessel of the Tang Dynasty, height 7.1 cm, mouth diameter 25 cm; unearthed from a shrine in Famen Temple, Fufeng County, Shaanxi Province, in 1987. It is said that the Famen Temple was first built in the Eastern Han. Additions were made in the Tang Dynasty. They included the stupa of the Huguo Dharmakaya and a shrine called a terrestrial palace housing Buddhist relics. Many of the relics in the palace were enshrined by Tang royal families. Among them, the "secret color" porcelain wares were products of the Yue Kiln made for exclusive use in the imperial palace. As the glaze color and shapes of the objects were unknown to most people, they were called "secret color" wares. Actually they were glazed in a misty bluish green, mixed with powdered agate, which produced a translucent and lustrous surface. 18 other objects were unearthed along with the porcelain bowl shown here; they included vases, bowls, plates and dishes. Most of them have been categorized as "secret color" porcelain. As the terrestrial palace was closed indefinitely in 874, 15th year of the Xiantong reign of the Tang Dynasty, "secret color" porcelains must have been made not later than the Xiantong years.

98

98. White porcelain vase with long neck Container of the Tang Dynasty, height 22.2 cm, mouth diameter 6.9 cm, bottom diameter 7.2 cm; unearthed from a Tang tomb in Shaan County, Henan Province, in 1957. In the Tang Dynasty, white porcelain articles were produced mainly in northern China. Those fired in the Xing kilns, in today's Lincheng and Neiqiu counties, Hebei Province, represented the finest products of the time. Their white porcelain articles glistened like snow or silver, and emitted a clear and melodious metallic sound when tapped. Kilns in Gong County, Henan Province, also produced white porcelain in impressive numbers and variety over a long period of time. Production was at its height in the eighth century. Relics of the Gong County kilns have been discovered among the ruins of Daming Palace and Western City of the Tang Dynasty in present-day Xi'an. The Quyang kilns in Hebei began firing white porcelain at a later date; their products were noted for their lily white bodies and lustrously white glaze. The Quyang kilns replaced the Xing kilns in late Tang. The white porcelain vase with long neck shown here is a rare object among the porcelain wares of the Tang Dynasty.

99. White porcelain spittoon Hygienic vessel of Tang, height 16.5 cm; unearthed from a Tang tomb in Shaan County, Henan Province. Spittoons were quite common in the Tang Dynasty. Those used by officials and aristocrats were very precious vessels; some were even made of gold. This white porcelain spittoon has a close-textured body with a lustrous, snow-white glaze. Exquisitely made, it is a nice-looking object to hold in the hand.

99

100. White porcelain lamp Lighting device of Tang, 30.5 cm tall; unearthed from a Tang tomb in Shaan County, Henan Province, in 1956. During the Warring States and the Qin and Han periods, lamps were mostly made of copper or pottery. Porcelain lamps became popular during the Wei and Jin. White porcelain made during the Northern Dynasties (AD420-581) was white but with a tinge of blue; it was still at an early stage. But the technique of making white porcelain improved appreciably during the Tang. The raw material used for making this white porcelain lamp was of very high quality, the workmanship is superb, and the glaze lustrous. The whole piece resembles a white jade lamp with a sturdy and well-balanced appearance.

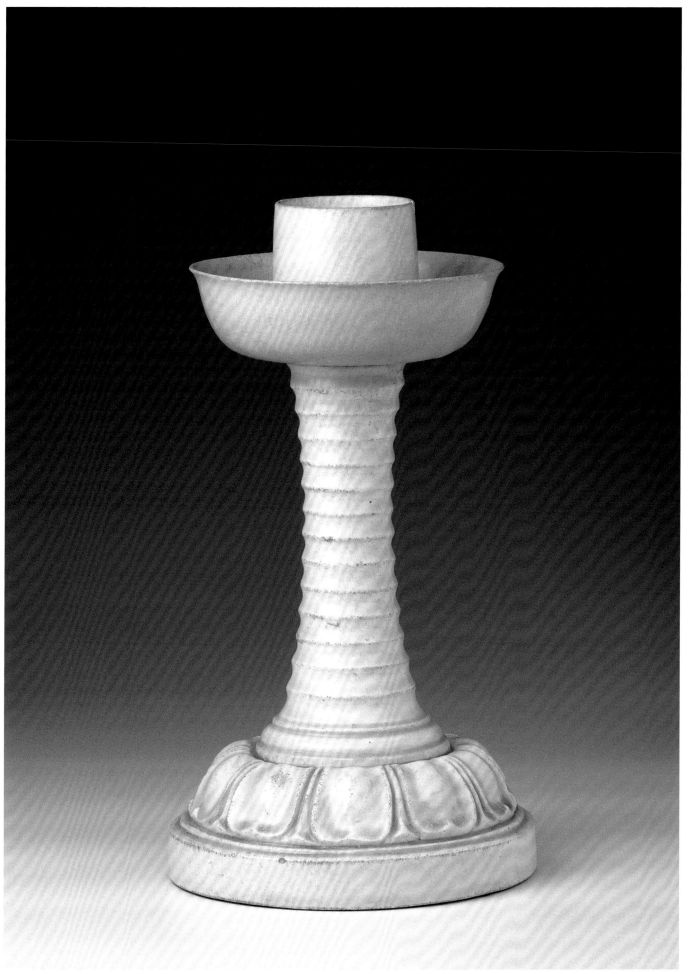

101. Porcelain pillow made with two-color twisted clay   Article for daily use, Tang Dynasty, height 7.7 cm, length 14.7 cm, width 10 cm; unearthed from a Tang tomb in Shaan County, Henan Province, in 1956. The pillow, a brick-shaped article decorated with a winding wood grain design, was a new and unique product of the Tang Dynasty. Its body was made of clay in two different colors, one dark, one light, twisted together, then glazed and fired. Shards of this kind of porcelain were discovered among the ruins of the kilns of Gong County, Yaozhou and Shouzhou. Articles made of such material unearthed from Tang tombs included cups, bowls, plates, jars and pillows. Rectangular pillows were most common. Documents record that wooden pillows with grain design were extremely beautiful, and porcelain pillows were made with wood grain design to simulate wooden pillows. A porcelain pillow made in this way is also called a "floral pillow".

102. Porcelain warmer, Shouzhou ware   Container of Tang, height 21.9 cm, mouth diameter 6.3 cm. It has a short neck and a straight belly resembling a tube. On its short spout is a six bowstring pattern. The whole vessel is covered with yellow glaze, under which are printed netlike designs. Shouzhou kilns were located in present-day Shangyao Town, Huainan, Anhui Province. Porcelains produced there were mostly glazed in yellow, done by firing in an outer flame. The flame was controlled in different ways to produce different shades of yellow, such as dark yellow, eel yellow and yellowish green. Usually, white clay was first applied to the surface of the body. Shouzhou wares included bowls, saggars, cups and water droppers, bowls being the most common.

103

103. Splash-glazed porcelain ewer   Water container of Tang, height 30.9 cm, bottom diameter 9.1 cm; unearthed from a Tang tomb in Shaan County, Henan Province, in 1956. Splash-glazed porcelain was made by splashing different tinges of glaze on the base glaze. The tinges were mostly sky blue or moon white, splashed on black, yellow or sky blue glaze. The craftsman who did this had to have a good command of the technique of mixing and applying glaze. This kind of porcelain, also called "floral porcelain" in Tang books, was the product of the Lushan Kiln. In the 1960's and 1970's kilns producing splash-glazed porcelain were discovered in Lushan, Neixiang, Jia and Yu counties of Henan Province and Jiaocheng of Shanxi Province. Vessels fired there included ewers, jars and waist drums. The making of splash-glazed porcelain was most popular during the mid-Tang. It was a new and significant achievement in ceramic production in the north.

104. Black glazed porcelain jar decorated with blue splashes   Container of Tang, height 38.3 cm, mouth diameter 16.1 cm. The jar is simple and solid in shape. It is covered with black glaze, on which are a few splashes of blue mixed with floating white, creating a smooth and natural appearance. This kind of porcelain was also called "Jun ware of Tang." The successful making of such porcelain during the Tang provided a sound technical basis for the production of the Jun ware and the maturity of splash-glazed porcelain in the Song Dynasty half a century later.

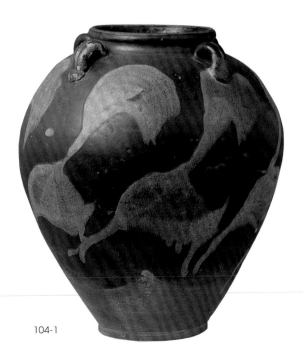

104-1

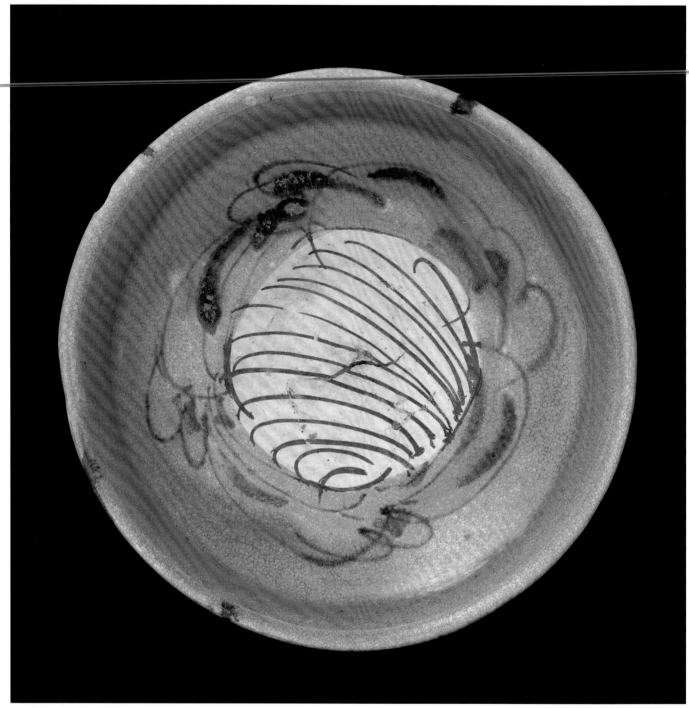

105-1

105-2

105. Bluish yellow glazed porcelain plate with orchid design   Food vessel of Tang, height 4.1 cm, mouth diameter 15.5 cm; unearthed at the site of the Tongguan Kiln in Changsha, Hunan Province, in 1978. The center of the plate is decorated with a round white figure, with brown orchids on and around it. The lines are smooth and curve freely. The Tongguan Kiln was located somewhere about 5 kilometers from present-day Tongguan Town and Shixu Lake in Wangcheng County, Henan Province. It was usually called the Changsha Kiln. There are no records of this kiln in any history books of the Tang Dynasty. It was not known until its

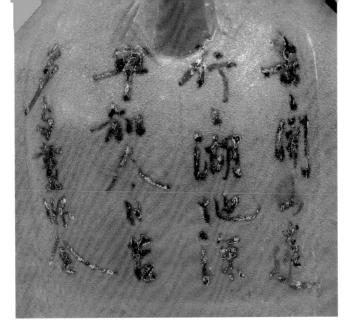

106-2

106-1

discovery in 1956, when people first learnt that it was a large kiln producing many varieties of porcelain with artistic features, and that it played an important role in the history of Chinese ceramics. The Tongguan Kiln was popular during the mid and late Tang Dynasty and its principal products were to meet the needs of daily life. It also produced porcelain stationery and sculptured toys. To avoid being formulistic, craftsmen made clever alterations in the mouths, necks, bellies, ears, handles or spouts of the vessels, creating new forms and patterns.

106. Blue glazed pottery ewer with poem inscribed in brown ink Container of Tang, height 19 cm, mouth diameter 9.5 cm, bottom diameter 9.5 cm; unearthed in Wangcheng County, Hunan Province, in 1983. Underglaze coloring was a major progress in the decorative technique of Chinese porcelain. The underglaze coloring in the Tongguan Kiln developed from pure brown to brown and green; its designs included human figures, birds and flowers, occult and auspicious beasts, and, in particular, inscribed poems, annotations and signatures, which were unique in style and enhanced the aesthetic value. Inscribed in brown ink on the belly of this ewer is a poem with five-character lines. Porcelain wares fired in the Tongguan Kiln were important export commodities in ancient China. They have been discovered time and again in coastal ports and on roads leading to the sea, as well as in Korea, Japan, and other countries and regions in southeastern and western Asia. On some of the wares are painted scenes of coconut trees, grapes, tigers and exotic dancers and musicians, which are in western Asian and Persian styles. Obviously they were designed to meet the aesthetic taste of foreign importers.

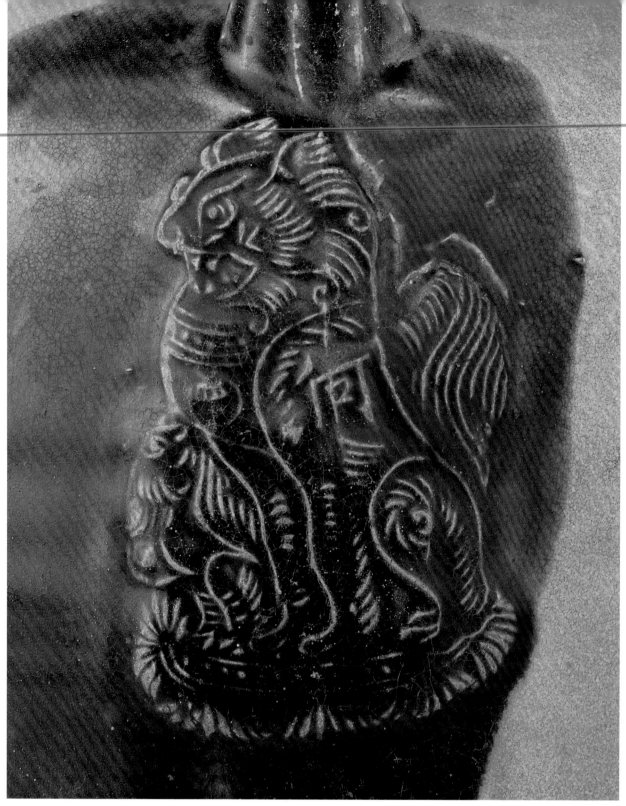

107. Yellow glazed porcelain ewer with applique designs of the character "何" in brown splashes Container of Tang, height 23.9 cm, mouth diameter 10.5 cm. Below the short spout and each of the two handles of this Tongguan Kiln ewer is a piece of brown glaze, on which is an applique stamped design of a mother lion and her cub and a cluster of leaves. All three designs bear the character "何". The underglaze coloring and applique stamped design show that products of the Tongguan Kiln had changed from stressing the beauty of glazed colors to painted decoration. To make an applique design, a mold must be made from an engraved pattern first. The design is stamped from this mold and then pasted on the body of the object. Sometimes a layer of brown glazed splashes is added before firing. The painting or design, protected by the layer of glaze, has a luster that never fades. The combination of color and convex applique design is very attractive.

108. Three-color glazed pottery rectangular cabinet Funerary object of Tang, 13.5 cm tall, 16 cm long, 12.1 cm wide; unearthed from a Tang tomb in Xi'an, Shaanxi Province, in 1955. This is a rare object among three-color glazed pottery ware, an imitation of a rectangular cabinet for daily use. A Tang three-color pottery object was made of china clay and coated with lead glaze. It was fired twice, the first time at a temperature of around 1100℃ before glazing. The biscuit was then painted and glazed and fired a second time to a temperature of 900℃. Although multicolored lead-glazed pottery had appeared in the Han Dynasty, its craftsmanship did not improve significantly until the Tang. Actually, so-called Tang three-color wares were not limited to three colors; they were multicolored objects. Using the technique of producing colors with metal oxides, craftsmen of the time mixed an appropriate amount of copper oxide with the glaze before firing to produce the color green. They mixed iron oxide with glaze to produce yellowish brown and cobalt oxide to produce blue. By applying the different mixtures alternately on the same object, they produced a variety of colors.

109. Blue glazed pottery donkey Funerary object of Tang, height 23.5 cm, length 26.5 cm; unearthed at Xiaotumen, Xi'an, Shaanxi Province, in 1956. On the donkey's back are a saddle, saddle blanket and reins. Its body is well proportioned. It appears to be in a moving posture, vivid and lifelike. The entire body, except the hooves, is covered with blue glaze, which is the most striking feature. Yellow, green and white were the three most common glaze colors of Tang three-color pottery; vessels in blue glaze were not common, and blue figures were even rarer. Blue glaze appeared during the prime Tang, and cobalt oxide was its principal ingredient. The appearance of blue glaze on Tang three-color pottery conduced to the use of blue and white glaze on Chinese porcelain in later periods.

110. Blue glazed pottery bowl Food vessel of Tang, height 4 cm, mouth diameter ll.5 cm, base diameter 4.6 cm; unearthed from a Tang tomb in Xi'an, Shaanxi Province, in 1955. Except for the base, the whole object is in blue glaze. The most common category of Tang three-color pottery are funerary objects. In fact, people used to believe that such pottery was not for practical uses. But among the increasing number of relics unearthed, a small number of Tang three-color pottery were definitely articles for daily use, such as bowls, plates, ewers, jars and cups for holding food and drink, inkstones and water droppers used in a study, and spittoons and incense burners. This blue glazed pottery bowl may have been an article for daily use.

110

111-2

111. Three-color twisted-paste pottery hunter on horseback

Funerary object of Tang, height 37 cm, length 27 cm; unearthed in Qian County, Shaanxi Province, in 1972. The object was made of twisted paste, a new technology in ceramic production in the Tang Dynasty. Most articles made of twisted paste were for daily use, and twisted-paste ornamental figurines like this one were rare. The hunter on horseback is holding an eagle as if about to feed it; there is a prey on the horse. Hunting was a fashionable activity among aristocrats in the Tang Dynasty, and it was a common theme of the Tang arts. This figurine was made by cutting into thin pieces a kneaded lump of two-colored china clay and sticking the pieces onto the pottery body, which was then glazed and fired. The workmanship was sophisticated and difficult, and articles made in this way were very valuable at the time.

112. Three-color ceramic pillow with flower-petal design

Funerary object of Tang, length 10.7 cm, width 8.7 cm, height 5.1 cm; unearthed from a Tang tomb in Luoyang, Henan Province, in 1987. China's ceramic pillows first appeared in the Sui Dynasty. The earliest pillow unearthed up to now is the one from Zhang Cheng's tomb in Anyany, Henan Province. The tomb dates back to 595, or the 15th year of the Kaihuang reign of the Sui Dynasty. Ceramic pillows since the Tang have been discovered in many places both in the north and the south. They include twisted-paste glazed pillows, three-color pillows, and blue and white porcelain pillows. As the size of the pillow shown here is small, some people think it was used as a hand-cushion by a Chinese traditional doctor when he was feeling a patient's pulse. Others hold that a ceramic pillow was unsuitable in clinical work, so it must have been a funerary object of an unusual size.

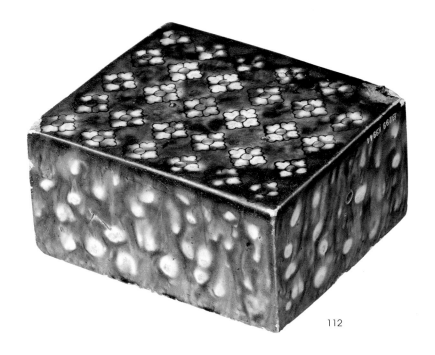

112

113. Three-color pottery horse Funerary object of Tang, height 54 cm, length 52.7 cm; unearthed from Xianyu Tinghai's tomb in Xi'an, Shaanxi Province, in 1957. The horse is white and has a saddle covered with a dark green blanket. Both its breast and its hindquarters are ornamented with belts strung with yellow flowers, from which hang golden bells. The colors contrast strikingly. Strong and vigorous in build, true to life in form, this is a vivid representation in miniature of a powerful saddle horse belonging to some high official or nobleman of the prime Tang. The modeling, coloring and glazing techniques of Tang three-color pottery created a new era in the history of Chinese ceramic technology. The horse shown here exemplifies the highest level of Tang pottery.

113-1

113-2

114-1

114. Silver plate with gilded lion design Food vessel of Tang, height 6.7 cm, mouth diameter 40 cm; unearthed northeast of Bafuzhuang, Xi'an, Shaanxi Province, in 1956. The term "silver plate with gilded design" appeared in books of the Tang Dynasty. Influenced by the gold and silver utensils of central and western Asia, silver plates decorated with gilded designs were very popular during the prime Tang (late 7th century to mid-8th century). From the mid-8th century to the early 9th century, handicraft industries making such plates were well developed in areas south of the Yangtze River. In the Tang Dynasty, common methods of processing gold and silver wares were cutting, polishing, welding, riveting, coating and carving. Simple hand-turned and foot-treadled lathes were in use, too. All these reflect the superb workmanship of making gold and silver wares at the time. This large silver plate is shaped like a sunflower. It has three legs and a single animal image in the center, with no designs around it. The rim of the plate is decorated with a loose flower design, a characteristic feature of silver plates with gilded designs during the prime Tang.

114-2

114-3

115-1

115-2

115. Ball-shaped gilded silver incense burner   Incense burner of Tang, diameter 4.8 cm; unearthed at Shapo Village, Xi'an, Shaanxi Province, in 1963. Ball-shaped incense burners were used to drive away insects and cleanse the air. When in use, they were usually hung at the side of an ox-cart or inside a mosquite net. Such a burner consists of two hemispheres, one above, the other below. Between the two is a clip for opening and closing the burner. Inside the lower hemisphere are two concentric rings and a small jar for holding incense. When in place, the axis of the jar and the diameter of the two rings intersect at right angles. The weight of the jar keeps it in a vertical position no matter how the ball turns, which prevents the incense from falling out. This principle is similar to that of the orientation device in a modern three-frame aero-gyroscope and its use in China over a thousand years ago deserves praise and admiration by people today. The outer shell of the burner is openwork, easy for smoke to disperse. There were many varieties of incense burners in ancient China, but none can surpass the fine workmanship of this ball-shaped silver incense burner of Tang.

116. Silver plate with gilded twin-fish design   Food vessel of Tang, height 3 cm, rim diameter 11.5 cm, base diameter 5.8 cm; unearthed in a cellar at Hejia Village, Xi'an, Shaanxi Province, in 1970. 265 pieces of gold and silver wares were unearthed in the cellar, an unprecedented discovery of such precious wares of Tang. Judging from the date, 19th year of the Kaiyuan reign, of the "silver coin paid for the *yong-diao* (labor and household) system of taxation in Jian'an" and the dates of other coins both Chinese and foreign unearthed from the same cellar, this batch of gold and silver wares must have been made during or before 756, the 15th year of the Tianbao reign of the Tang Dynasty. The plate shown here is one of the silver wares in the batch. The two fishes at the center are swimming in the same direction.

116-1

117. Silver bowl with gilded flower-and-bird design   Food vessel of Tang, height 4.3 cm, mouth diameter l5.5 cm, weight 203.1 grams. The mouth of this bowl is shaped like a sunflower. It has a flat belly and a ring foot. Its inside wall and bottom are engraved with gilded designs. On the bottom are two birds flying amidst flowers, encircled by bowstring, cord and flower-petal designs. The inside wall is decorated with patterns of jade pendants and gilded flowers and leaves, in pairs facing each other. Along the rim is a pattern of petals, alternately facing different directions.

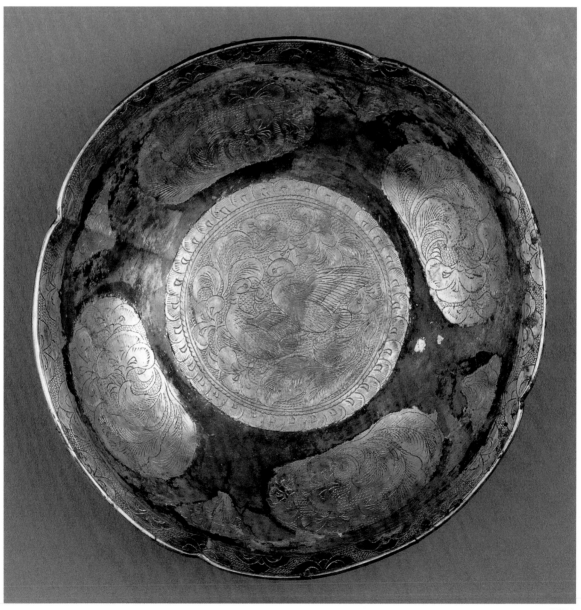

117-1

117-2 ▷

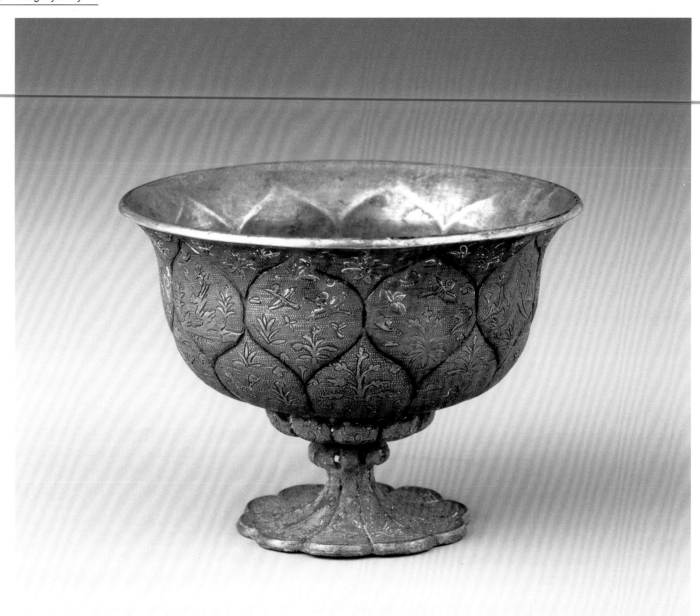

118

118. Silver stemmed cup with lotus-petal and bird design Wine vessel of Tang, height 5 cm, mouth diameter 7.2 cm; unearthed from a cellar at Shapo Village, Xi'an, Shaanxi Province, in 1963. The cup consists of two parts, upper and lower. The upper part is the body of the cup, which is shaped like a deep bowl. The lower part is the stem, which has a ring base and a disk above supporting the cup like a tray. In the middle of the stem is a joint shaped like the bead of an abacus. The base is shaped like a flower with nine petals, a pattern seldom seen on traditional Chinese tableware. Obviously, it was influenced by Western gold and silver wares. A total of 15 pieces of gold and silver ware were unearthed from the cellar at Shapo Village. Their style suggests they were made before the mid-eighth century.

119. Silver bowl Food container of Tang, height 7.6 cm, mouth diameter 17.7 cm, base diameter 9.2 cm; unearthed from a cellar at Hejia Village, Xi'an, Shaanxi Province, in 1970. The bowl has a seamed belly and plain surface. On the bottom of the cup are six characters written in ink which read in translation: "ll.l taels plus". The seamed belly was a popular model of Western pottery and gold and silver wares. It had a great effect on the shape of Chinese gold and silver wares. In the early eighth century, even some Chinese three-colored pottery articles were imitations of gold and silver wares with seamed bellies. This bowl dates from the late seventh century or early eighth century. The characters in ink indicate the weight of the bowl. They show how the Tang people managed gold and silver wares, and provide a basis for studying the weight

system of the Tang Dynasty. According to tests made, a Tang tael averaged 42.798 grams, which is a bit smaller than a modern tael, which is 50 grams.

120. Silver strainer Utensil of Tang, length 25.5 cm, weight 93.3 grams; unearthed at the ruins of Guangqi Palace of the Tang Dynasty in Xi'an, Shaanxi Province, in 1958. The characters inscribed on the handle say that the strainer was made in Guangqi Palace in the first month of the third year of the Qianfu reign and that it weighed 2.33 taels. This shows that the strainer was an article used in the imperial palace in the mid-ninth century.

119-2

119-1

120-1

120-2

121-1

121. Bronze mirror with twin-phoenix design Relic of Tang, diameter 24.2 cm. Auspicious, supernatural animals such as the green dragon, white tiger, scarlet bird and mythical tortoise—the four spirits of the north in Taoism—and the 12 animals that represent a 12-year cycle were the principal designs on bronze mirrors of the early Tang. Later, the phoenix became just as important as auspicious animals as decoration on mirrors. By the prime and middle Tang, auspicious animals were basically replaced by birds and flowers, and this led to the production and development of bird-and-flower mirrors in the post-Tang era. Mirrors with twin-phoenix designs were among the most beautiful mirrors of Tang. On the back of the mirror shown here are two phoenixes facing each other across a knob, their wings spread and their tails sticking up. Each bird holds a silk ribbon in its beak. As the Chinese character for silk has the same pronunciation as the character for longevity, the design is a representation, by analogy, of long life. Besides phoenixes, other objects such as birds, beasts, flowers were usually added above and below the knob on the mirror.

122. Bronze mirror with design of traditional lotus-like flowers Relic of Tang, diameter 23.2 cm. The mirror is in the shape of a blossom. On the back is a knob encircled by patterns of lotus-like flowers called *baoxianghua*, which differ greatly in shape. During the prime Tang, floral patterns, instead of playing secondary roles, became the main theme in mirror decoration. Use of lotus-like flowers, auspicious flowers and pearl-like flowers created greater variety in the artistic styles of Tang mirrors. Along with this, Tang mirror decoration completed its thematic evolution from auspicious beasts to birds and finally to floral patterns.

122

◁ 121-2

123

123. Bronze mirror with flying-immortal design Relic of Tang, diameter 25.3 cm; unearthed from a Tang tomb in Xi'an, Shaanxi Province, in 1955. From the Han to the Tang Dynasty, the use of immortals as the theme of designs on bronze mirrors never ceased. People in the Han Dynasty wished they could become immortals with wings on their shoulders and live forever. Therefore, images of immortals like the Queen Mother of the West, Prince of the East, etc, appeared frequently on bronze mirrors. In the Tang Dynasty, portrayals of immortals became more and more fantastic. Some were depicted riding a crane or a beast; some were shown soaring into the sky on clouds; some were dancing in the moon; and some playing reed pipes to summon phoenixes. The immortals shown on this mirror are in the act of flying up to the sky. Lines like floating clouds and flowing water make up the graceful patterns on their clothes. Clouds and mountains below enhance the feeling of being high above the earth.

124

124. Burnished bronze mirror inlaid with gold-and-silver floral design

Relic of Tang, diameter 19 cm; unearthed in Xi'an, Shaanxi Province, in 1955. During the Tang Dynasty, many innovations were made in the techniques of casting bronze mirrors. There appeared so-called "mirrors cast by special techniques," such as burnished mirrors with gold-and-silver designs, mirrors inlaid with mother-of-pearl and mirrors with applied gold and silver designs. The technique of making gold-and-silver burnished mirrors is called *pingtuo*. The first step in the process is to glue pieces of gold and silver onto the back of the mirror to form the design. The whole surface is then coated with several layers of lacquer. When the lacquer is dry, the surface is polished carefully until the design is level with the lacquered surface and clearly exposed. This technique appeared in China at a fairly early date but it was not used in the making of bronze mirrors until the Tang. Most of the designs on such burnished mirrors are of birds and flowers. Because gold and silver are lustrous metals, the designs are unusually bright and glittering.

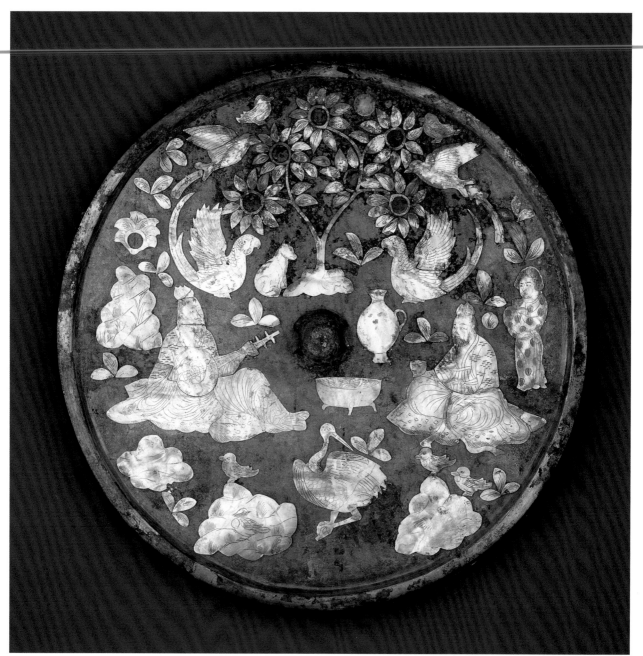

125-1

125. Bronze mirror with shell-inlaid design depicting a nobleman's feast
Relic of Tang, diameter 23.9 cm; unearthed from a Tang tomb in Luoyang, Henan Province, in 1955. The design is made by sticking thin pieces of shells with lacquer onto the back of a mirror. Some of the shell pieces are openwork; others are carved with fine lines. The technique of

inlaying dates back to the eleventh to eighth centuries BC, but use of the technique in decorating bronze mirrors started in the prime Tang. The dress adornments of the figures and the feathers of the birds are delineated clearly, and the natural luster of the shells helps to produce a unique artistic effect. This is a rare specimen of Tang mirrors.

126

127

128-1

126. Bronze mirror with design of a scene in the Moon Palace   Relic of Tang, diameter 19 cm. "Chang'e Flies to the Moon" is a widely known legend among the Chinese people. As the legend goes, Chang'e's husband, Houyi obtained the elixir of immortality from the Mother Queen of the West, but his wife secretly swallowed it, became a fairy and flew up to the moon. According to some folk tales, after Chang'e flew into the Moon Palace, she turned into a toad, an incarnation of the moon spirit, and pounded medicine in a mortar. But most of the moon-palace mirrors made in the Tang Dynasty show a luxuriant osmanthus tree and the beautiful Chang'e soaring into the sky, her long sleeves fluttering amid colored ribbons and floating clouds. Additionally, there is a white rabbit with a pestle pounding medicine and a jumping toad.

127. Bronze mirror with design of Prince Qiao playing a reed pipe to summon the phoenix   Relic of Tang, diameter 12.2 cm. This is a round mirror with a unique pattern. On its back is a scene of landscape and figures in bas-relief, with rolling hills and flowing waters. The knob of the mirror is a part of the hills and rocks. To the right of the knob is a man sitting sidewise on a rocky slope, his two hands holding a reed pipe; to the left is a phoenix with its wings spread. The whole picture conveys a tranquil atmosphere in a scene of motion. Such a technique of expression was rare in Tang mirrors. It is said that the scene represents the story of Prince Qiao playing a reed pipe to summon the phoenix. Ancient books say that Qiao, the crown prince of King Lin of Zhou, was able to imitate the singing of phoenixes with a reed-pipe. So real did the imitation sound that phoenixes actually flew in when they heard it. While on a tour around the area of Yi and Luo rivers, the prince was taken by a Taoist to Mt. Songgao, where he stayed more than 30 years and finally became an immortal. One day he flew away on the back of a white crane.

128. Bronze mirror with coiled-dragon design   Relic of Tang, diameter 19.5 cm. The dragon was a popular theme in the Sui and Tang dynasties. It appeared not only on stone carvings and murals, but also on many utensils. Mirrors with coiled-dragon designs were typical works of the time. The one shown here has the design of a solitary dragon whirling among the clouds. Its fangs are bared, it is brandishing its claws, and its head is turned back towards the knob in the act of swallowing a pearl. The atmosphere is lively and buoyant, conveying a keen sense of motion, and the dragon, this creature of the human imagination, is depicted with unusual power, enchantment and mystery. The most famous mirror with a dragon design was the one presented as tribute to Tang emperor Xuanzong from Yangzhou in 744, the third year of his reign titled Tianbao. It was so dazzlingly bright and shiny and the dragon so vividly portrayed that the emperor was astounded on seeing it. Mirrors with dragon designs were frequently mentioned in Tang poetry. The expression "coiled-dragon mirror" can be found in the works of some of the greatest Tang poets such as Li Bai and Meng Haoran, which is further evidence of the popularity of the coiled dragon as the theme of mirror designs.

129

129. Printed thin silk with brown background   Relic of Tang, remnant length 37 cm, width 23 cm; unearthed in Turpan, Xinjiang Uygur Autonomous Region, in 1967. Quite a lot of printed fabrics have been found among the Tang silks unearthed at excavation sites. The printing technique used in ancient China was mainly resist-dyeing. In the Tang Dynasty wax-resist dyeing, tie-and-dye and sandwich-dyeing were widely used, as well as a method of printing by basichromatin. The tie-and-

dye method flourished during the Tang; it included tie-sewing, tie-dyeing, and knotting. The sandwich-dyeing method was a rather complicated process among the printing and dyeing techniques.

130. Brocade with design of small flowers   Relic of Tang, remnant length 26.3 cm, width 14.2 cm; unearthed from a Tang tomb in Turpan, Xinjiang Uygur Autonomous Region, in 1960. The brocade was woven by the warp-patterned technique. It consists of

alternating small flowers and cross patterns, with no direct connection between them. The small flowers contain a pistil in the center surrounded by petals. The cross patterns also have a pistil in the center, from which leaves radiate in all directions. Designs like this, consisting of unconnected patterns, scattered dots, and a balanced symmetrical layout are often seen on silk fabrics of the Tang.

Commerce and Transportation

The progress of agriculture and handicraft industry in the Tang Dynasty promoted the development of commodity economy. Many important cities emerged and shops engaged in the same kind of business increased. This gave rise to the formation of guilds—feudal organizations of people of the same trade. Along with the development of commodity exchange, the demand for coins increased too. Both land and water transportation in the country were well developed. All this provided good conditions for the development of commerce, strengthened economic ties between different parts of the country, and promoted economic and cultural exchange with countries and regions abroad.

131

131. *Kaiyuan tongbao* coin Currency of Tang, diameter 2.4 cm, weight 4 grams. According to the *History of the Tang Dynasty*, the inscription on *kaiyuan* coins was composed and written by the calligrapher Ouyang Xun. In 621, the Tang government abolished the five-*zhu* coin of the previous Sui Dynasty and replaced it with the *kaiyuan* coin. The *kaiyuan tongbao*, a denomination of *kaiyuan* coins, was the most important currency of Tang and in circulation the longest. It occupied a particularly important position in the history of Chinese currency. Nearly all the coins used before the Tang Dynasty had

133

134

names that signified their weight. From the Tang Dynasty on, this practice was changed. Tang coins were variously called *bao*, *tongbao* and *yuanbao*, which were unrelated to their weight, and the names were prefixed by the reign title of an emperor. *Kaiyuan*, however, is not a reign title; it means the opening of a new era; and *tongbao* means money in circulation. The *kaiyuan* coin is an imitation of the five-*zhu* coin of the Han Dynasty. Ten such coins weighed one tael. The coin has a raised, impressive border and characters that are dignified and well proportioned. On the back of some *kaiyuan* coins are star and moon designs.

132. *Qianfeng quanbao, qianyuan zhongbao, dali yuanbao, jianzhong tongbao* and *huichang kaiyuan* coins
Currencies of Tang. In addition to the *kaiyuan tongbao* coin, which was in circulation for nearly 300 years, the Tang imperial court minted seven or eight other kinds of coins. The *qianfeng quanbao* coin was mintd in 666, the first year of the Qianfeng reign of Emperor Gaozong, but it was withdrawn from circulation in

less than a year. *Qianyuan zhongbao* and *dali yuanbao* coins were minted in 758 and in 769 respectively. The *jianzhong tongbao* was issued between 780 and 783. It was lighter and smaller than the *dali yuanbao*. In 845 a new *kaiyuan* coin was issued. On the back of the coin were the names of provinces of the country. The coin was called *huichang kaiyuan* in history. There were different political and economic backgrounds to the issue of all these coins, but none could fully replace the *kaiyuan tongbao*.

133. Bronze ruler with dragon design
Measure of Tang, length 29.71 cm, width 2.3 cm, thickness 0.2 cm; unearthed from a Tang tomb in Wuhan, Hubei Province, in 1958. Rulers in the Tang Dynasty were made of bronze, wood, ivory or iron; they were carved, perforated, gilded or inlaid with designs of figures, flowers, birds and beasts. In some Tang graves, rulers and iron scissors were found; evidently they were articles the occupant of the grave had used when he was alive. The obverse of the ruler shown here is divided into two equal sections. One section is subdivided

into five *cun* (one *cun* is 3.333 centimeters); on the other section is the figure of a dragon. There is a small hole at one end of the ruler.

134. Silver coated bronze ruler with flower design
Measure of Tang, length 31 cm, width 2.2 cm; unearthed in Xi'an, Shaanxi Province. Measures of the Tang Dynasty—*chi* (ruler), *dou* (a unit of dry measure for grain, equivalent to one decalitre) and *chen* (weight)—had two units each, big and small. A big ruler was equivalent to 1.2 small rulers, a big *dou* to 3 small dou, and one *liang* (0.0625 catty) of a big weight to 3 *liang* of a small weight. Small rulers were used to measure implements that regulate musical instruments, and to measure the shadow cast by the sun on a dial, and the pot for decocting herbal medicine. Studies show that one big Tang ruler is about 29.5 cm and one small Tang ruler about 24.5 cm. Most of the Tang rulers that have been preserved or unearthed are big ones, whose length is between 29 and 31.4 cm. The bronze ruler shown here should belong to the category of big rulers.

135

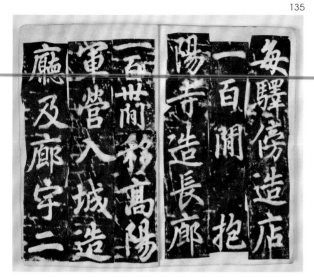

135. Rubbing from a tablet in Yizhou
(section)   Relic of Tang, height of tablet 322.3 cm. The original tablet was erected in Yi County, Hebei Province, in 739. The text of 18 lines on the tablet explained why and how the tablet was erected. From the notes at the end of the text, one can make out the following: "Three postal roads were built at Beishan, where three counties had been set up. Around each courier station were 100 inns and four threshing grounds where water-powered rollers were used." The record casts light on the development of commerce and transportation in those days. According to the *Six Codes of the Great Tang*, there were 1639 courier stations in the country at the time, of which some were built on water routes, some on land routes, and some on both land and water routes. They were built to meet the needs of public functions and the development of commerce. Yizhou was an important communication hub at the time. The tablet may serve as a supplement to the accounts in historical books concerning the location of courier stations and inns.

136. Three-color pottery
donkey   Funerary object of Tang, length 16.5 cm, height 15.6 cm; unearthed in Xi'an, Shaanxi Province, in 1955. In the Tang Dynasty, a network of courier routes was set up with Chang'an the capital as the center. Besides providing services to the government, the courier routes also served merchants transporting their goods and ordinary people coming and going. Along the routes were many private restaurants and inns, and quite a few shops kept "courier donkeys" for rent to travelers. These donkeys were fast and could easily cover a journey of several dozens miles. This three-color saddled donkey is an exact image of a courier donkey.

137. Blue and white glazed pottery ox-
drawn vehicle   Funerary object of Tang, height 11.6 cm, length 8.9 cm; unearthed from a Tang tomb in Sanmenxia, Henan Province, in 1957. The driver of this exquisitely made pottery vehicle is walking in front of the carriage, in which a young woman sits upright. In the Tang Dynasty horses, donkeys and mules were the main draft animals, but there were also ox-drawn vehicles used mainly by women. Two murals of ox-drawn vehicles were found in the tomb of Li Shou, a cousin of Li Yuan, Emperor Gaozu, in Sanyuan County, Shaanxi Province. One vehicle had a railed body, the other a planked one, in which was seated a woman. They show that ox-drawn vehicles, which were popular during the Wei and Jin dynasties, were still used in the early Tang. Later, because horse-riding was so much in vogue, ox-drawn vehicles, too, were replaced by horses.

136

137-1

137-2 ▷

International Relations

In the Tang Dynasty, China was one of the richest and most civilized countries in the world and it had a strong appeal for other countries. Its social production developed at an unprecedented rate, its foreign trade showed a rapid increase, and its external relations were frequent and cordial. In the course of its exchanges with foreign countries, the Tang empire was able to dissiminate its culture far beyond its borders and at the same time, with an open mind, bring in the cultures of other countries to enrich its own.

The Silk Road Busier Than Ever Before or Since

The united and strong Tang empire exported its silk, tea and other commodities to the West through the Silk Road which started from the Tang capital Chang'an (today's Xi'an, Shaanxi Province) in the east, passed through the heartlands of Asia and terminated at Constantinople (now Istanbul, Turkey), capital of the Eastern Roman Empire in the West. Along the same route, jewels, medicinal herbs, and perfumes of the West were introduced into China in an endless stream. After the mid-Tang, thanks to progress in shipbuilding and navigation technology, maritime trade routes developed rapidly and many popular commodities like silk and ceramics were now exported in large amounts by sea.

138. Pottery camels　Funerary objects of Tang, height 27-29 cm; unearthed from Xianyu Tinghui's tomb in Xi'an, Shaanxi Province, in 1957. The Silk Road passed through a large expanse of the Gobi Desert where there were fierce sandstorms, making traveling very difficult. Camels are docile animals; they can withstand thirst and hunger, and can carry heavy loads over long distances. Called "ships of the desert," they were the principal means of transport on the Silk Road.

139. Pottery figurine of a traveler from Tajik Funerary object of Tang, height 27 cm; said to have been unearthed in Xi'an, Shaanxi Province.

140. Yellow-glazed pottery figurine of a traveler from Tajik, holding a bottle Funerary object of Tang, height 29 cm; said to have been unearthed in Xi'an, Shaanxi Province.

139

140

141. Three-color pottery figurine of a traveler from the Western Regions
Funerary object of Tang, height 29 cm; unearthed from a Tang tomb at Hanshenzhai, Xi'an, Shaanxi Province, in 1955.

142. Yellow-glazed pottery figurine of a camel driver   Funerary object of Tang, height 42.4 cm;unearthed from Xianyu Tinghui's tomb in Xi'an, Shaanxi Province, in 1957. In the Tang Dynasty large numbers of foreign merchants, diplomatic missions, students and religious people came to China by land or water. Most of them stayed in Chang'an, Luoyang and other important commercial cities. Among archaeological relics, images of foreigners are often seen. These blue-eyed, high-nosed aliens played a part in promoting trade between China and other countries. They were envoys in the exchange of ideology, religion, art, science and technology between China and the outside world.

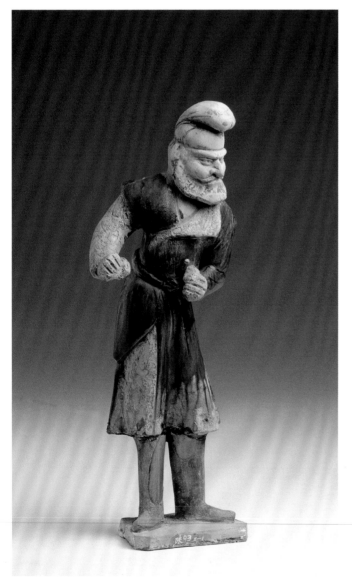

141

142-1

142-2

143. Brocade with hoopoe and phoenix design   Silk fabric of Tang, length 19 cm, width 14 cm; unearthed in Turpan, Xinjiang Uygur Autonomous Region, in 1969.

144. Brocade with pearled deer design Silk fabric of Tang, length 19.5 cm, width 16.5 cm; unearthed in Turpan, Xinjiang Uygur Autonomous Region, in 1966.

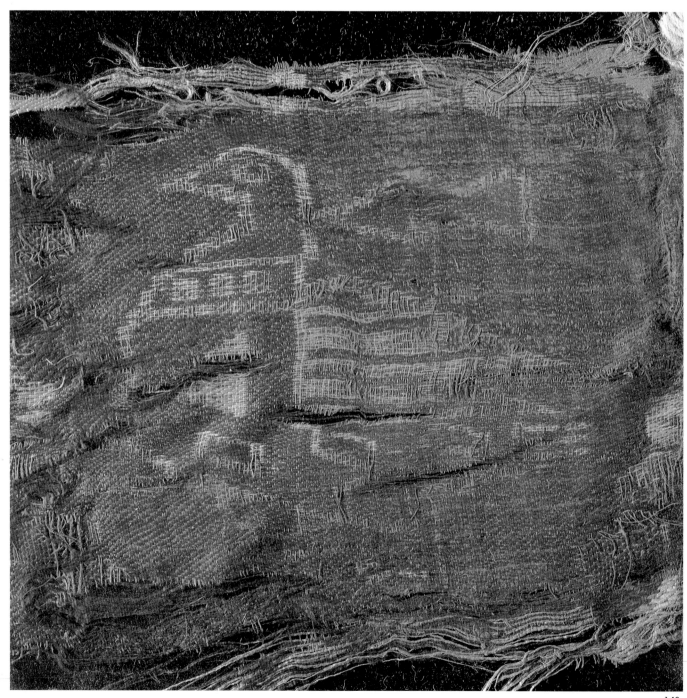

145. Printed silk gauze with hunting design on dark green background Silk fabric of Tang, length 35 cm, width 18 cm; unearthed in Xinjiang Uygur Autonomous Region, in 1968.

146. Red Silk Silk fabric of Tang, length 45 cm, width 16 cm; unearthed in Turpan, Xinjiang Uygur Autonomous Region, in 1967.

147. Batik with green background Silk fabric of Tang, length 50 cm, width 14 cm; unearthed in Turpan, Xinjiang Uygur Autonomous Region, in 1967.

In the Tang Dynasty, silk fabrics were produced in large quantities and in many varieties. There was a precise division of labor in the silk-weaving industry. The techniques of weaving, printing and dyeing were superb. In the weaving of brocade and its designs, the techniques and styles of Persian brocade were absorbed. For instance, the designs on different sections of the fabric were partitioned with rings of pearls, and images of pig-heads, phoenixes, deer, and pairs of birds and beasts were added. Along the open and unobstructed Silk Road, large quantities of silk fabrics made their way to the Western Regions, central and western Asia and Europe, where they were warmly received and sold quickly. The numerous Tang fabrics found in Xinjiang and other places are evidence of the thriving trade along the Silk Road at the time.

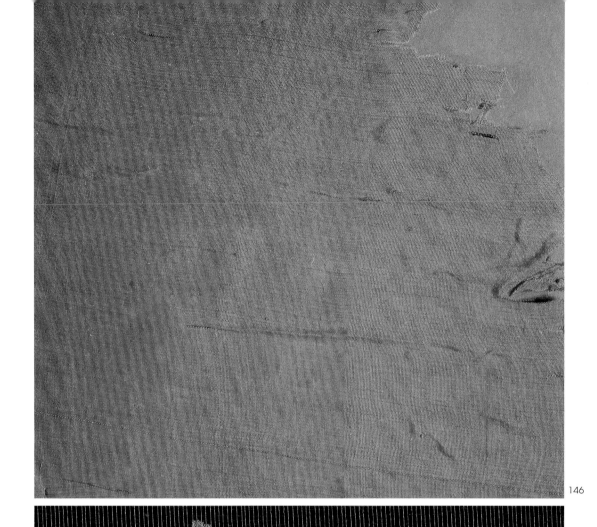

146

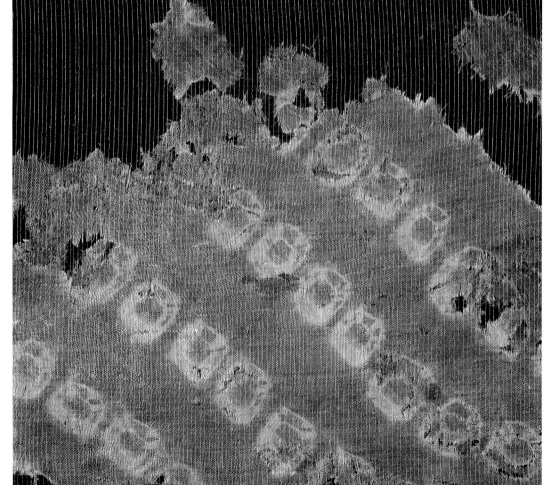

147

Economic and Cultural Exchange between China and Other Countries

The Tang royal court maintained friendly ties with many countries, especially with its neighboring countries in Asia. Diplomatic missions, trade cavarans and travelers came and went in an endless stream and Sino-foreign economic and cultural exchange was on an unprecedented scale. The rich culture of the Tang Dynasty, in particular its advanced techniques of paper-making and textile weaving, were introduced into countries of Asia and Europe, and Western culture, arts and religion were brought into China.

149-1

148. "Music from Piao" Poem by Bai Juyi, a well-known Tang poet; selected from the Ming edition of *Changqing Collection of Bai Juyi*. In 801, the 17th year of the Zhenyuan reign of the Tang Dynasty, Yongqiang, a king of Piao (Burma), sent a cultural and art mission that included 35 musicians, led by his son, Prince Sumanto, to the Tang Empire to perform Piao music and promote friendly relations. They were warmly received upon their arrival in Chang'an (now Xi'an, Shaanxi Province). Piao music had reached a high level at that time; and the excellent performances given by the mission produced a great sensation in Chang'an. "Music from Piao" is a poem written by Bai Juyi after he attended a performance. It was a vivid depiction of the grand performance and a tribute to the friendly relations between the two countries at the time. It also shows the Tang royal court's readiness to absorb the essence of foreign culture.

149. Curly haired pottery figurine
Funerary object of Tang, height 28 cm, said to have been unearthed in Xi'an, Shaanxi Province. Kunlun was a general term used in the Tang Dynasty in reference to countries bordering the South China Sea (in southeast Asia); and the people there were called Kunluns. In the eyes of the Tang people the Kunluns had curly hair and dark skin. Southeast Asia played a major role in sea transportation in ancient times; it was a medium in the economic and cultural exchange between East and West. The Kunluns were active in China, India and western Asia. This pottery figurine is the image of a Kunlun man who visited China.

149-2

150

151

151. *Collection of Works of Cui Zhiyuan*
Hand-copied edition of Qing; the author was Cui Zhiyuan of Silla. The Tang royal court had very close ties with Silla. There were frequent economic and cultural exchanges between the two countries. The government of Silla sent large numbers of students to study in China. Cui Zhiyuan came to China at the age of twelve. Later, he passed the Tang imperial examinations and was appointed a military officer at Lishui County (in what is now Jiangsu Province) and given other official posts. In 879, the 6th year of the Qianfu reign, Gao Pian took up the post of provincial governor in central Anhui Province. He appointed Cui Zhiyuan to be secretary in charge of documents. *The Collection of Works of Cui Zhiyuan* contains many of his poems and essays, most of which were documents he drafted on behalf of Gao Pian. Many of them were prose writings in

150. Rubbing from the inscription on the tombstone of the wife of Su Liang, née Ma Relic of Tang, length 39.5 cm, width 35.5 cm; unearthed in Xi'an, Shaanxi Province, in 1955. The inscription was written in two languages, Chinese and Pahlavi(mid-Persian). It says that Su Liang and his wife, née Ma, were descendants of the royal family and aristocrats of Persia's Sasanian Empire (226-651), who fled to China after the empire was overthrown. They were both believers of Zoroastrianism, a religion founded in the sixth century BC, which became the national religion of the Sasanian Empire in the 3rd century AD and was introduced into China during the Northern Dynasties. As the Tang Dynasty adopted a lenient policy towards religion, Zoroastrianism was allowed to spread widely in China. The government set up special organizations and employed special persons to administer its affairs, and permitted the establishment of Zoroastrian churches in Chang'an and Luoyang. This epitaph is evidence of the propagation of Zoroastrianism in China; it is of high academic value.

parallel style, showing that Cui was deeply read in Han culture.

152. Celadon pot with phoenix-head design   Container of Tang, height 18.7 cm, mouth diameter 1 cm, bottom diameter 7.6 cm; unearthed in Guangzhou, Guangdong Province, in 1954. Guangzhou was an important foreign trade city in the Tang Dynasty. Large quantities of Chinese commodities, and ceramics in particular, were sold through Guangzhou to southeastern and western Asia and North Africa. This celadon pot is very similar to the white porcelain pot unearthed in Sulawesi Selatan of Indonesia, evidence of the trade activities mentioned above.

153. Rubbing from a stele marking the spread of Nestorianism to China   Relic of Tang, stele height 2.36 meters, width 0.86 meter, thickness 0.25 meter; unearthed in Zhouzhi (today's Zhouzhi County, Shaanxi Province), in 1623. The stele is now housed in the Stele Museum in Xi'an, Shaanxi Province. In 428 after it split with Orthodox Christianity, the state religion of the Eastern Roman Empire, Nestorianism gradually spread eastward, becoming popular in western and eastern Asia. In 635, the ninth year of the Zhenguan reign of the Tang Dynasty, it was introduced into China. The text of the stele was written by Adam, a Nestorian priest, and it recorded briefly how the basic principles of Christianity and Nestorianism spread to China during the 140 years between the reigns of Emperors Taizong and Dezong. It is an important material for the study of the religious and cultural exchange between the Tang royal court and the Eastern Roman Empire, and of the history of communications between China and the West. It reflects some of the notable features of the rich and powerful Tang Empire, its opening up to the outside world and its lenient policy towards religion.

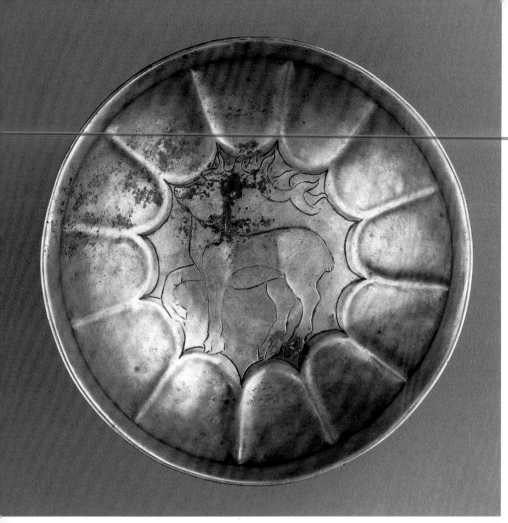

154-1

154-2

155. Bronze mirror with sea-beast-and-grape design Relic of Tang, diameter 21 cm; unearthed from a Tang tomb in Shaan County, Henan Province, in 1956. The mirror is decorated with a design of a sea beast and grapes. The beast symbolized auspiciousness and was carved vividly in high-relief. Why did people in ancient times call this auspicious animal a sea beast or sea horse? Why was the beast depicted together with grapes? With these questions in mind, some scholars regarded the mirror as "a reflection of riddles" or "a mirror that embodies the civilizations of Europe and Asia." The second statement shows the linkage of the mirror with the cultural exchange between China and the West, and provides an explanation for the combination of the auspicious beast with grapes. In the Tang Dynasty Western patterns that combined animals and grapes were introduced into China. We may presume, therefore, that some mirror casters in China were inspired by the exotic patterns and decided to put the traditional auspicious beast together with grapes on their mirrors, forming the sea-beast-and-grape design. Such mirrors were popular at the end of the 7th century. They were generally of fine workmanship, containing intricate designs with interlocking branches and hanging leaves.

154. Silver bowl with twelve U-shaped and deer designs Food vessel of Tang, height 4 cm, mouth diameter 14.7 cm; unearthed in a cellar at Shapo Village, Xi'an, Shaanxi Province, in 1963. The vessel was shaped by hammering and has a level design. There are twelve U-shaped figures carved on its outer wall. In the center of the bottom is the image of a standing deer with curved antlers. Inscribed under the rim is a line of characters which are hard to identify. The U-shaped figures are similar in style to the silver wares of the sixth century found in central and western Asia. Deer were used as decorative patterns both in ancient China and in foreign countries, but with different images. The curved antlers on the vessel shown here were common on Western vessels, but are quite different from the flat antlers that appeared on gold and silver wares of the late Tang. Therefore, some scholars think this bowl was made by Sogdians who lived in the valleys of the Amu Darya and Syr Darya.

155-1

155-2

156. Ivory sculpture of a bodhisattva riding an elephant Buddhist sculpture of 7th century India, height 15.8 cm, thickness 7.5 cm; relic of Yulin Cave, Anxi County, Gansu Province. The sculpture is made from a single piece of ivory; it can be opened and closed. When closed, the article is of an image of a bodhisattva riding an elephant with a pagoda in its hand. When opened, each side consists of 25 squares, on which are carvings of the Jataka story about Sakyamuni's earlier incarnations, containing a total of nearly 300 figures, carriages, horses, pagodas, etc. The whole sculpture was ingeniously conceived and is of high artistic level. To judge from the shapes of the figures, animals, and Buddhist pagodas, it must be a Buddhist sculpture of ancient India. And the artistic style suggests it may be a product of the 3rd or 4th century. In the Tang Dynasty many Chinese monks went westward to India to study Buddhist doctrines. The Buddhist sculpture shown here was probably brought to China by those monks and enshrined in the Yulin Cave.

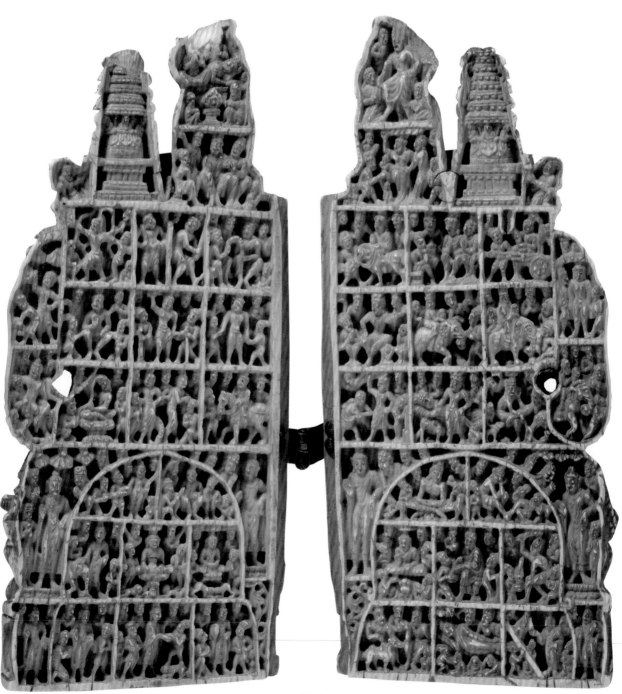

156-1

156-2

157. *Records of the Western Regions During the Tang Dynasty* Hand-written copy of Tang, oral account by Xuanzang written down by Bianji; discovered in the Mogao Grottoes, Dunhuang, Gansu Province. Xuanzang was a high-ranking Buddhist monk of the Tang Dynasty. He went westward to India to further his study of Buddhist doctrines in 627, and stayed there for 18 years, returning to China in 645. In the following year, on the orders of Emperor Taizong, he wrote the book *Records of the Western Regions During the Tang Dynasty*, describing what he had seen and heard on his trips. The book consists of 12 volumes, introducing the physical geography, politics, economy, religion, culture, habits and customs of 138 countries and cities Xuanzang had visited. It is an important material for the study of countries in central and southern Asia and of communications between China and the West in medieval times. Thanks to Xuanzang's naratives, the sites of the famous Nalanda Monastery and Rajagrha in Indian history have been discovered. The hand-written copy of the Records is the earliest edition extant, but only three of the 12 volumes are available; they are in the British Museum in London and the National Library in Paris.

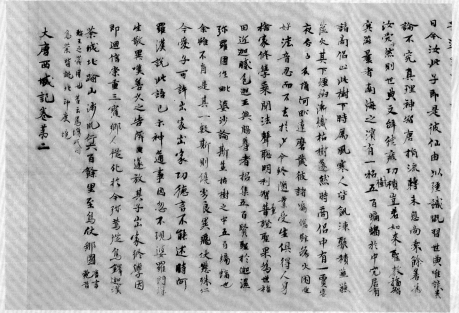

157

158. Stone seat of the Buddha inscribed with the name of Xuanzang Buddhist consecrated object of Tang, height 36 cm, diameter of upper part 49.5 cm; unearthed at the ruins of Yuhua Palace, Tongchuan, Shaanxi Province, in 1977. On one side of the base is an inscription of 20 characters, which says that the consecrated statue of Sakyamuni was made by Xuanzang, Master of Tripitaka, in the second year of the Longshuo reign of the Great Tang. Yuhua Palace was built in 624, the seventh year of the Wude reign of Tang, and was expanded during the reign of Emperor Taizong. It was one of the temporary abodes for the emperor during his tours. The palace was turned into a temple in 651, and renamed Yuhua Temple. In 659, in order to concentrate on the translation of Buddhist scriptures, Xuanzang moved from Chang'an to Yuhua Temple. The stone Buddhist seat is a relic left by him during his stay at the temple.

159. *Biographies of Famous Tang Pilgrims to Western Regions* by Yijing Copy printed from engraved blocks by the China Buddhist Seminary in Nanjing, in 1932. Yijing was another high-ranking Buddhist monk in the Tang Dynasty after Xuanzang. Between 671 and 695 he travelled to India and the region of the South China Sea (southeastern Asia) to study Buddhist doctrines. The book records what the author saw and heard about 60 Chinese monks who went to India to study Buddhist doctrines in the early Tang Dynasty, including an autobiography of the author himself. In the early Tang, Buddhism developed on a large scale in China and Buddhism in India was also at its zenith. Under such circumstances, a great number of Chinese monks went to India to study Buddhist doctrines, forming a high tide of travels to the west. The book also records the major routes between China and India.

160. *Records of Buddhist Practices Sent Home from the South Sea* by Yijing Copy printed from engraved blocks by the Buddhist Scriptures Printing Office in Tianjin in 1924. In the early Tang Dynasty, Buddhism developed fast in China thanks to the encouragement and support of the

government. But as religious discipline was loose at that time, unhealthy practices and scandals often appeared in the temples. So when Yijing studied in India and other places, he paid special attention to Buddhist commandments and rules and to monastic order. Before he returned to China, he wrote a book in Sriwidjaja (now Sumatra, Indonesia)and mailed it back to China, which is why it was called *Records of Buddhist Practices Sent Home from the South Sea*. In the book the author recorded the rules and regulations formulated by Buddhism in India, in hopes of correcting the misdoings of Buddhism in China at the time.

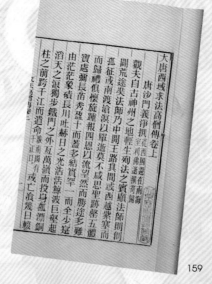

159

160

161. Map showing High Monk Jianzhen's eastbound trips to Japan Jianzhen (687-763) was a high-ranking monk of the Vinaya Sect of Buddhism in the Tang Dynasty. In 742, he was invited by the Japanese monks Yoei and Fusho to give lectures on Buddhist teachings in Japan. He made five attempts to go east without success, and meanwhile lost his eyesight. It was not until 753, on his sixth attempt, that he succeeded in arriving in Heijaukyo, (today's Nara, Japan), where he taught monastic rules and was respected as the founder of the Vinaya Sect in Japan.

He introduced to Japan China's advanced techniques in architecture, sculpture and mural painting, and supervised the building of the Toshodai Temple in Nara. Possessing a good knowledge of medicine, he taught the Japanese people the art of healing and was credited with the founding of Japanese medicine. Even the techniques of the Japanese bean-curd, catering and brewery industries are said

to have been taught by Jianzhen. He died at the Toshodai Temple in May 763.

162. *Wado Kaizhen* silver coin Ancient coin of Japan, diameter 2.4 cm; unearthed from a cellar in Hejia Village, Xi'an, Shaanxi Province, in 1970. This silver coin was cast in Japan between 708 and 714, during the Wado reign of Ganmei Mikado of Nara Ojau. As Japan attached great importance to learning and absorbing the advanced culture of the Tang Dynasty, this coin is entirely the same as the Tang *kaiyuan tongbao* coin in shape and weight. The character "珎" on the coin means "treasure" and "开珎" (*kaizhen*) was shortened from "开元通宝"(*kaiyuan tongbao*). There is also a great resemblance in the character "开" on the two coins. Moreover, some Tang *kaiyuan tongbao* coins were made of silver. These similarities show how Tang coins influenced Japanese coins.

Map Showing High Monk Jianzhen's Eastbound Trips to Japan

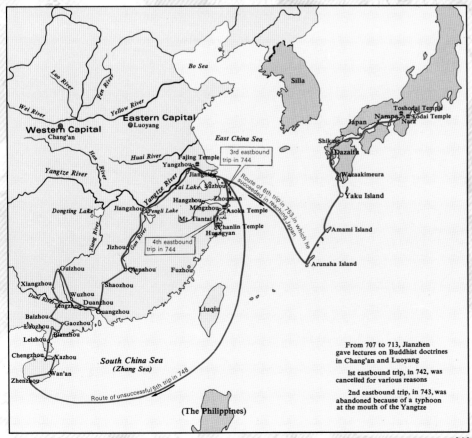

From 707 to 713, Jianzhen gave lectures on Buddhist doctrines in Chang'an and Luoyang

1st eastbound trip, in 742, was cancelled for various reasons

2nd eastbound trip, in 743, was abandoned because of a typhoon at the mouth of the Yangtze

161

162

Science, Culture and Social Life

The Tang Dynasty was the heyday of feudalism. Apart from inheriting the traditions of the Northern and Southern Dynasties, Tang culture absorbed generously the essence of foreign cultures. Imbued with a great vision, it had a far-reaching influence on later generations. In the field of science and technology, major breakthroughs and numerous innovations were made in astronomy, geography, medical and pharmaceutical science, as well as block printing. In literature and art and, in particular, in poetry, calligraphy, painting, sculpture, music and dance, great achievements were made and notable artists and men of letters emerged in large numbers. With the prosperity of cities, great changes took place in social life such as recreation, costumes, tea and wine drinking, reflecting a flourishing, free and open culture.

Science and Technology

Block printing was gradually popularized in the Tang Dynasty and it played an important role in the dissemination and development of Chinese culture. In astronomy, the most outstanding achievement was a ground survey of the meridian line for the first time in human history. In geography, the *Map of Chinese and Alien Peoples Within the Country*, drawn by Jia Dan, set an example of reform in mapmaking. *Illustrated History of Prefectures and Counties During the Reign of Yuanhe* by Li Jifu is the earliest extant historical account of local administrations. In medical and pharmaceutical science, *A New Compendium of Materia Medica* by Su Jin and others is the first government-authorized pharmacopoeia in the world. Medical works by Sun Simiao had a tremendous impact on the development of China's medical and pharmaceutical science.

163. Buddhist Dharani Charm, printed copy by Bianjia of Longchifang, Chengdu County, Chengdu Prefecture Religious object of Tang, length 31 cm, width 34 cm; unearthed from a Tang tomb at Wangjianglou, Chengdu, Sichuan Province, in 1944. The technique of block printing was developed from seal carving and stone rubbing. As Buddhism was popular at the time, block printings were mostly of Buddhist portraits and scriptures. The charm shown here was printed sometime after 757. Buddhists believe that people who read the charm could escape misfortune and diseases and those who kept it would be protected by the Deity. This printed charm was taken out of a silver bracelet worn on an arm of the grave owner. After the 12th century the technique of block printing was introduced into Europe via central Asia.

163-1

Sketch Map Showing Monk Yixing's Survey of the Meridian

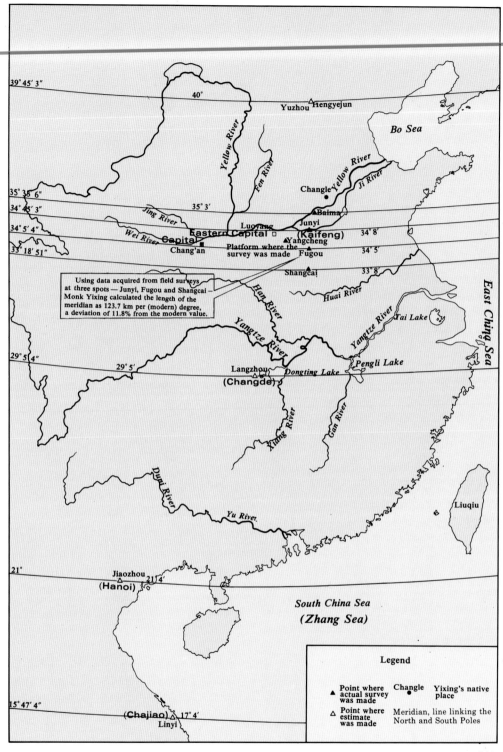

Using data acquired from field surveys at three spots — Junyi, Fugou and Shangcai — Monk Yixing calculated the length of the meridian as 123.7 km per (modern) degree, a deviation of 11.8% from the modern value.

Legend

▲ Point where actual survey was made

● Changle Yixing's native place

△ Point where estimate was made

Meridian, line linking the North and South Poles

164

164. Sketch map showing Monk Yixing's survey of the meridian   Monk Yixing (683–727), originally named Zhang Sui, was a famous astronomer of the Tang Dynasty. In ancient China astronomy was closely related to the calendar and mathematics. Therefore an astronomer was also an expert in calendrical science and mathematics. The bronze armillary sphere made by Monk Yixing could monitor quite precisely the movements of the sun, moon, and stars. Most importantly, the monk took charge of surveying the meridian line from the earth. In 724, the 12th year of the Kaiyuan reign of Tang, he directed a survey in the Henan area to measure the length of the sun's shadow and the altitude of the North Pole. Based on the results of the survey he concluded that one degree on the meridian line was 351.27 Tang *li* in length, equivalent to 123.7 kilometers. Though the figure was not very exact, it was the first ground measurement of the meridian line on record. Learning from the discoveries of earlier astronomers, he also took charge of the making of the Dayan calendar, the national calendar of the Tang empire.

165. Portrait of Sun Simiao, and his medical works *Precious Prescriptions for Emergencies* and *Supplement to Precious Prescriptions* Sun Simiao (581–682) was an outstanding Tang pharmacologist and a native of Huayuan, Jingzhao Prefecture(today's Yao County, Shaanxi Province). When young, he was often ill, so he started to learn medicine. He was good at summing up the achievements of his predecessors and his own experiences based on practice. His works *Precious Prescriptions for Emergencies* and *Supplement to Precious Prescriptions* contained detailed descriptions of ways of diagnosing and treating diseases, and knowledge concerning nutrition and hygiene. In these books, gynecological and infantile diseases were listed for the first time. He initiated the classification of diseases by *zang* and *fu*. In traditional Chinese medicine, the five *zang* organs refer to the heart, liver, spleen, lung and kidney, and the six *fu* organs to the stomach, gallbladder, triple energizer, urinary bladder, large intestine and small intestine. His writings have contributed immeasurably to Chinese medical science. After his death, Sun Simiao was honored as the "Master of Pharmacology."

165-1

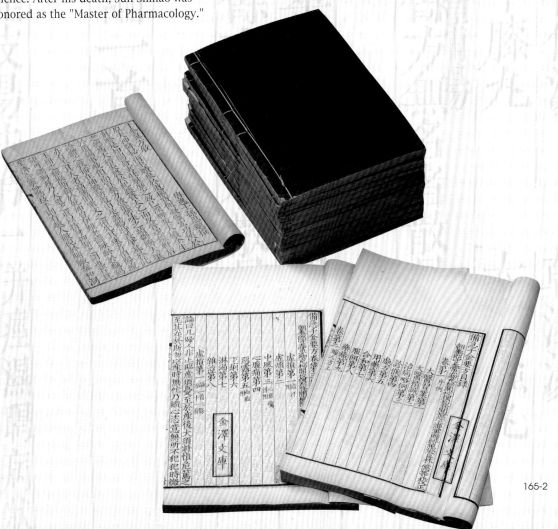

165-2

166. *A New Compendium of Materia Medica*　Compiled and written by Su Jing and others. Hand-copy edition from Mori's collection in Japan. The original Chinese for the term "materia medica" as used here is *bencao,* which means herbs but has become a general term for all drugs used in traditional Chinese medicine. While jade and other minerals and even insects and parts of animals can be found in Chinese medical prescriptions, by far the most common kinds of medical ingredients are herbs. *A New Compendium of Materia Medica* is also called *The Tang Materia Medica.* Made public in 659, the fourth year of the Xianqing reign of Tang,

the book was the first government-authorized pharmacopoeia in China. It is based on the *Annotations to Emperor Shen Nong's Materia Medica* by Tao Hongjing of the Liang Dynasty, and lists over 800 kinds of drugs, of which 114 were not included in the Annotations. Containing pictures of specimens of medicines, it is the earliest illustrated medical book. It was originally in 54 volumes, namely 2 volumes of tables of contents, 20 of materia medica, 25 of illustrations of medicinal specimens, and 7 of illustrations of channels. Now only 11 volumes of materia medica are extant, all the others being lost.

167.　Silver medicine box with a lid
Medicine container of Tang, height 2.9 cm, mouth diameter 4.3 cm; unearthed from a cellar at Hejia Village, Xi'an, Shaanxi Province, in 1970. In the center of the lid are two openwork petals in cross shape. The lid and the box are carved with designs. A total of 28 gold and silver medicine containers were unearthed from the cellar of Hejia Village; some were gold boxes of various sizes; some were silver boxes with plain surface; and some were gilded silver boxes with carved designs. On the inside of some lids were inscriptions in ink. In those days, it was considered proper to keep medicines in

gold and silver boxes. Historical records say that the Tang rulers bestowed on their subordinates gold or silver boxes containing rare readymade medicines, spiced medicines or cosmetics. The large number of gold and silver medicine boxes discovered in the cellar of Hejia Village casts some sidelight on the frequent use of medicine boxes by the Tang royal family and officials.

168. Silver pot with a loop handle Tang vessel for decocting medicinal herbs, gross height 18.5 cm, mouth diameter 19.3 cm; unearthed from a cellar at Hejia Village, Xi'an, Shaanxi Province, in 1970. The pot has a wide rim, flared mouth and round bottom. It was shaped by hammering and has a plain but glittering body. Four silver pots each with one loop handle and one silver pot with two handles were

unearthed from the cellar. The bottoms of some pots are inscribed with ink characters meaning l.25 catties. Many medical books of the Tang Dynasty mention that silver wares like pots or *diao* (small vessels with handle and spout) had to be used for decocting herbal medicine. When silver wares were not available, bronze or porcelain wares could also be used, but silver wares were the first choice. Records show silver pots were also used for refining so-called pills of immortality.

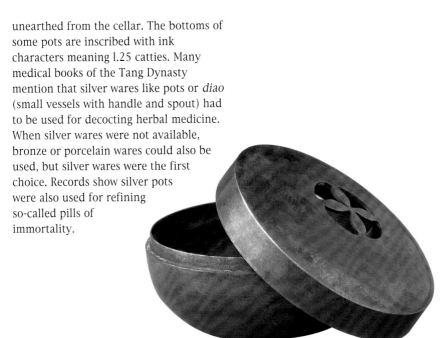

167

168

169. Portrait of Li Bai and *Collected Poems of Li Bai* Li Bai(701-762), styled Taibai, one of the greatest Tang poets, was a native of Changlong, Mianzhou (today's Jiangyou County, Sichuan Province). He lived in the prime Tang, and travelled to many places during his lifetime. His poems are noted for their sincerity, boldness and absence of constraint. Imbued with imagination and exaggeration, and careless of the rules and forms of classical poetry, he expressed his love for his land and people freely, vividly and incisively. About 1,000 of his poems have been preserved down to the present. "Hard Is the Road to Shu," "Hard Is the Way of the World," "Mount Skyland Ascended in a Dream," "Thoughts on a Silent Night," and "Leaving White Emperor Town at Dawn" are on the lips of every lover of Chinese poetry.

170. Portrait of Du Fu and *Collected Poems of Du Fu* Du Fu (712-770), styled Zimei, a native of Gong County (northeast of present-day Gong County, Henan Province), was a famous poet of the Tang Dynasty. He experienced the transition from prosperity to decline of the Tang empire and suffered during the Rebellion of An Lushan and Shi Siming, drifting from place to place in a sea of frustration. He had a profound insight into the social life of his time. Many of his poems are expressions of sorrow over worldly problems and describe his concern and worries about his country and people. Therefore, his poems have been called "history in verse." They are solemn and

Literature and Art

In Tang literature, the greatest achievements were in poetry. Nearly 50,000 Tang poems are extant. There were numerous schools, each with its own style, and a great number of famous poets during the Tang. Legends or romances were a new form of literature, which had a great influence on the drama and novel of later generations. In calligraphy, the new style of regular script emerged. Most of the later students of calligraphy followed the Tang style. Depictions of figures were the most successful in Tang painting, and landscapes brought in new techniques such as paintings in gold and green and in beaten ink. Flower painting developed gradually, and birds-and-animals became more realistic. In sculpture, Buddhist images were the main theme; they represented a special Tang style of beauty—full and round, charming and kindly. The mural paintings, stone and clay sculptures in the Mogao Grottoes of Dunhuang, and Longmen Grottoes of Luoyang, are the best-known examples of Tang painting and sculpture. Music and dance also blossomed with renewed splendor through the blending of Chinese and foreign styles.

169-1

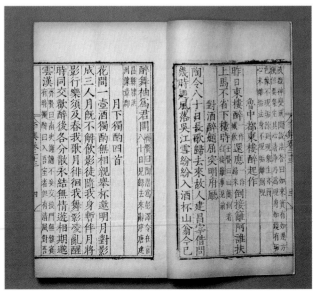
169-2

serious, vigorous in style, concise in language and strict in rhythm. His extant poems number over 1,400, the most representative being "Song of the War Chariots," "Song of Fair Ladies," the three partings— "Lament of the New Wife, " "The Old Couple Part" and "The Homeless," and the three conscripting officers—"The Conscripting Officer at Xin'an," "The Conscripting Officer at Shihao," and "The Conscripting Officer at Tongguan." Du Fu was as famous as Li

Bai, both men have had a profound influence on the literature of later periods.

171. Portrait of Bai Juyi, *Collected Works of Master Bai in the Changqing Reign*   Bai Juyi (772-846), courtesy name Letian, from Xiagui (present-day Weinan County, Shaanxi Province), advocator of new Music Bureau poems and songs in the mid-Tang period. In contrast to the old-theme poems and songs of the Music Bureau of the Han Dynasty, new Music

Bureau poems and songs used new themes to write on current events. By the time of Bai Juyi, a realistic poems and songs movement was formed. Bai Juyi lived after the Rebellion of An Lushan and Shi Siming, a time of upheaval and misery for the people. Most of his outstanding works were allegoric poems reflecting reality, including 50 new Music Bureau poems. His poems and songs were clear and easy to understand, and were circulated widely among the people.

170-1

171-1

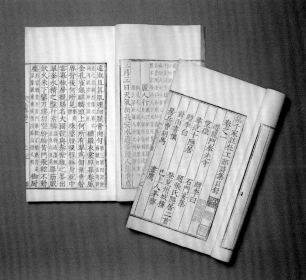

170-2

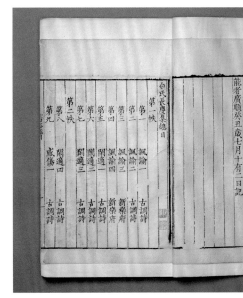

171-2

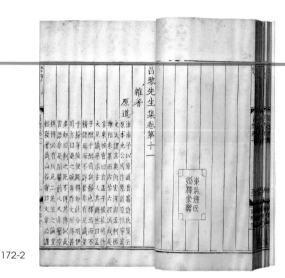

172-2

172-1

172. Portrait of Han Yu, *Collected Works of Master Changli* Han Yu (768-824), courtesy name Tuizhi, from Heyang, Henan (present-day Meng County, Henan Province), writer and thinker in the mid-Tang period, one of the leaders of the Tang-dynasty ancient literature movement. Han Yu advocated the use of prose (ancient style prose) of the Qin, Western and Eastern Han dynasties to replace the parallel prose prevailing at that time. The style gradually became the main-stay of the literature of the time. The reform of the literary style that ocurred at this time played an important role in the development of Chinese literature. Han Yu also advocated the restoration of Confucianism to its ancient form, started the tendency of collaboration between Confucianism, Taoism and Buddhism, and exerted great influence upon the Neo-Confucianism of the Song and Ming dynasties.

173. *Chunyu Fen* Written by Li Gongzuo; a Ming-dynasty edition. The *Chunyu Fen*, also known as *Biography of the Prefect of Nanke*, is one of the representative collections of Tang-dynasty tales. Using the dream of Chunyu Fen, a Tang official, as its vehicle the story exposes the dissipated, pleasure-seeking life that marked officialdom in those days, and sneers at the pursuit of position and wealth by people of the time. The tales were based on earlier stories describing strange events in the six dynasties; they were short stories written in classical Chinese. Tales such as these belonged to Tang popular literature and occupied an important position in the history of Chinese literature. Li Gongzuo was a productive writer of tales in the Tang Dynasty. *Chunyu Fen* was his representative work.

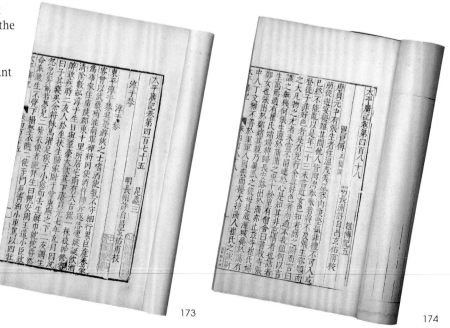

173

174

174. *The Story of Yingying*
Written by Yuan Zhen; a Ming-dynasty edition. *The Story of Yingying* tells about the love affair of a young man and a young woman. It reflects the maturity of Tang-era stories. It has been repeatedly adapted for traditional operas and other art forms, since the Tang Dynasty. The *Western Chamber* adapted by Wang Shipu of the Yuan Dynasty is still performed in China today. Yuan Zhen (779-831) was a friend of Bai Juyi, and the two frequently exchanged poems.

175. Rubbing from Inscription about Sweet Spring in Jiucheng Palace
Calligraphy of Ouyang Xun; original stele kept in the Forest of Steles Museum in Xi'an, Shaanxi Province. The rubbing is 32.8 cm long and 20 cm wide. This representative calligraphic work of Ouyang Xun (557-641) was done in 632, the sixth year of the Zhenguan reign of the Tang Dynasty. Ouyang Xun's style was influenced by the calligraphers of the Jin period. His calligraphy used powerful strokes, was compact in structure, and had a unique characteristic of its own, called the "Ouyang style". He was one of the four master calligraphers of the early Tang period and had great influence on the calligraphy of later ages.

唐故通議大夫行薛王友柱國贈祕書

176. Rubbing from Yan Family Ancestral Temple Stele   Calligraphy of Yan Zhenqing; original stele kept in the Forest of Steles Museum in Xi'an, Shaanxi Province. The rubbing is 27 cm long and 13.4 cm wide. Yan Zhenqing (709-785) was a celebrated calligrapher of the Tang Dynasty, leaving examples of several dozen kinds of calligraphy and stele carvings for posterity. He adopted many of the strong points of others in his calligraphy, while also bringing about a change in the ancient style of writing. His style is bold, vigorous, dignified in structure, dense in layout, and imposing, thanks to the strength of his wrist as he wielded the writing brush. His regular script is considered a classic one and is known as the "Yan style". The Yan Family Ancestral Temple Stele was carved and erected in 780 (the first year of the Jianzhong reign of the Tang Dynasty) to honor his father Yan Weizhen when he was 71. The carving was representative of the calligraphic works in his later years.

177. Rubbing from Xuanmi Pagoda Stele   Calligraphy of Liu Gongquan; original stele kept in the Forest of Steles Museum in Xi'an, Shaanxi Province. The rubbing is 38 cm long and 23 cm wide. Erected in 841, the first year of the Huichang reign of the Tang era, it was written by Liu Gongquan when he was 64. Liu Gongquan's calligraphy was bold in style, delicate in essence. He left over 10 stele carvings for posterity. All in regular script, they are considered classics. The style of the regular scripts of Yan Zhenqing and Liu Gongquan had a far-reaching influence on the art of calligraphy. In learning regular script, people of later generations have "started with the Liu style and achieved perfection with the Yan style".

178

178. Mural of maid Decorative picture from a Tang-dynasty tomb chamber, 113 cm high, 54 cm wide; unearthed from a tomb in Dizhangwan, Xianyang, Shaanxi Province, in 1953. Most of the Tang paintings that have been preserved are murals. The murals in grottoes and temples focused on Buddhist themes, while the murals in tomb chambers mainly depicted secular figures. Compared with the tomb chamber murals of the Han Dynasty, those of the Tang are much less mythological in theme and richer in their depiction of life. The maid in the mural is a young girl with a plump round face; she appears innocent and beautiful. The lines of the drawing are simple and smooth, typical of the painting style of the Tang Dynasty.

179. Mural of a dancing girl clad in red Decorative picture from a Tang-dynasty tomb chamber, 116 cm high, 70 cm wide; unearthed from the tomb of Zhishi Fengjie in Guodu Township, Chang'an County, Shaanxi Province, in 1957. It is a picture of a dancing girl with a red scarf draped over her body. In the ancient dance called "scarf dance", the dancer held the scarf in her hand and waved it, letting it follow her own posture and movements. The ritual dances of the Tang Dynasty were divided into civil and martial ones. The civil dances extolled the political achievements of the time; the martial dances eulogized the military achievements. As these two kinds of dance were relatively large in scale, they were staged mainly during large sacrificial rites and grand banquets in the palace. The small-scale dances of the Tang Dynasty were divided into the "vigorous dance" and "soft dance" forms. The former were brisk, powerful, with sprightly rhythms and a heated feeling to them, while the latter was gentle, lithe and graceful, with slow, unhurried rhythms and fine, smooth movements. These two kinds of dance were widely popular in palaces, the residences of the nobility and among the people. Some were solo dances; others were meant for two people. The scarf dance belonged to the small-scale "soft dance" category.

179

180-1

180. Rubbings from a so-called dented-line stone carving of beautiful women
Tang Dynasty; 155 cm high, 60 cm wide; unearthed from the tomb of Princess Yongtai in Qian County, Shaanxi Province, in 1961. Stone-carved line drawings were an art form unique to China, usually found on tomb walls, the inner and outer parts of coffins, epitaphs or steles. The contents of the stone-carved line drawings in Tang tombs mostly portrayed the life of the tomb occupant. These two drawings of beautiful women were selected from those carved on the outer stone coffin found in the tomb of Princess Yongtai. The lines of the drawing are smooth, clear and pithy. The women are graceful in bearing. They are surrounded by flowers, plants and flying birds, which add life to the picture.

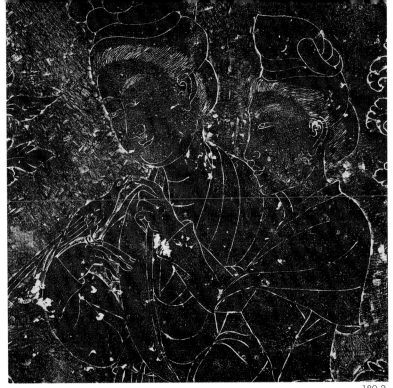

180-2

180-3

180-4

181

Tang Dynasty; 107 cm tall; unearthed from the ruins of the Ten-Thousand Buddha Temple outside the West Gate of Chengdu, Sichuan Province. Stone-carving during the Tang Dynasty stressed Buddhist themes. The images in the Ten-Thousand Buddha Temple, including Buddha, Bodhisattva, the Heavenly King and warrior, were all carved from fine sandstone. This Tang-era stone-carved image of the Heavenly King is plump and graceful, skillfully carved in a style that combines the unsophisticated traditions of the Yellow River Valley with local traditions. The Heavenly King is the guardian of Buddha. His image usually reflects great power and grandeur, is neatly armored, and tramps upon ghosts and evil spirits. In the wake of the secularization of Buddhism that occurred in the Tang Dynasty, the exaggerated aspects of the Heavenly King image were gradually reduced and the image became more realistic. This stone-carved image of the Heavenly King looks much more like a mortal general than a god.

181. Gilded warrior figurine carved from stone Tang-dynasty burial object; 40.3 cm tall; unearthed from the tomb of Yang Sixu in the southern suburbs of Xi'an, Shaanxi Province, in 1958. Wearing the typical dress of a man in the Tang Dynasty, the figurine carries three weapons, a crooked sword, bow and sabre. One of the sets, painted and gilded, is more exquisite than the others. It was apparently for the master. The others were for the warrior himself. The figurine, which looks young, soldierly and respectful, presumably represented the guard of the tomb occupant. Yang Sixu, the tomb occupant, was a eunuch who was eventually promoted to the high rank of general due to his meritorious military service. The figurine was carved from a whole piece of white marble. The work was done with meticulous care to the figure and dress as well as the weapons. It is lifelike and natural. Originally, it was painted and gilded all over, but now more than half of the paint has peeled off. The figurine is considered representative of stone-carving at the height of the Tang era.

182-1

183. Three-color glazed pottery figurine of a camel and rider Tang Dynasty; 39.4 cm tall, 47 cm long; unearthed from the tomb of Xianyu Tinghui in Xi'an, Shaanxi Province, in 1957. The figurine presents a man of the northern tribes sitting atop a crouching camel, pulling the reins and about to set off. It is typical of the camel sculptures of the Tang period, as well as a portrayal of real life in those days. The figurine is well-shaped with beautiful glazed colors; it is a fine example of the tri-colored pottery of the period. The methods of applying color to pottery figurines in past dynasties had differed. Some applied a layer of white powder to the surface of the article after biscuiting, then painted meticulously; others painted first then baked. The tri-colored pottery was a new technology, developed in the Tang Dynasty; such pottery was very popular due to its shining, colorful glaze.

183-1

◁ 183-2

184. Three-color figurines of the Heavenly King Tang-dynasty burial objects; 52 cm and 53.5 cm tall respectively; unearthed at Hansenzhai Village, Xi'an, Shaanxi Province, in 1955. The figurines of the Heavenly King were just one type of pottery tomb guardian. There were also animal figurines and warrior ones. An important burial object in the Tang Dynasty, the Heavenly King figurines were usually buried in pairs, placed on both sides of the tomb's gate and thought to have the role of warding off evil. Such burial customs started in the sixth century, originally with a pair of warrior figurines. By the Tang Dynasty, under the influence of Buddhist thinking, the warrior figurines were gradually replaced by images of the Heavenly King. The image of the Buddhist Heavenly King tends to be realistic, but the Heavenly King burial figurines were terribly exaggerated. The spirits under the feet of these two Heavenly Kings appear ferocious, yet they are moaning and struggling, showing the deterent force of the Heavenly King.

184-2

185-1

185. Black glazed three-color terracotta horse figurine   Tang-dynasty burial object; 66.5 cm tall; unearthed from Guan Lin Temple, Luoyang, Henan Province, in 1971. Horse sculptures of the Tang era had changed from the primitive, crude form of the Qin and Han dynasties into one that used a livelier raised-head posture. The three-color horses unearthed from Tang tombs, though varied in posture, all have small heads, round buttocks, and well-balanced bodies that are plump and sturdy, reflecting the typical characteristics of the horses of the Western Regions in those days. This terracotta horse figurine was completely glazed in black, except for its face, mane, tail and hoofs which were glazed in white. It is something rarely seen among Tang pottery samples. Moreover, its shape is robust, its glaze even and its posture natural, making it a rare, fine example of the period.

185-2 D

186-1

186. Three-color pottery tomb animals Tang-dynasty burial objects; 63.2 cm and 67.5 cm tall respectively; unearthed from the tomb of Xianyu Tinghui in Xi'an, Shaanxi Province, in 1957. The two animal tomb guardians are squatting. One was a human face, the other the face of an animal with a horn on its head. Exquisitely made, they are ferocious but beautiful, typical of such items at the height of the Tang Dynasty. Usually, such animal statues were placed at the entrance of the tomb to ward off evil and guard the soul of the deceased. They were intentionally made to look ferocious, in order to achieve a deterrent effect. Tomb animals were first seen in graves of the third century; in the beginning only one was used; later they were placed in pairs. The faces of the tomb animals in the Tang Dynasty were even more ferocious, and the differences between those with human faces and those with animal faces diminished. By the later part of the Tang era, pottery tomb animals had gradually disappeared.

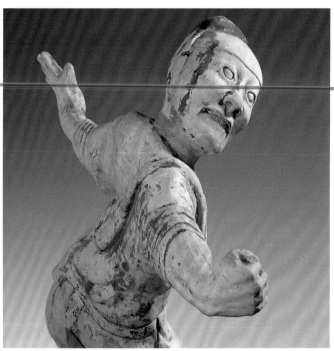

187-1

187. Pottery figurine of a horse and tamer   Tang-dynasty burial object; the tamer is 36.8 cm tall and the horse 40 cm high. The appearance of this set of figurines is lifelike and dynamic. The horse is rearing. He appears stubborn and unwilling to proceed. The tamer has his mouth open as if shouting and is pulling the reins forcefully with his right arm. The surface of the article was originally painted, but the paint has peeled off. Tang figurines were mostly moulded, then painted, and finally baked in a kiln. The moulding was mostly a combination of split patterns. The tamer and horse in this set were first made separately, then glued to each other.

187-2

188-1

188. Pottery figurine of a weeping woman Tang-dynasty burial object; 10.5 cm tall; unearthed from the tomb of Wang Chen in Changzhi, Shaanxi Province, in 1954. The female figurine bends down and holds her knees as she weeps. Perhaps to mourn the occupant of the tomb. The whitewash originally applied on her body has mostly peeled off. The figurine is a forceful one, expressing strong emotion while embodying the aesthetic characteristics of China's ancient art. Both essence and artistic conception are stressed.

188-2

189-1

189. Three-color figurines of musicians on horseback Tang-dynasty burial object, 36-37 cm tall; unearthed from the tomb of Li Zhen in Liquan County, Shaanxi Province, in 1972. In the early stage of the Tang era, burial objects in the tombs of the nobility often represented an outing, frequently with a group of entourage figurines used to depict an outing in the

real life of some member of the Tang nobility. These figurines of musicians on horseback were a part of such an entourage. Such sets usually included drummers and other percussionists, plus figures playing other types of musical instruments. Sometimes there were also singers. Some drums or drum racks have survived, slung round the necks or shoulders of a few horses, but the majority of the musical instruments have been lost and it is impossible to determine what they were. Judging by the gestures of the players, this was presumably a drum and wind instrument band on horseback, namely, the so-called "sound band" sometimes included in a Tang-dynasty entourage.

189-2

190. Pottery ensemble of musicians and dancers   Tang-dynasty burial object; 11-11.5 cm tall; unearthed from a tomb in Xi'an, Shaanxi Province, in 1955. These musicians and dancers are all kneeling or sitting cross-legged, holding in their hands such ancient musical instruments as the *konghou* (stringed), clappers, bamboo flute, multi-tube flute, or *pipa* and vertical flute, as if performing. The performing arts in the Tang palace combined the music and dances of many Chinese and foreign nationalities. New compositions and dances were also very popular. After Emperor Gaozong (650-683) of the Tang Dynasty, the compositions were regrouped, in accordance with their performance scale, into two categories, "sitting performers"and "standing performers", each having a fixed scope. A performance by the "sitting performers" was composed of six dances. They played in a hall while sitting, accompanying 3-12 dancers, on traditional stringed and woodwind instruments. The style of performance was elegant and the musicians' skills were relatively high. The performances by the "standing performers" were done on a larger scale and included eight dance numbers with 60-180 dancers. The dancers were accompanied by drums and bell-shaped percussion instruments. The overall effect was rather grand but the skill of the performers was actually a little inferior to that of the "sitting performers". This is a group of pottery "sitting performers".

190-2

Social Life

The social life of the Tang Dynasty was rich and varied. Many new changes took place in such things as dress, the utensils used in daily life and recreation. By absorbing foreign elements, the patterns of traditional dress were broken, and new styles and designs appeared. The appearance and use of tall pieces of furniture such as tables, chairs and stools replaced the ancient practice of sitting on the ground. The appearance of new types of tea sets and sets of drinking cups, and their gradual use for special purposes, marked a change in the way people drank tea or wine. With respect to the recreation of the Tang people, in addition to hunting, chess-playing, horsemanship and the earlier ball games, polo became fashionable for a while in the Tang era.

191. Pottery three-color figurine of a warrior   Tang dynasty burial object; 89 cm tall; unearthed form the tomb of Dugu Sizhen in Xi'an, Shaanxi Province, in 1958. The warrior figurine is somewhat exaggerated, yet its dress is basically realistic. The armor of the Tang Dynasty was mainly "Mingguang armor", which included a helmet with earflaps, a gorget, a single-piece backplate, left and right breastplates each with a round chestplate in the center, and straps that tied the breastplates to the backplate at the shoulders. The armor-straps were tied in the shape of a cross, their upper part revealing the round tasse. Below the belts there was a kneepiece on both the left and right sides, and under the kneepieces the war robe. The brassard had two layers, an upper one in the shape of a beast head swallowing the shoulder and the lower one stretching to the wrist. There was also another kind of robe with a round collar but no pants and a slit under the hip. As such a robe was comfortable to move around in and good for riding and shooting, it was popular in the army.

192. Pottery three-color figurine of a civil official   Tang-dynasty burial object; 72 cm tall; unearthed from the tomb of Xianyu Tinghui in Xi'an, Shaanxi Province, in 1957. The figurine holds a tablet with both hands before his breast, and wears an open-collared, wide-sleeve robe and clothes hanging to the knee. It also wears a wide girdle around its waist, with the end of girdle hanging behind the waist to the feet, a rectangular hemmed "knee cover "in front of the waist as well as upturned square-headed "red shoes". This kind of clothing was the court dress worn by officials of the fifth rank or higher in

191-2

court ceremonies. The ranks of the officials were distinguished by their style of hat, color of dress, quality of cloth and ornaments. While in court dress, an official was supposed to wear many ornaments. In addition to a sword, silk sash, streamer, double pendants and small bag, he could also wear such articles as a waist sword, knife, whetstone, needle tube, firestone bag, fish, fish bag, tortoise and tortoise bag. The style may have been influenced by the dress worn by the northern tribes. The wearing of such ornaments as a fish, fish bag, tortoise and tortoise bag originated in the Tang Dynasty and continued all the way into the Song and Ming dynasties.

191-1

192

193. Three-color pottery figurine of a groom Tang-dynasty burial object; 45.3 cm tall; unearthed from the tomb of Xianyu Tinghui in Xi'an, Shaanxi Province, in 1957. The figure wears a scarf on its head and a light yellow narrow-sleeve robe with a turndown collar. It is an example of one of the dresses of the northern tribes that prevailed in the Tang Dynasty. The scarf was actually a kind of hat used by men in the Tang period. It was a piece of black cloth or gauze wound around the head, and its shape could be changed at will. In the early Tang period, the top of the scarf hat was low and flat; later it became high, round or sharp, with its two ends hanging down.

In the mid and late Tang periods, a lining was added inside the scarf hat to facilitate it wearing and taking off. The two ends of the scarf hat changed from soft ones to hard ones and gradually evolved into horizontal, straight ones that stuck out on each side.

193-1

194-1

194-2

194. Pottery figurine of a man

Tang-dynasty burial object; 52.5 cm tall; unearthed from the tomb of Yang Sixu in Xi'an, Shaanxi Province, in 1958. Influenced by foreign cultures, the dress of men in the Tang Dynasty changed from the traditional loose gown worn with a wide girdle, high hat and leather shoes to the most popular form of wearing a scarf hat, round-collared robe and high boots. This was called "informal dress". Except for important ceremonies, emperors, nobles, common people and slaves all wore such outfits. The figurine is wearing the informal dress. The basic features of such a dress included its round collarband, narrow sleeves and the front of garment unhemmed and reaching the feet or below the knees. After the mid-Tang era, dresses gradually became loose. The use of a scarf hat, robe and boots in the Tang Dynasty influenced the dress of the Song and Ming dynasties, and also had an important influence on the dresses of Japan and Korea.

195. White porcelain inkslab

Tang-dynasty writing utensil; 7.2 cm high and 14.8 cm in diameter; unearthed from a tomb in Shan County, Henan Province, in 1957. The Tang Dynasty was an important period for the development of inkslabs in China. The time-honored famous inkslabs made in Duanxi and Shexian appeared at that time. The stone used in Duanxi was usually purple in color, while that in Shexian was black. As the demand for the inkslabs was big, stone inkslabs, pottery inkslabs and porcelain ones were all used. As for porcelain inkslabs, the three-legged ones of the Wei and Jin periods were still used, the number of legs of the inkslab increased and the grinding surface was raised. The bottom of the white porcelain inkslab is a hollowed-out ring foot composed of 21 legs, shaped like animal hoofs.

195

196. White porcelain three-legged water receptacle

Tang-dynasty writing utensil; 4.5 cm high, 3.5 cm in diameter; unearthed from a tomb in the city of Sanmenxia, Henan Province, in 1958. The receptacle is melon-shaped and glazed on both its inner and outer sides. It was used for holding water to be dropped onto an inkslab. There were a great deal of white porcelain water receptacles in the Tang Dynasty. During the early Tang, they were usually found in the shape of a contracted mouth and flat bottom. At the height of the Tang period straight mouths and four legs were more common, while in the late Tang they were covered with a lid. As the Tang Dynasty culture flourished, water receptacles of this kind were in great demand.

196

197. Pottery female figurines wearing double hair-buns and a high hair-bun

Tang-dynasty burial objects; 31.4 cm and 31.6 cm tall respectively. The female figurine wearing the double hair-buns is clad in a round-collar, narrow-sleeved upper garment with her neck exposed. The one wearing the high bun is clad in a narrow-sleeved short jacket, long skirt, with a long belt around her waist and a piece of silk draped over her shoulders. Women's dress in the early Tang era followed the style of the Sui Dynasty, with tops that were short and fitted and fell to the waist and long, slim skirts that hung from the waist or chest to the ground. They reflected the aesthetic awareness of women in this period and an emphasis on elegance. The popularity of narrow sleeves resulted from the cultural influence of the Western Regions. At the height of the Tang period, sleeves gradually became wider and female styles began to change. There were a great variety of hair-styles worn during the Tang Dynasty. Most noble women wore fake hair-buns done up in various ways. In the early Tang, hair-buns were relatively low and small and simple and unadorned, while at the height of the Tang period, high buns were favored and garlands added. In the mid and late Tang, buns were high and inserted with such ornaments as hair clasps, hairpins and colorful combs. The effect was a stately appearance for the woman who wore such a hair-style.

198. Silver hair clasp, silver hairpins

Tang-dynasty articles for binding hair; the phoenix-shaped hairpin is 33 cm long, the fan-shaped one 29.6 cm long, and the fan-shaped hair clasp 29 cm long. The hair-buns of Tang women were varied and complicated, as were the tools for binding hair. Gold and silver hair clasps and hairpins were all the more gorgeous. In addition to their practical use, they were ornaments. Hair clasps and hairpins were made of gold, silver, jade or copper. They came in various styles, with designs of flowers and birds engraved on them or featured pendants and, in some cases, were inlaid with exquisite jewels. These hairpins and clasps added splendor to the unique hair-buns of the Tang women.

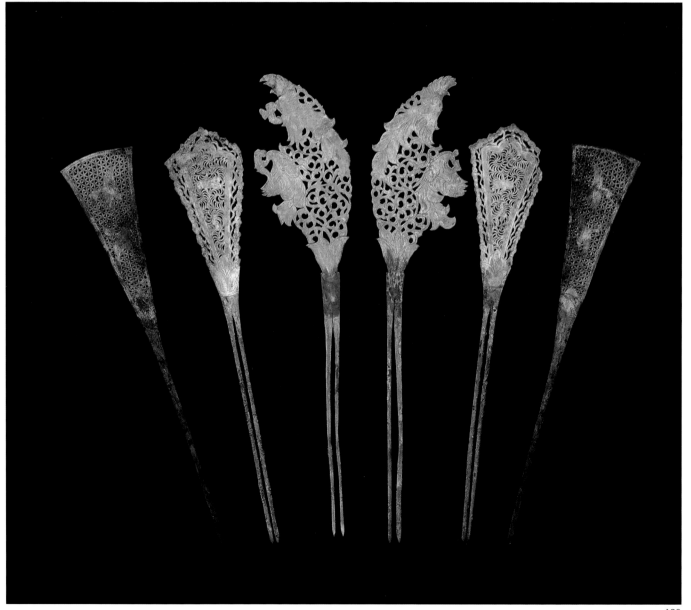

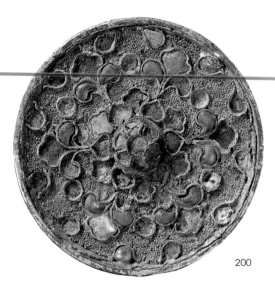

200

199. Three-color figurine of a woman
Tang-dynasty burial object; 45.2 cm tall; unearthed from the tomb of Xianyu Tinghui in Xi'an, Shaanxi Province, in 1957. The figurines of women in the most flourishing period of the Tang Dynasty changed from the elegant style of the early Tang to a full-figured style reflecting the change in aesthetic standards. In line with this change, the sleeves of women's tops and their long skirts became increasingly broad. Thanks to progress in the methods of spinning and weaving, embroidery, printing and dyeing, the color, pattern and workmanship of garments also became increasingly exquisite and luxurious. By the time of the mid and late Tang, broad-sleeved, loose tops and wide, pleated skirts had become fashionable. Several emperors attempted to limit the width of the sleeves and skirts, but failed. The figurine pictured here was unearthed from a tomb of the most flourishing Tang period. It appears plump in figure, and its hairstyle and dress are considerably different from those of the female figurines in the early Tang period.

200. Gilded bronze mirror inlaid with green and white beads   Tang-dynasty cosmetic article; 4.8 cm in diameter; unearthed in Xi'an, Shaanxi Province, in 1955. This is a "palm mirror". It is handy and can be taken out at any time to apply cosmetics, even by a woman on an outing. The mirror is small, yet it demonstrates the high level of handicraft skill achieved in the Tang Dynasty. The luster of its gold-plate and the green and white inlaid beads add further radiance.

199-1

201

201. Pottery figurine of a woman
Tang-dynasty burial object; 51 cm tall; unearthed from the tomb of Yang Sixu in Xi'an, Shaanxi Province, in 1958. Women dressed in men's clothes was a popular sight in the Tang Dynasty, especially in the heyday of the Tang. It was a fashion seen regardless of the social status of the woman. When doing so, a woman usually wore a scarf or a hat of the northern tribes on her head, round-collar robe, dark leather boots and a leather girdle around her waist, just like a man. This pottery figurine of a woman was unearthed from the grave of a member of the nobility who died in 740, the 28th year of the Kaiyuan reign, i.e. during the most flourishing Tang period. It wears high double hair-buns, a round-collar robe, waist belt and boots. Except for the absence of scarf hat, it is the typical dress of a Tang man.

202. Three-color sitting female figurine   Tang-dynasty burial object; 28.5 cm tall; unearthed from Baijiakou in Xi'an, Shaanxi Province, in 1953. This female figurine wears an upper garment with a low neck, narrow sleeves and long skirt. A piece of silk is draped around her shoulders and hangs down. Gorgeously dressed, she is the image of a young noble woman of the Tang Dynasty. The figurine sits on a round stool which has a slender waist, showing that the people of the Tang era changed from sitting on the ground to sitting with dangling feet. The stools of the Tang Dynasty were crescent-shaped, round and slender, or rectangular. Chairs were called "rope beds" in the early Tang period and mainly used in temples. A chair had four legs, a back and an armrest on each side. They were wide so a monk could sit on them cross-legged. "Rope beds" were later called "leaning beds"; the name "chair" was not used until after the mid-Tang period.

202

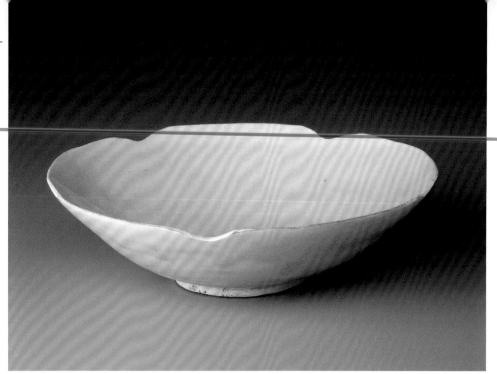

203

203. White porcelain bowl with sunflower-shaped mouth and shallow bottom

Tang-dynasty tea set; 4.3 cm high, diameter 14.3 cm. Tea-drinking is a time-honored activity in China and its popularization took place after the mid-Tang period. During that period, the Chinese character meaning "tea"came into existence, books on tea appeared and a tea tax was levied for the first time. The barter of tea for horses also occurred in border trading. The tea set at that time was mainly a bowl, *zhan* (small cup) and regular cup, usually bowls. The tea bowls in the early and at the peak of the Tang era were simple, thick and heavy in appearance. In the mid-Tang period tea bowls with open mouths, sloping sides, jade sides or with ring bases appeared. The best-quality tea bowls were the white porcelain bowls from the Xingyao Kiln in the north and caledon bowls from the Yueyao Kiln in the south. The bowl pictured here is a fine porcelain one from the Xingyao Kiln. There are circular traces of rubbing on the glaze inside the bowl, presumably the result of stirring the tea with a tea brush or tea spoon for a long time.

204. Gilded silver saucer with lotus-petal design

Tang-dynasty tea set; 4 cm high, 17.4 cm in diameter; unearthed from the ruins of the Pingkang workshop in the Tang capital of Chang'an, now Xi'an, Shaanxi Province, in 1957. In its early stage, the bottom of the tea saucer was concave and surrounded by a raised edge for holding it. This silver tea saucer exactly reflects such a pattern. Inside its foot were inscribed Chinese characters saying "The tea depot in the residence of a commander of the imperial guards". The raised edges of another seven gilded silver saucers unearthed at the same time were relatively lower. In the late Tang period, the raised edge of the tea saucer became higher, as if a small bowl had been added to the saucer. This type of tea saucer was discovered in Tang tombs in Hunan, Zhejiang and Hubei provinces.

204-1   204-2

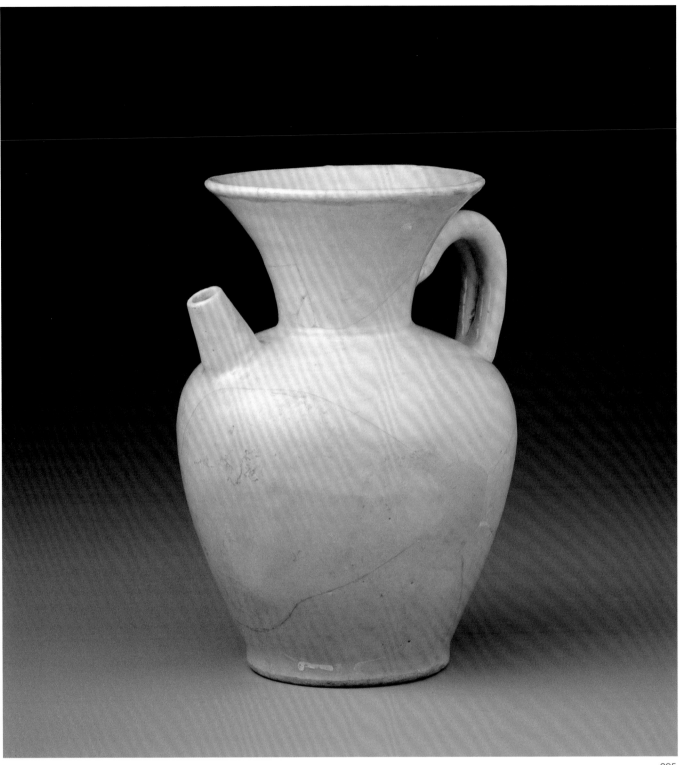

205

205. White porcelain tea vase Tang-dynasty tea set; 16.7 cm high, 9.6 cm in diameter; unearthed in Liujiaqu, Shan County, Henan Province, in 1956. Tea vases were also called "hot water bottles". The shape of this tea vase is similar to the one unearthed from the tomb of Wang Mingzhe of 829, the third year of the Taihe reign of the Tang Dynasty, in Xi'an, Shaanxi Province. It was used for holding boiling water while making tea. After the mid-Tang period, greater attention was paid to the way tea was drunk, and a series of special tea sets were developed. The development of tea vases came rather late, signaling the beginning of making tea with boiling water. This method of tea-making was very popular in the late stage of the Tang Dynasty, and tended to replace the older method of "simmering tea".

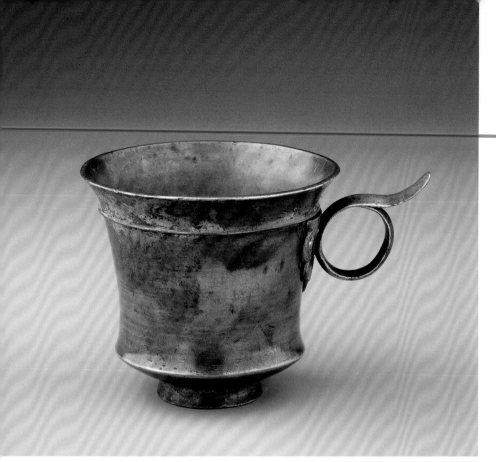

206. Ring-handled silver cup

Tang-dynasty drinking utensil; 6.3 cm high, 7 cm in diameter; unearthed from a cellar in Shapo Village, Xi'an, Shaanxi Province, in 1963.This cup is a drinking vessel. There was a great variety of Tang cups, which included the high-foot cup used for drinking wine. In the early stage of the Tang Dynasty, special drinking utensils such as gold and silver cups with a small circular foot or a single ring handle, or even with several lobes or ridges, were popular. This was appearently due to the influence of the drinking set used in Central Asia. At that time ring-handled porcelain cups that imitated gold and silver wares also appeared, along with other drinking vessels. The bottoms of some of them were set on a special wine platform. The relation between the wine cup and wine platform was similar to that between the tea saucer and tea cup, indicating a mutual influence between special-purpose tea sets and drinking vessels.

207. Silver ladle with duckbill handle

Tang-dynasty drinking utensil; 26.4 cm long; unearthed from a Tang tomb in the city of Sanmenxia, Henan Province, in 1957. In the early stage of the Tang Dynasty, a zun (cup) was used to hold wine, and a silver zun had to be matched with silver ladle. Currently, the two silver ladles extant overseas both have the ends of their handles in the shape of a bird's head. Tang narratives describe such other kinds of ladles as those in the shape of a goose neck or the head of a duck, all similar to the shape of extant cultural relics. It appears that it was the prevailing custom in those days to make the end of the handle of a wine ladle in the shape of some sort of fowl.

208. Melon-shaped celadon ewer from the Yueyao Kiln

Tang-dynasty drinking utensil; 22.6 cm high, 10.2 cm in diameter; unearthed in the city of Ningbo, Zhejiang Province, in 1974. Wine ewers were a new type of drinking vessel which appeared after the mid-Tang period; they were known as "wine pots" or simply "pots" . Before the appearance of the wine pot, the traditional wine vessel was mainly the zun matched with its silver ladle. The zun and ladle were used at banquets till the Jin and Yuan dynasties. Following the development of distilled liquor, the zun and ladle were gradually replaced by the wine pot. In the Tang Dynasty, there was a kind of wine vessel, the hu (foreign)vase, which was made under the influence of the wine vessels of the Sasanian Dynasty of ancient Iran. It had a handle but no spout, similar to the form of the wine pot. It was difficult to distinguish the shape of the wine pot from a tea vase in the Tang Dynasty. Both vessels were labelled, some were inscribed with the character meaning "wine" and others with the one for "tea" . Others had no inscription at all. It seems that the difference between the wine pot and tea vase was not apparent at this stage. The evolution of such vessels was as follows: in the early stage it was short with a big belly and short spout; in the late stage it became slender with a long spout. This ewer belonged to the type used in the late Tang period.

209. Celadon bowl from the Yueyao Kiln

Tang-dynasty drinking utensil; 5.8 cm high, 12 cm in diameter; unearthed at Heyi Road, Ningbo, Zhejiang Province. The people of the Tang Dynasty drank wine from bowls. Generally speaking, a bowl could be used to drink either wine or tea, it could be determined to be a wine vessel or a tea vessel only by the inscription on the vessel, i.e. by the character meaning "wine" or meaning "tea". It is relatively easy to identify a tea bowl which was used for a long time from the tea stains or scratches on it. The structure of this celadon bowl is obviously different from the shallow bowl with an open mouth found in mid-Tang period. With its higher ring foot slanted outward and its relatively deep belly, the bowl appears to be a wine drinking vessel of the late Tang period.

209

210. High-legged silver cup with hunting design Tang-dynasty wine vessel; 7.4 cm high, 6.3 cm in diameter; unearthed from a cellar in Shapo Village, Xi'an, Shaanxi Province, in 1963. The cup was shaped by hammering and its decorative pattern is flat. Four horse-riding hunters are chasing deer, hares and foxes in a setting of trees and flowers. Emperors and officials of the Tang Dynasty were fond of hunting and portrayals of such scenes have not only been found on gold and silver vessels, but also on bronze mirrors and murals. The shape of this cup has the features of a Western goblet, while the dresses of the figures in the design are in the Tang style. This reflects the fact that gold and silver vessels of the Western style had, in those days, gradually developed into a Chinese style.

210-2

211

211. Stone record of Hanguang Hall "polo field"   Tang-dynasty stone record; 53.5 cm both in length and width; unearthed from the ruins of the Daming Palace in the city of Chang'an, now Xi'an, Shaanxi Province, in 1956. It is believed by some that polo originated in Persia and was later introduced into China via the Western Regions; others say the sport was introduced to the inland regions from Tubo (Tibet) in the first year of the Tang Dynasty. Promoted by Li Shimin, Emperor Taizong of the Tang Dynasty, polo became popular first in palace and then gradually circulated amog the people. According to records, many "polo fields" or "polo

pavilions" were built in the imperial city of the Tang Dynasty. On this stone record were inscribed Chinese characters meaning "Hanguang Hall and polo field, etc., built in the year *xin hai* (831)in the Dahe reign of the Tang Dynasty". It indicates that a polo field was built in the Hangunag Hall of the Daming Palace. Moreover, many nobles in the city of Chang'an in the Tang Dynasty built polo fields at their private residences. Polo was at first fashionable in the capital, and then spread to garrison posts, becoming popular in the army. Usually, wherever the army went, polo prevailed.

212. Painted pottery polo players Tang-dynasty burial objects; 32-36 cm tall; unearthed in Xi'an, Shaanxi Province, in 1958. There are quite a few images of polo players on horseback left from the Tang Dynasty. Polo players were usually divided into two teams, each player riding on horseback and holding a polo stick over one meter in length with a crescent end. The ball was as small as a fist and made of hollowed-out light, hard wood. There were two types of goals, one being a board on one side of the field with an opening under the board to form the goal post. A net covered the opening to form a bag. The side which hit the ball into the bag won. The other way was to have a goal on each side of the field, the two teams would contend to hit the ball and the side which hit the ball into the goal won. The polo field was spacious and smooth, and the two teams, riding on horseback, contended for one ball in a very strenuous competition. These five polo players on horseback wear close-fitting dresses and their postures and expressions as they fight for the ball are vivid, though their polo sticks are missing.

212

213. Mural of musicians playing

panpipes Tang-dynasty decorative picture from coffin chamber; 195 cm tall, 93.5 cm wide; unearthed from a Tang tomb at Dizhangwan in Xianyang, Shaanxi Province, in 1953. The graves of the Tang imperial family, their relatives and civil and military officials usually included a courtyard and coffin chamber, reflecting the residence of a wealthy person of the time. On the walls of the tomb passage, entrance, court yard, paved path and coffin chamber murals were usually painted, which depicted such things as a procession, watch tower, city walls, servants and maids, hunting scenes, polo games and dances. They reflected different aspects of the social status and life of the tomb occupant. Most of the nobility and rich people in the Tang Dynasty maintained singers and dancers. This mural thus portrays a common social occasion.

214. Pottery figurines of the twelve zodiac animals Tang-dynasty burial objects; 36.5-42.5 cm tall; unearthed at Hansen Village, Xi'an, Shaanxi Province, in 1955. The so-called Ten Heavenly Stems and Twelve Earthly Branches were used to designate the years, months, days and hours as early as the Shang Dynasty in China. In the Han Dynasty, 12 kinds of animals were matched with the Twelve Earthly Branches. They were called the "twelve animals symbolic of the year of birth", namely, *zi* (rat), *chou*(ox), *yin* (tiger), *mao* (hare), *chen* (dragon), *si* (snake), *wu* (horse), *wei* (sheep), *shen* (monkey), *you* (cock), *xu* (dog) and *hai* (hog). Only later did the concept emerge that the animal denoting the year of birth affected the fate of a man. During the period of the Southern and Northern Dynasties, figurines of the zodiac animals were buried together with the deceased to ward off evil spirits. By the Tang Dynasty, images of the twelve symbolic animals were often found on bronze mirrors, gold

214-1

and silver vessels and tombstones. Thus, a considerable number of such figurines have been unearthed from graves. Usually, they are of three types: the symbolic animal held in the arms of a man, a symbolic animal head with the body of a man, the symbolic animal lying prone on a man's head. This group of 12 figurines are standing haman figures with the heads of animals.

Five Dynasties and Ten Kingdoms Period

(907—960)

Table of the Rise and Fall of the Five Dynasties and Ten Kingdoms

Name of Dynasty and country	Founder	Time	Exterminated by
Later Liang	Zhu Wen	907-923	Later Tang
Later Tang	Li Cunxu	923-936	Later Jin
Later Jin	Shi Jingtang	936-946	Qidan
Later Han	Liu Zhiyuan	947-950	Later Zhou
Later Zhou	Guo Wei	951-960	Song
Wu	Yang Xingmi	902-937	Southern Tang
Southern Tang	Xu Zhigao (*Li Bian*)	937-975	Song
Wu Yue	Qian Liu	907-978	Song
Chu	Ma Yin	927-951	Southern Tang
Min	Wang Shenzhi	909-945	Southern Tang
Southern Han	Liu Yan	917-971	Song
Early Shu	Wang Jian	907-925	Later Tang
Later Shu	Meng Zhixiang	934-965	Song
Nanping	Gao Jixing	924-963	Song
Northern Han	Liu Min	951-979	Song

The Rebellion of An Lushan and Shi Siming, which broke out in 775, weakened the centralized state power of the Tang Dynasty. It was followed by a period marked by separatist regimes set up by military governors, internal strife among factions, arrogation of all powers by eunuchs and all sorts of complicated situations. A large-scale peasant uprising led by Huang Chao broke out in 874; that was followed by the collapse of the Tang court. After the downfall of the Tang Dynasty, China entered a historical period of Five Dynasties and Ten Kingdoms. During the period from 907 to 960, the Yellow River valley came under the rule of several

relatively short successive dynasties, namely, the Later Liang, Later Tang, Later Jin, Later Han and Later Zhou. These were collectively called the Five Dynasties. At the same time, south China and Shanxi were ruled by ten separatist political regimes one after another, namely, the Early Shu, Wu, Min, Wu Yue, Chu, Southern Han, Nanping, Later Shu, Southern Tang and Northern Han. These were to become known in history as the Ten Kingdoms. During that period, the north was plagued by frequent warfare and its political situation turbulent, while the south was relatively stable with a fairly developed society and economy. The kingdoms in the south generally attached importance to irrigation which played a vital role in the development of agriculture. On the basis of that agricultural development, considerable progress was made in such crafts as salt-making, tea-processing, shipbuilding, paper making, ceramics, smelting, weaving and dyeing. Commerce prospered and a number of commercial cities emerged.

215. Kaiping tongbao coins
Later Liang currency diameter 3.5 cm
Tiancheng yuanbao coins
Later Tang currency diameter 2.35 cm
Tianfu yuanbao coins
Later Jin currency diameter 2.2 cm
Hanyuan tongbao coins
Later Han currency diameter 2.4 cm
Zhouyuan tongbao coins
Later Zhou currency diameter 2.45 cm
During the Five Dynasties, due to tangled warfare over a long period of time, the economy in the area of the middle and lower reaches of the Yellow River was devastated. The monetary system in those days was also chaotic, as manifested by the lack of coins, frequent illegal minting of coins of inferior quality of many small galvanized-iron coins. The currency irregularities reflected the disruption in the economy, and at the same time seriously hindered the development of commerce.

216. Datang tongbao coins
Southern Tang currency
diameter 2.3 cm
Qianheng zhongbao coins
Southern Han currency
diameter 2.4 cm
Tianhan yuanbao coins
Early Shu currency
diameter 2.3 cm
Guangzheng tongbao coins
Later Shu currency
diameter 2.2 cm
Tiance fubao coins
Chu currency
diameter 4.4 cm
Yonglong tongbao coins
Min currency
diameter 3.5 cm
During the period of the Five Dynasties and Ten Kingdoms, there was less warfare among the kingdoms in the south and the political situation there was relatively stable. The kingdoms undertook new water conservancy projects and the reclamation of wastelands, resulting in the growth of agricultural production to varying degrees. The planting of such commercial crops as mulberries and tea became increasingly popular. Handicrafts such as silk weaving, porcelain making, tea-processing, and shipbuilding became more and more developed. Commerce was also active and various kinds of coins were circulated.

217. Iron pledge for Qian Liu
Tang-dynasty written contract; 52 cm long, 29.8 cm wide, 0.4 cm thick. This is a document bestowed by an emperor upon a meritorious man to exempt the latter from the death penalty or confer on him other special privileges. The iron pledge for Qian Liu is the only iron pledge of the Tang Dynasty currently preserved in China. It was bestowed by Emperor Zhaozong in 897, the 4th year of the Qianning reign, on Qian Liu, the military governor of Zhenhai and Zhendong prefectures and the founder of the Wu Yue Kingdom in the period of the Five Dynasties and Ten Kingdoms. Shaped like an overturned tile, the iron pledge was inscribed with a 333-character imperial edict in gold. The edict lists the rank and title, government post and feoff of Qian Liu and the feats for which he was enfeoffed. It also specifies that Qian Liu could be excused nine times for a capital offence, and his descendents could be excused three times. Should they violate other laws of the country, the officials concerned were not supposed to have a hand in the affair.

Five Dynasties and Ten Kingdoms Period 215

維乾寧四年歲次丁巳八月甲辰東朔

四日丁未皇帝若曰咨尔鎮海鎮東

等軍節度浙江東西等道觀察處置

營田招討等使薫兩浙諸道鐵判置發

運等使開府儀同三司撿校太尉兼

中書令使持節潤越等州諸軍事

潤越等寺州刺史上柱國等彭成

邑五千戶食實封一百戶

銘節隮之言經州太夫德今

事美名董昌僑僑蒿氏餞水狂謀西貫

所者

218. Celadon bowl with carved lotus-petal design   Kingdom of Wu Yue vessel; 7.4 cm high, diameter 4.5 cm,

218

base diameter 5.9 cm; unearthed in Ningbo, Zhejiang Province. The present-day Zhejiang Province belonged to the Kingdom of Wu Yue in the period of the Five Dynasties and Ten Kingdoms. Of the ten kingdoms, Wu Yue was relatively stable politically, had a developed production, prosperous economy and its ceramics making was well-developed, with the celadon produced in the Yueyao Kiln exquisite and even famous in the outside world. This celadon bowl is regular in shape, its glaze shining and clean and its outer wall decorated with plump lotus petals, believed to be related to the worship of Buddhism.

219. Celadon box with carved design of seven children   Kingdom of Wu Yue vessel; 3.8 cm high, diameter 12.4 cm, base diameter 7.6 cm; unearthed in Furun Township, Sheng County, Zhejiang Province. This celadon box is composed of a box-like body and a lid, buttoned by snap fasteners. In the center of the lid are carved seven children. Innocent and naive, they reflect the Chinese tradition that more children mean more blessings. On the outside of the lid is carved an auspicious expression "long life from generation to generation".

220. Gilded bronze statue of *guanyin*   Kingdom of Wu Yue Buddhist statue; 53 cm high; unearthed from the base of the Ten-Thousand Buddha Pagoda in Jinhua, Zhejiang Province, in 1958. The statue of *guanyin* (the Goddess of Mercy) sits on a rockery; she is peaceful and serene, graceful and natural. The pagoda style originated in India to house the relics of Sakyamuni, the founder of Buddhism, and later spread into China with Buddhism. When a pagoda is erected, a container to hold relics, musical instruments for worship and alms is usually buried in its base. After the period of the Five Dynasties, it was common to place stone pillars inscribed with Buddhist scriptures and images of Buddha in the base of a pagoda. The leaders of the Wu Yue regime that ruled present-day Zhejiang Province during the Five Dynasties were Buddhists. The regime built Buddhist temples on a wide scale, and cast or printed a large number of Buddha images to be distributed to the temples for worship.

219

220 ▷

221. Melon-shaped white porcelain water receptacle Five Dynasties writing utensil; 6 cm high, 2.8 cm in diameter, 4.5 cm at its base; unearthed in Yangzhou, Jiangsu Province, in 1976. During the Sui and Tang dynasties, the white porcelain of the north and celadon of the south kept abreast of each other in development. During the Five Dynasties new progress was made in the production of white porcelain which featured fine bases, spotless white glaze and exquisite workmanship, thus preparing an excellent background for the development of painted porcelain in later ages.

222. White porcelain pillow Kingdom of Wu daily-use item; 17.8 cm long, 12.5 cm wide, 10.4 cm high; unearthed from the Wang family tomb on the Yudai River in Lianyungang, Jiangsu Province, in 1956. The surface of this rectangular porcelain pillow is slightly concave to suit the needs of a sleeper. Porcelain pillows first appeared in the Sui Dynasty. After the Tang Dynasty, they became increasingly common and their shape and design all the more interesting.

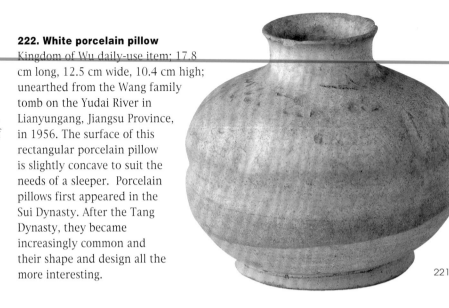

221

222

223. Gilded brass knocker Early Shu, door part; 37.8 cm high, with the diameter of the animal-mask 29.4 cm; unearthed from the tomb of Wang Jian in Chengdu, Sichuan Province, in 1942-1943. This knocker was a component of the door of a building in ancient China. Usually a round base was made of brass or iron with a knocker fixed on it to be used for opening, closing or knocking on the door. The base was usually made in the shape of an animal mask with a knocker held in its mouth. The decorative effect is very good. Wang Jian was an emperor of the Early Shu, and the gilded brass knocker on the door of his tomb is a splendid and complete decoration which shows a relatively high level of technology.

225

224. Pottery figurine of a female dancer   Southern Tang burial object; 49.5 cm tall; unearthed from the mausoleum of Li Bian in Jiangning County, Jiangsu Province, in 1950-1951.The female figurine is dancing with her body bent and sleeves raised, in a lifelike gesture. During the period of the Five Dynasties and Ten Kingdoms, the Southern Tang ruled the whole province of Jiangxi and a part of today's Anhui, Jiangsu, Fujian and Hubei provinces. It was thus a relatively powerful kingdom in the south. Marked progress was made in its agriculture, handicraft and commerce, and the country was rich. It launched an imperial examination system, set up schools and emphasized culture. Meanwhile, its literature and art flourished, topping those of all other regimes of the time. The Southern Tang regime considered itself the successor of the Tang Dynasty and imitated the latter to a very great extent in institutions like the civil service system, the law, imperial examinations, ceremonies, music and dress. In sculpture, it also inherited and developed the style of realism begun in the Tang Dynasty.

225. Bronze mirror from government copper workshop   Southern Tang cosmetic article; 17.6 cm in diameter, 0.3 cm thick; unearthed from the tomb of Jiang Mei Po in Hefei, Anhui Province, in 1957. The back of the mirror is plain, except for the Chinese characters meaning "Government copper workshop craftsman Fang Zong" and "official". The copper workshop was a handicraft work shop run by the government and its products were mainly for the use of society's upper classes. The reason for casting the name of its maker was to establish clear responsibility and ensure the quality of products. The character meaning" official" precisely indicates that it is the product of an official workshop.

夫馬
備爵得　　　　　　　　　拜
否拜尸　　　　　　　　　造
　其功　　酒酢酒
　酌于　巳巳真之者　非主人
　　之　　　　　　　　　　　馬
　王人
馬　　王人

226. Stone inscription of classics carved in Later Shu Relic of Later Shu; remnant 29 cm high, 21.5 cm wide, 7.5 cm thick; said to have been unearthed in Chengdu, Sichuan Province, in 1938. This stone inscription of classics is modelled on the Confucian classics which were carved on stone tablets. Since the stone inscriptions of the classics carved in the Xiping reign of the Eastern Han Dynasty, the carving of the classics on stone had continued down through the various dynasties. The Later Shu ruled the area of present-day Sichuan, an area relatively developed in economy and culture for its time. During the reign titled Guangzheng of Meng Chang, the last ruler of the Later Shu (938–965), Prime Minister Wu Zhaoyi proposed carving of the Confucian classics on stone. The inscriptions of ten classics were completed, namely, *The Classic of Filial Piety, The Analects of Confucius, Er Ya (Near to Correctness), The Book of Changes, The Book of Poetry, The Book of History, The Rites, The Book of Rites, The Rites of Zhou* and *Zuo Qiuming's Commentary on the Spring and Autumn Annals.* In the Song Dynasty, *The Biography of Gongyang, The Biography of Guliang* and *Mencius* were also carved, forming a complete series of thirteen Confucian classics. There are annotations under the stone inscriptions of Confucian classics done in the Later Shu, making them unique among such works.

227. Celadon jar with six loop handles Southern Han vessel; 19.5 cm high, 6.9 cm in diameter, 8.1 cm in diameter at the base; unearthed from a tomb of the Southern Han period in Panyu County, Guangdong Province, in 1954. The jar has a lid and six ears. According to research, the tomb in Panyu might be the Zhaoling Mausoleum of Liu Sheng, Emperor Zhongzong of the Southern Han. The tomb had been robbed in earlier years, and only around 200 pieces of ceramics and stone carvings were left behind. The celadon unearthed is exquisite, unconventional, with glaze evenly applied and glittering. It was a fine piece of celadon for its time and probably produced in government kiln of the Southern Han.

227

228. Peacock blue glazed pottery vase with three loop handles　Later Tang vessel; 75 cm high, 17 cm in diameter, 16 cm at the base; unearthed from the tomb of Liu Hua in the suburbs of Fuzhou, Fujian Province, in 1965. This olive-shaped pottery vase is glazed all over in peacock blue, with its belly overlaid with a semicircular arc design. In the period of the Five Dynasties and Ten Kingdoms, the Kingdom of Min made full use of the fine natural harbors of Fuzhou and Quanzhou to develop overseas trade and had commercial exchanges with such regions as South and West Asia. The pottery vase unearthed from the tomb of Liu Hua is the same as the glazed pottery Islamic-style vases of the 9th-10th centuries discovered in present-day Iran, in terms of shape, the color of its glaze and the design on its belly.

229. Painted pottery figurine of a civil official　Later Tang burial object; 62.5 cm tall; unearthed from the tomb of Liu Hua in the suburbs of Fuzhou, Fujian Province, in 1965. The Kingdom of Min was the regime governing present-day Fujian in the time of the Five Dynasties and Ten Kingdoms. Liu Hua was the wife of Wang Yanjun, the king of Min (later King Huizong of Min). At that time, though the Kingdom of Min nominally submitted itself to the rule of the Later Tang regime, it was in fact an independent kingdom. The tomb of Liu Hua had been robbed in earlier years, yet 43 pottery figurines were unearthed, mainly images of ladies in waiting, female officials and civil officials, all reflecting the illustrious position and extravagant life led by Liu Hua.

230. Pottery figurine of a woman with high hair-bun and both hands folded　Later Tang burial object; 100 cm tall; unearthed from the tomb of Liu Hua in the suburbs of Fuzhou, Fujian Province, in 1965. This painted figure of a woman wears a high fan-shaped bun. Both hands are folded before her chest inside her long sleeves. The figurine has a plump carriage and her shape copies the style of the Tang Dynasty. The modelling of her face in particular maintains the Tang style of plumpness. The workmanship of the entire piece is very professional, its proportions are precise and the expression of the figure is serene. Altogether, it demonstrates the relatively high level of sculpture of the Kingdom of Min.

228

230

229-1

229-2 ▷

231. Stove and tea pot
overall height 15.6 cm

232. Tea vase
9.8 cm high, 4.3 cm in diameter

233. Tea mortar
3.1 cm high, 12.2 cm in diameter

234. Dregs cup
9.5 cm high, 11.3 cm in diameter

These are burial objects of the Five Dynasties period modelled in the style of a tea set said to have been unearthed in Tang County, Hebei Province. The tea pot and stove were used to simmer tea, i. e., to heat water in the tea pot itself over the stove, and when the water was boiling, add a measure of tea dust to the water and stir it with a chopstick. After the tea floated to the surface of the pot, the tea was poured into a bowl for drinking. In the later stage of the Tang Dynasty, simmering tea was gradually replaced by the method of pouring boiling water on to the tea. That was the reason why whole sets of stoves and tea pots are rarely seen from those days. This set of tea utensils, includes both the tea pot and a tea vase, evidence of the transition from simmering tea to making tea by boiling water. Blocks of tea, prepared with care were popular in the Tang Dynasty. In either method of making tea, part of the block had to be ground into dust before use, and a tea mortar was the implement used to grind the tea dust. A dregs cup, also known as a spittoon, was used for holding the dregs of the tea, and was usually included in a tea set.

231

232

233

234

235

235. Porcelain figurine of Lu Yu Five Dynasties burial object; 10 cm tall; said to be unearthed in Tang County, Hebei Province. The figurine was unearthed at the same time as a tea set, so it is known to be a figurine of Lu Yu, the tea-god. The book held in his hand symbolizes the *Book of Tea*. Lu Yu (733-804) was an advocator of tea drinking in the Tang Dynasty. His *Book of Tea* was the first on the subject and systematically summarized the rich history of the beverage. Vivid analysis and description are given in the book with regard to the places of production, shape and characteristics of tea plants, along with information about their cultivation; the methods of picking, evaluating the quality and processing tea, as well as the implements for brewing it; plus descriptions of tea sets and ways of drinking tea. Owing to the wide influence and circulation of the *Book of Tea*, Lu Yu has been regarded as the tea-god and worshipped since the later part of the Tang Dynasty. According to records, from those days, a figurine of Lu Yu would be given to a buyer of several dozen tea sets.

Northern and Southern Song Dynasties

(960—1279)

The Northern and Southern Song Dynasties, which lasted from the sixties of the 10th century to the seventies of the 13th century, was an important period in the feudal history of China. It inherited the past and ushered in the future. The Song Dynasty founded in 960 lasted 320 years, ruling first from Kaifeng and then Hangzhou. The Song Dynasty which made Kaifeng its capital until 1127 is usually called the Northern Song Dynasty, and the Song regime which moved its capital to Hangzhou after 1127 has been called the Southern Song Dynasty. Along the periphery of the Song Empire, where the Han made up the principal ethnic group, a few minority regimes co-existed side by side for a long time. These included the Liao founded by Qidan, the Western Xia founded by Dangxiang and Jin founded by Nuzhen. All of them waged war with the Song court, yet there was also a relatively long period of peaceful co-existence. During this period, frequent trade exchanges and the spread of agricultural technology promoted the gradual merging of the northern tribes with the Han people. The rapid increase of large and medium-sized cities, the unprecedented briskness of trade and the extensive circulation of paper money marked the economic development achieved by the two Song dynasties. During this period, the population increased to 100 million and the focus of the economy shifted to the south. Along with the increasing popularity of land-leasing, the privatization of land became more serious with each passing day. A large class of tenant farmers as well as industrialists and merchants emerged.

During this period new progress was made in science and technology. The use of

the compass in navigation enhanced overseas trade; the extensive spread of printing spurred the compilation and circulation of all kinds of books. Tremendous achievements were scored in the fields of philosophy, history, literature and art. The rise of a class of urban inhabitants and the development of popular literature for storytelling and ballad-singing open the way to an era in which opera and fiction would one day flourish.

The Simultaneous Existence of the Song, Liao, Western Xia and Jin

In 960, the Song Dynasty was founded to replace the Later Zhou and Kaifeng was made the capital, a period called the Northern Song Dynasty by historians. The Northern Song court eliminated the eight separatist regimes south of the Yangtze River and in north Shanxi one by one, ending the split of the country and bringing about partial unification. The minority ethnic regimes that existed side by side with the Northern Song were the Liao in the northeast, the Western Xia in the northwest, and Tubo and Dali in the southwest. Repeated warfare took place between the Liao, Western Xia and Song. Later, peace treaties were concluded and border trade opened, permitting a relatively long peace to ensue. At the beginning of the 12th century, the Nuzhen tribe founded the Kingdom of Jin, which

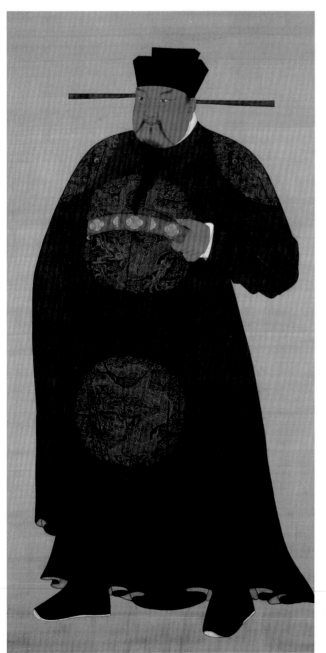

eliminated the Liao and Northern Song at a time and occupied the area north of the Huaihe River. The Song court moved its capital to Hangzhou and is called the Southern Song by historians. In the early years after the founding of the Southern Song Dynasty, the Jin regime frequently invaded the south and the Song court also carried out repeated northern expeditions. Following a peace treaty, the long period of confrontation ended.

Founding of the Northern Song and Mid-Term Reform

In 960, Zhao Kuangyin, a high-ranking military leader of the imperial guards of the Later Zhou, staged a mutiny, seized power and founded the Song Dynasty. The Northern Song Dynasty unified step by step the vast area from the places south of the Five Ridges (covering present-day Guangdong and Guangxi) to the Yellow River valley. In order to strengthen the centralization of authority, Zhao Kuangyin removed power from a number of high-ranking military leaders and sent civil officials from the capital to be prefects and magistrates. In order to resolve the serious social contradictions and financial crisis, in the time of Emperor Renzong of the Song Dynasty, Fan Zhongyan pursued a new but unsuccessful policy. In the time of the Song Emperor Shenzong, Wang Anshi introduced reforms and achieved some results.

236. Portrait of Zhao Kuangyin Zhao Kuangyin, Emperor Taizu of the Song Dynasty (927-976), from Zhuozhou Prefecture (present-day Zhuo County, Hebei Province). Originally the supreme commander of the imperial guards of the Later Zhou Dynasty, in 960 he staged a mutiny at Chenqiao and founded the Song Dynasty. He basically accomplished the unification of the south and north, ending the disruption that had marked the period of the Five Dynasties and Ten Kingdoms. To strengthen imperial power, he compelled a number of high-ranking military leaders to resign and recruited local crack soldiers to replenish the imperial guards and protect the capital. At the same time, he sent civil officials to serve as prefects and magistrates, so that local military power, financial power and political power—were all recovered by the central authorities. He set up the posts of deputy prime minister, Privy Councilor and directors of three financial departments, in order to break up the power of the prime minister and place more direct control in his own hands.

237. Copper seal of a "*gongsheng* deputy commander" Northern Song Dynasty; 5.5 cm long, 5.4 cm wide, 5.7 cm high. This copper seal was one of the official seals of the imperial guards. In order to

strengthen the emperor's direct control over the imperial guards, no supreme military commander was named. The imperial guards were divided into two parts: the *dianqiansi* (palace guardian forces) and *shiweisi* (garrison forces). The former were placed under the control of a commander and the latter under the control of two commanders, one for infantry and the other for cavalry. The three commanders were all appointed by the emperors. The *gongsheng* was one of the divisions of the cavalry under the *shiweisi*. It was set up by Emperor Taizong and was composed of 21 *zhihui* (units of 500 soldiers) with the duty of protecting the capital. This was the seal of a deputy commander of the *gongsheng*.

238. Copper seal of "5th *du* under the 2nd *zhihui* of the 4th *jun* under the left *xiang* of the *shenwei* army" Northern Song; 5.5 cm long, 5.3 cm wide, 4.2 cm high. An inscription on the back of the seal indicates it was "cast in the year 981. *Shenwei* was one of the infantry main units of the imperial guards of the Northern Song, belonging to the *shiweisi*. A "du" was the basic unit of the imperial guards. It was composed of 100 men. Five *du* made up one *zhihui*, 5 *zhihui* made up one *jun*, and 10 *jun* made up one *xiang*. Each *xiang* was divided into a left *xiang*

237

238

and right *xiang*. This copper seal was the seal of the 5th *du* under the 2nd *zhihui* of the 4th *jun* of the left *xiang* of the shenwei army.

239. Map of the Eastern Capital of the Northern Song The Northern Song Dynasty established four capitals with Kaifeng, the Eastern Capital, as the capital of the entire country. The Eastern Capital had an outer city, an inner city and an imperial city. The Bianhe, Caihe, Jinshuihe and Wuzhanghe rivers flowed through the city. With a population of over one million at its most flourishing time, the city was the largest and busiest metropolis in the whole country in those days. After the downfall of the Northern Song, the Eastern Capital waned, and after repeated inundations of the Yellow River, the greater part of the city proper was buried under present-day Kaifeng.

Map of the Eastern Capital of the Northern Song

239

240

240. Brick from Song city wall   Northern Song Dynasty building material; 32.2 cm long, 15.4 cm wide, 5 cm thick; unearthed in Kaifeng, Henan Province. As Kaifeng was located on a plain and had no tenable mountains for defence, an outer city was built encircling the old city. Following exploration and excavation, it has been initially verified that the outer city of the Eastern Capital was about 6, 990 meters long from south to north and about 7, 600 meters wide from east to west, the circumference was nearly 30 kilometers and the city wall over 8 meters in height. This piece of Song city wall brick was discovered among the ruins of the west wall of the outer city.

241. Brick from the Fan Pagoda showing a Tang monk's pilgrimage   Northern Song Dynasty building material; 30.2 cm long, 30 cm wide, 11.5 cm high. The Fan Pagoda, also known as the Tianqing Temple Pagoda, is located in Tianqing Temple south of the Eastern Capital. A hexagonal 9-story brick pagoda build in a pavilion style, it was erected in 990, the first year of the Chunhua reign of the Northern Song Dynasty. Mounting the pagoda, one can look into the distance for over 5 kilometers. It was a nice place for worshipping Buddha as well as a tourist spot. Owing to the devastations of war and fire, only three stories remained in the Yuan Dynasty. A small 6-story pagoda was built on the third floor of the original one, during the Qing Dynasty. The extant Fan Pagoda is 31.67 meters high. On its inner and outer walls are mounted hundreds of glazed and decorated bricks. Most of the reliefs on them are Buddha images, while some of them depict Buddhist stories.

241-1

241-2 ▷

242. Iron Pagoda with unicorn design
Northern Song Dynasty building material; 35.5 cm long, 20 cm wide, 6.8 cm thick. The Iron Pagoda is also known as the Kaibao Temple Pagoda; it is located in the Kaibao Temple in the city of the Eastern Capital. Originally a wooden pagoda, which later burnt down, it was first built in 982, the 7th year of the Taiping Xingguo reign of the Song Dynasty. It was rebuilt as a brick pagoda in 1044, the 4th year of the Qingli reign. That version was an octagonal 13-story structure, 55 meters in height, which imitated a timber one with a bracket system and protruding eaves. There is a winding stairs leading directly to the top of the pagoda. As the outer wall of the pagoda is mounted with brown bricks carved with designs of a lion, flowers and plants, a unicorn, Bodhisattva and flying Asparas, and glazed tiles, the color of the pagoda is close to that of iron. Hence the name of Iron Pagoda.

243. Jiayou copper weight Northern Song Dynasty measure; 30 cm high, 20 cm thick, 64 kilograms heavy; unearthed in Xiangtan County, Hunan Province, in 1975. A copper norm was a standard measure issued by the government. The whole body of the copper norm is carved with a fine posy design. There are inscriptions on its front and back. On one side the Chinese characters say "cast in the first year of the Jiayou reign", namely, the year of 1056; the other side says "weight of the copper norm 100 catty". Calculating on the basis of the actual weight of the norm, one catty in those days equalled 640 grams.

243-1

244. Copper and iron coins of the Northern Song Northern Song Dynasty currency. Following the development of industry and commerce, the demand for currency greatly increased. The Northern Song government minted more than five million strings of coins every year, equivalent to 20 times the coins minted by the Tang government every year. At that time, copper coins were circulated in most regions, and iron coins were only used in the Sichuan region. There were over 50 kinds of Song coins, mainly distinguished by reign titles. There were also different forms in each category of coins with reign title; in terms of script, regular script, official script, cursive script and seal script; in terms of nomenclature, *"yuanbao"*, *"tongbao"* and *"zhongbao"*. In addition, the Song Emperor Taizu minted *"songyuan tongbao"*, Emperor Renzong minted *"huangsong tongbao"* and Emperor Huizong minted *"shensong yuanbao"* and *"shensong tongbao"*. The copper and iron coins of the Song Dynasty were the most numerous in variety and most complicated that China has had through the ages.

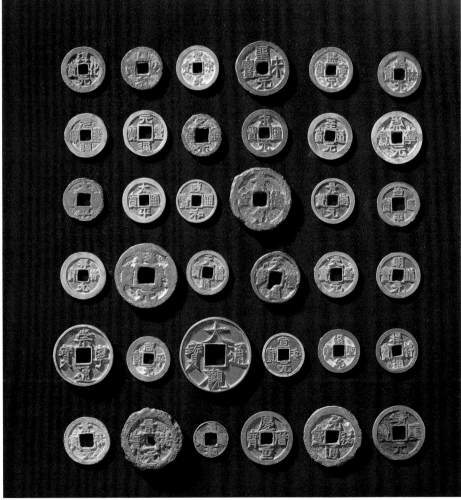

244

245. Part of the "Illustration of Imperial Guards of Honor"   Northern Song Dynasty illustration; 51.4 cm long, 1,481 cm wide. During the Song Dynasty, there were four categories of imperial guards of honor. The illustration shows the imperial guards of honor of the first category used for the grand ceremony in the southern suburbs. In order to facilitate the drill of officials and soldiers for such an occasion, the Song Emperor Taizong had three "illustrations of Imperial Guards of Honor" drawn and carefully preserved. At the time of Emperor Renzong, Song Shou reformulated the system of the imperial guards of honor and drew 10 illustrations

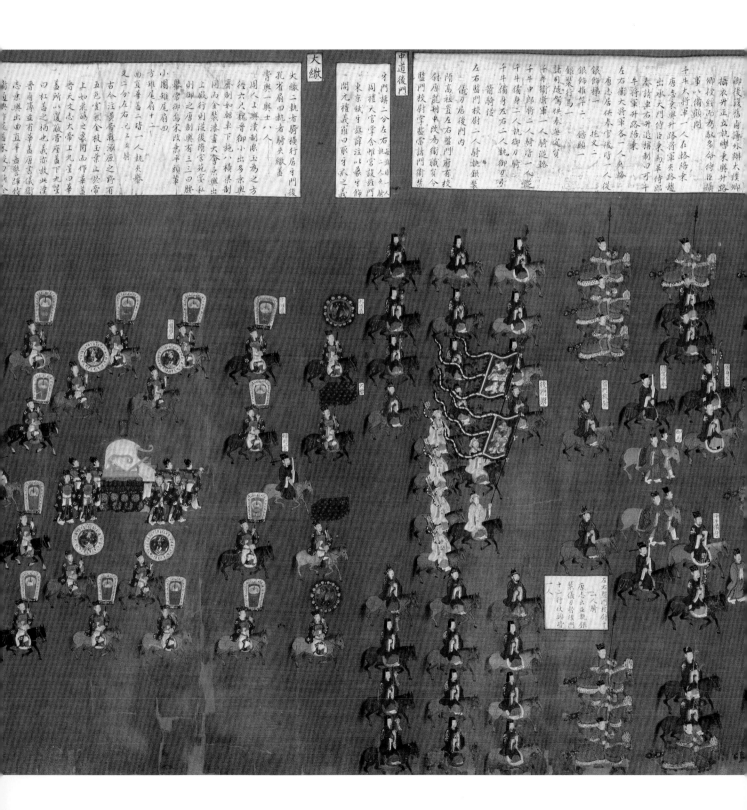

accordingly. This illustration was accomplished on the basis of Song Shou's works. Some 5,481 officers and soldiers, 61 carriages, 2,873 horses, 36 oxen, 6 elephants, 1,701 musical instruments and 1,548 weapons, were drawn to illustrate the magnificent scene when the emperor proceeded to Qingcheng to the south of the city to offer sacrifices to heaven and earth. The drawing was probably done between 1053, the 5th year of the Huangyou reign, and 1065, the 2nd year of the Zhiping reign. It is a visual aid for studying the system of the Song Dynasty with respect to carriage, dress, guard of honor, weapons and musical instruments.

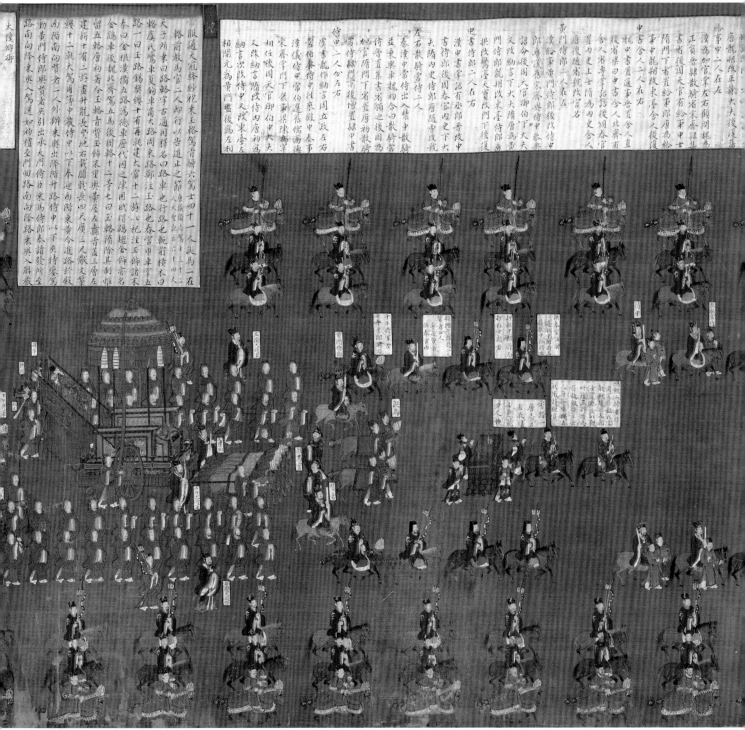

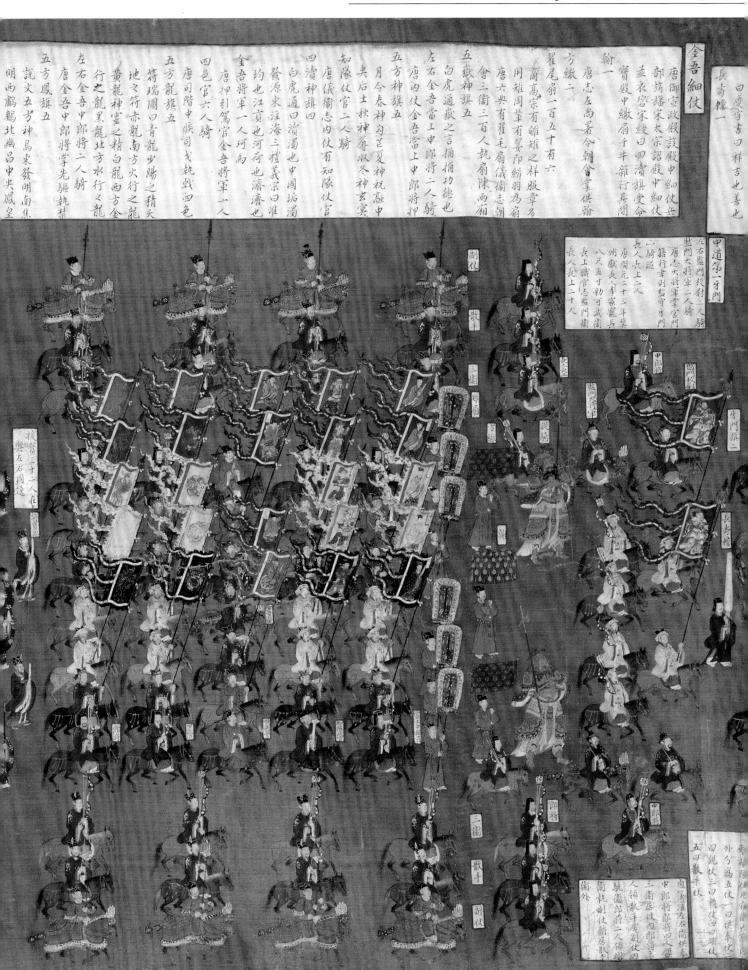

246

247

246. Portrait of Fan Zhongyan

Fan Zhongyan (989-1052), courtesy name Xiwen, from Wu County of Suzhou (present-day Jiangsu), was an outstanding politician and man of letters in the Northern Song Dynasty. In 1043,Fan Zhongyan was appointed deputy prime minister. He proposed 10 reform measures, including the rectification of local administrations, stressing agriculture and seri-culture, and the introduction of a legal system. Emperor Renzong issued an imperial edict to implement these measures, which were called the "new policies of the Qingli reign". The new policies limited some of the prerogatives of the big bureaucrats and big landlords, and were strongly opposed by the conservatives. They were soon abolished. Fan Zhongyan was good at poetry and prose, his writings rich in political content and clear and lucid in style. His *Collected Works of Fan Wen Zheng Gong* was handed down to posterity.

247. Portrait of Wang Anshi

Wang Anshi (1021-1086), courtesy name Jiepu, from Linchuan, Jiangxi, was a noted politician and man of letters in the Northern Song Dynasty. He was appointed deputy prime minister in 1069, and was made prime minister the following year. With the support of Emperor Shenzong, Wang Anshi carried out a series of reforms for the purpose of making his country rich and powerful. The reforms included measures to regulate the market and support the needs of the country, measures to adjust the taxation and labor systems; and measures to strengthen the army and consolidate government rule. After implementing the political reforms for over 10 years, there were some achievements while abuses were also exposed. In 1086, Sima Guang was appointed prime minister and the new policies were abolished. The prose of Wang Anshi was vigorous in style, and his poetry pure and fresh.

248. Bronze plate of the "4th general of the Fuyan Command"

Northern Song Dynasty; 6 cm high, 4.2 cm wide. In the reforms of Wang Anshi, one of the important measures was the reform of the military system, including the introduction of a system of command. With the exception of the imperial guards in the capital and a part of the imperial guards stationed in other places, all remaining imperial guards were to mix with local forces to form *jiang* (commands). A general was appointed in each command area to drill soldiers, and the long-existing practice of transferring imperial guards was abolished. The reforms were first implemented in areas around the capital and in Hebei and Shaanxi before being spread to the south. Fuyan was a strategically important command area in the northern part of Shaanxi with its seat in present-day Yan'an. This is the bronze plate worn by an officer under the 4th general of the Fuyan command area.

249. Rubbing from Steles on the Yuanyou clique

Southern Song Dynasty; 142 cm long, 79 cm wide. After the death of Emperor Shenzong, 10-year-old Emperor Zhezong ascended the throne and changed the reign title to Yuanyou. In 1086, the conservative Sima Guang completely abolished the reforms of Wang

248

Anshi and removed supporters of the new policies from the capital. After Emperor Zhezong took over the reins of government, he demoted those who had opposed the new policies. When Emperor Huizong ascended the throne, Cai Jing, his prime minister, while pretending to hold in esteem the new policies, labelled his political opponents and those opposed to the new policies as the "treacherous clique of Yuanyou", listing 309 men including Sima Guang, and carving the names on stone posts for public display. Later, Emperor Huizong thought this inappropriate and ordered all the steles destroyed. By the time of the Southern Song, it was already difficult to see the Steles on the Yuanyou Clique, and someone went to the trouble to carve new steles based on old rubbings. The two extant Steles on the Yuanyou Clique were carved in the Southern Song period. The rubbing in the picture is from Rongshui, Guangxi, carved in 1211.

元祐黨籍

皇帝嗣位之五年雄
別淑慝明信賞刑黜
元祐害政之臣廉有
俟罰乃命有司考
罪狀弟其首惡與其
附麗者以聞得三百
九人
皇帝書而刊之石置
文德殿門之東壁
又詔臣京書之天下
漏之天下臣為雄
大者昆子之戒
檀固何受王藏
安燾呂希純梁燾
張集黃庭堅范柔之
周詖孫琮

司馬光 文彥博 呂公著 呂大防
劉摯 范純仁 韓忠彥 蘇轍 曾布
韓維 孫固 范百祿 胡宗愈

文臣曾任宰臣執政官
王巖叟 蘇軾 王存
鄭雍 傅堯俞 趙瞻

右元祐姦黨

命仰承
陛下李惟繼述之志
司空尚書左僕射兼
門下侍郎臣蔡京謹
書

249

Liao

The Qidan tribe was a minority nationality in the north of ancient China, which originally lived in the area south of the Xilamulen River, on the upper reaches of the Liaohe River and north of the Laoha River, leading a nomadic life by hunting and fishing. In 916, Yelu Abaoji, the chieftain of an alliance of Qidan tribes, abolished the election system of the clan and implemented the dynastic system of the Han nationality. Claiming to be the emperor, he founded the Kingdom of Qidan (later changed to the Liao) and made his Upper Capital, Linhuang Prefecture (present-day Balin Zuoqi, Inner Mongolia Autonomous Region), the capital of the kingdom. The Liao court ruled the northern tribes and the Han people separately. "Southern officials" and "northern officials" were appointed. The "northern officials" were Qidan nobility, who administering the affairs of the people of Qidan and other nationalities, while the "southern officials" included both Han and Qidan officials who administered the Han people. The Liao Dynasty created Qidan characters by imitating the strokes of the Chinese ones, and formulated written laws. In their long contact with the Han, the Qidan nationality was influenced by the advanced culture of the Han people and made marked progress in the political, economic, military and cultural fields as well as in the arts. Powerful and prosperous in the 10th century, the Liao regime controlled the vast area south and north of the Mongolian Desert, the Heilongjiang River valley and the northern part of present-day Hebei and Shanxi. It existed along with Northern Song and Western Xia, and was destroyed in 1125 by the Kingdom of Jin.

250

250. *Dakang tongbao* coins   Liao currency. Made of copper, the coins were minted in the Dakang reign (1075-1084) of Liao. Copper was produced in Liao and copper coins were minted by Liao itself right after the founding of the kingdom. There were as many as 18 kinds of coins minted by Liao:the *tianzhan tongbao* minted in 922, the first year of the Tianzan reign, and other coins minted by subsequent emperors. All bore titles of reigns, such as the *qingning yuanbao* and *tonghe yuanbao*. These copper coins and the coins in the area of the Han people were identical in shape and structure. Liao coins all used Chinese characters, but the level of the minting was relatively low.

251. Bronze pot made in Songde Palace   Liao measuring tool; full length 27.2 cm, height 8.4 cm, weight 1000 grams; unearthed from a tomb at Qinghe Gate in Yi County, Liaoning Province, in 1950. It was a standard measure cast by the government and a partition part way up the pot separates it into two vessel-shaped containers. The upper container has a capacity of 1047 milliliters, and the lower one 500 milliliters. An inscription on the outer wall of the bronze pot reads, "Made in the Songde Palace, weight one catty-third day".

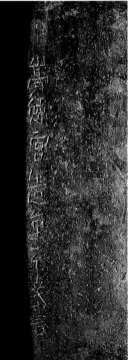

251-1   251-2

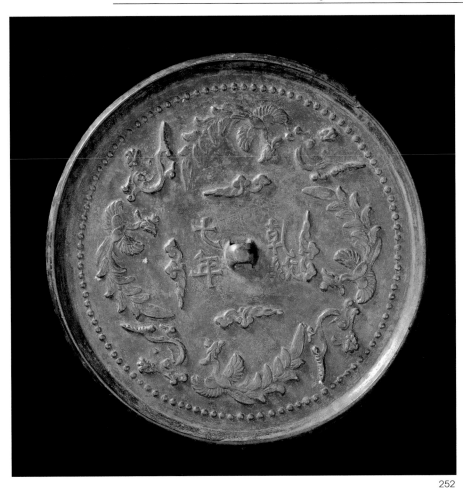

252

252. Bronze mirror with design of four phoenixes Liao cosmetic utensil; diameter 19 cm, edge thickness 0.7 cm, weight 650 grams. On the back of the mirror there is a knob around which is the design of four clouds, phoenixes and flying dragons. The decoration is encircled by a pearl-bordered medallion. Also cast are the Chinese characters meaning "the 7th year of the Qiantong reign" (1107). In addition, there are carved Chinese characters indicating the mirror was made under the supervision of the government.

253. Iron shovel Liao; total length 51 cm, the face of the shovel is 19 cm long and 21 cm wide; unearthed from the tomb of the son-in-law of a Liao emperor in Chifeng, Inner Mongolia Autonomous Region, in 1954. In the tomb there were over 1,000 burial objects, most of which were exquisitely made. The iron shovel was buried together with other implements. As there were three decorations with the design of rolled straw on the handle, the shovel does not look like an ordinary production tool. It might be a thing used by the son-in-law of the Liao emperor, or a specially made burial object.

254. Flatiron Liao daily-use article; full length 37.7 cm, diameter 20.5 cm, height 6.5 cm; unearthed in Ju Ud League, Inner Mongolia Autonomous Region. The flatiron, which was heated by a charcoal fire inside, can be used to press clothes. There is a handle on the side.

253   254

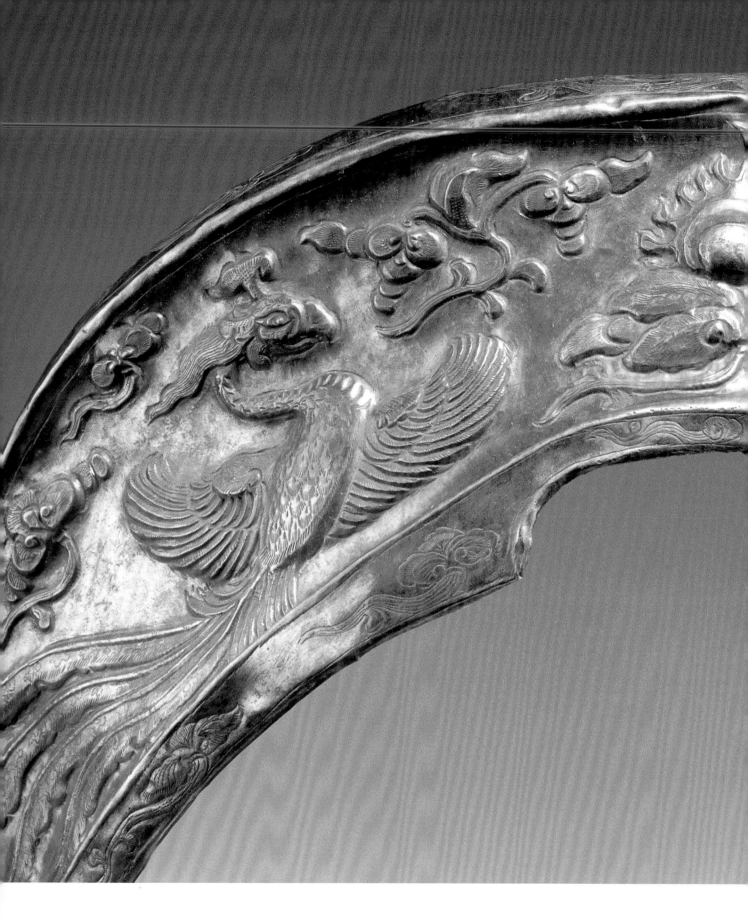

255. Gilded silver cantle   Liao horse gear; unearthed from the tomb of the son-in-law of a Liao emperor in Chifeng, Inner Mongolia Autonomous Region, in 1954. This gilded silver cantle was an ornament laid over the saddle. A cantle is composed of six pieces, the biggest piece is 35 cm high, 22 cm wide, and 0.1 cm thick. It includes the fore and rear parts of the cantle, embossed with the design of two phoenixes playing a ball among designs of flowing clouds and flowers. All the edges are gilded. The two of knife-shaped and crescent parts of the silver cantle are well-balanced on the left and right and embossed with a design of peonies and flowing clouds. This cantle set was exquisitely made, pleasing to the eye and

255-2

255-1

reflected a very high technological level. The Qidan people could hardly do without horses and treasured horses and saddles very much.

256-2

256. Gilded silver pot in the shape of cockscomb Liao water container; 26.3 cm high, 5.5 cm in diameter, 21.2 cm at its base; unearthed in Chifeng, Inner Mongolia Autonomous Region. The pot handle is cockscomb-shaped, and the pot lid is connected to the body of the pot by a silver chain. On the lid is a carved design of four symmetrical petals and on the outside brim are eight flowers with four petals each. The pot neck is relatively high with the design of a peony carved on all sides. On both sides of the full body of the pot are carved delicately rhombus designs of a deer surrounded by a fairyland formed by a rockery, *ling zhi* (a mythic plant of long life) and sea. The front of the pot is triangular with the three edges decorated with a cord pattern. Qidan was considerably influenced by the Tang Dynasty in the technology of making gold and silver wares, yet the shape and design of such goods still reflected the style of a people on horseback. The cockscomb-shaped gilded silver pot is one of the finest examples of the wares of the Liao period ever discovered.

257. Silver pot with fish scale design Liao water container; 10.7 cm long, 7.2 cm in diameter, length of chain 41 cm; unearthed from the tomb of the son-in-law of a Liao emperor in Chifeng, Inner Mongolia Autonomous Region. There is a band pattern around the belly of the pot with a fish scale design above and below that ring, and a bow-shaped loop handle on the fore and rear knobs of the shoulder. The central part of the pot lid is raised with a knob, and the lid is fastened to the front knob on the shoulder by a silver chain. The silver pot is beautifully shaped, reflecting high skill-level attained by the Qidan people in the production of gold and silver wares.

258-1

258-2

259

258. Three-color long dish shaped like a begonia flower with impressed fish design Liao vessel; 2.1 cm high, 27.6 cm long; unearthed from a Liao tomb in Ningcheng County, Inner Mongolia Autonomous Region, in 1959. The long dish is shaped like a begonia flower. White pottery coating was first applied on its rough and hard base before applying the yellow, white and green glaze. The glaze cover has traces of broken ice crackles. The outer wall was yellow-glazed, its edge green-glazed, and on the white-glazed background of its bottom was painted a design of fallen flowers and fish. The glaze colors are lustrous and the shape of the dish attractive and in good taste. It is a fine work in tricolors of the Liao period.

The Liao learned the technology used for glazed pottery on the central plains, and produced a great many pieces of tricolor pottery with their own national characteristics. The pieces were comparable to the Tang tricolors.

259. Three-color square dish impressed with peony design Liao vessel; length of side 12.5 cm, height 2.8 cm; unearthed from a Liao tomb in Ningcheng County, Inner Mongolia Autonomous Region, in 1959. On the sides of the dish is impressed a floral design. The inside of the dish is decorated with a round design of a chrysanthemum with leaves on four corners. The whole body is glazed in three colors-yellow, green and brown. The

colors are lustrous and beautiful with small crackles. The overall design of the dish is artistic and in good taste, the colors of glaze harmonious. It is a fine example of a Liao tricolor.

260. Three-color round plate with impressed peony design Liao vessel; 6.2 cm high, 25 cm in diameter. The plate was made with light yellow pottery base. In the center of the plate is impressed the design of chrysanthemum and around it double-belt peony design. The white background is glazed in three colors and the glaze is bright. Both Liao tricolors and Tang tricolors were low-temperature glazed pottery, the former relatively brighter and the latter more lustrous.

261. Yellow glazed long neck porcelain vase   Liao water container; height 35.1 cm, diameter 10 cm, base diameter 7.5 cm. The pottery base of this vase is rough and hard, the glazed colors clean with a very strong luster. The yellow glaze was painted only up to the middle part of the vase, which looks like the pear-shaped vases used in the area of Han nationality. This is a practical utensil for holding water, so its body is long and its belly full in order to hold more water. The neck is slender to avoid an overflow.

262. Green glazed porcelain phoenix-head vase   Liao water container; height 52 cm, diameter 11.6 cm, belly diameter 17.5 cm; unearthed from No.2 tomb of the Xiao Shenwei ancestral graveyard at Qinghe Gate, Yi County, Liaoning Province, in 1950. The shape of this vase resembles a phoenix with protruding neck and wings held back, hence its name. Such utensil shapes were popular in the Western Regions and there were similar utensils in the Tang Dynasty called "*hu* vases" (*hu* meaning "foreign"). There were a large number of phoenix-head vases in the Liao period, probably due to the influence of the nationalities in the Western Regions such as the Tujue (Turk) and Huihe (Uighur).

263. Brown glazed porcelain stirrup-shaped pot   Liao utensil for carrying water; 24 cm high; unearthed at Fuxing Gate, Beijing, in 1956. This utensil looks like a stirrup, hence its name. The base of this pot is crude and hard, glazed all over in brown; the glaze is relatively thick and glittering. On both sides of the pot are wave designs, imitating the leather bags with which nomadic horsemen carry water. The appearance of the pot is the same as a leather bag, and even the imitation knots and buttons of the leather straps used to sew leather pieces together appear remarkably close to the real things.

261

262

264. Porcelain pillow glazed in hawksbill color   Liao daily-use article; 20 cm long, 12.4 cm wide, 15.8 cm high. The porcelain pillow is in the shape of a saddle, hollowed-out, with an oval surface and glazed all over. The design of the glaze is very similar to the smooth design on the back of a hawksbill, hence the name.

265. Lotus-petal-shaped white porcelain tray inlaid with copper buckles   Liao vessel; height 4.9 cm, diameter 22.2 cm, base diameter 9.1 cm; unearthed from the tomb of the son-in-law of a Liao emperor in Chifeng, Inner Mongolia Autonomous Region. The rim of the plate is in the shape of lotus petal, inlaid with copper buckles, with which its ring base is also inlaid. The tray is white glazed all over with broken ice crackles. The shape and the color of the glaze look somewhat like the white porcelain trays produced by the Dingyao Kiln in the Song Dynasty. The Dingyao white porcelain was usually baked in an overturned position in the

264

sagger, so copper buckles were inlaid to cover the burr on the rim of the tray. Such lotus-petal-shaped tray rims were not frequently seen among the Song porcelain to be found in the Liao period, yet the influence of the Song Dingyao white porcelain was still apparent.

266. White porcelain ewer with lotus-petal design in relief   Liao water container; height 17.5 cm, diameter 4.7

cm, base diameter 8.3 cm. The ewer has a bulging belly to hold more water. The upper part of the belly surface is decorated with a wave design and the lower part with lotus petals. The mouth of the ewer is cylindrical, the spout and the handle are curved. The ewer has a ring base. Its overall appearance is novel and somewhat staid. It is a fine example of white porcelain in the Liao Dynasty.

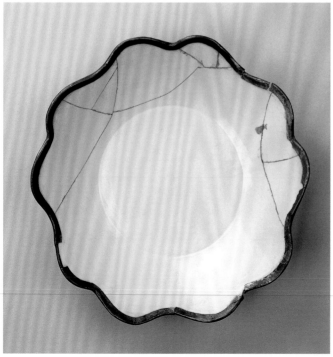

265

266

267. Sectional drawing of wooden pagoda in Yingxian County Liao. The name of the pagoda is the Sakya Pagoda, located in the Buddhist Palace Temple in Ying County, Shanxi Province. It was built in 1056, the second year of the Qingning reign of the Liao Dynasty. With a total height of 67.31 meters, the pagoda is an octagonal building whose lowest floor is 30 meters in diameter. The base of the pagoda, 4.4 meter high, is surfaced with brick and stone. The pagoda itself is 51.41 meters high, and the iron top of the pagoda is 9.91 meters high with a 1.86-meters high brick-surface seat. The pagoda is multieaved in style, with five stories and six eaves obvious on the outside and four hidden stories, comprising nine actual stories in all. It is supported by a framework of columns, positioned to form two concentric octagons with two *cao* (grooves) strengthened by beams, trusses and brackets. A total of 54 kinds of brackets and over 60 different kind of supports, beams and short columns were used to ensure the stability of the building. During more than 900 years after its completion, the pagoda is still towering despite earthquakes, the ravages of wind and rain and the devastation of war. It is the most ancient and tallest pagoda-style building extant in China.

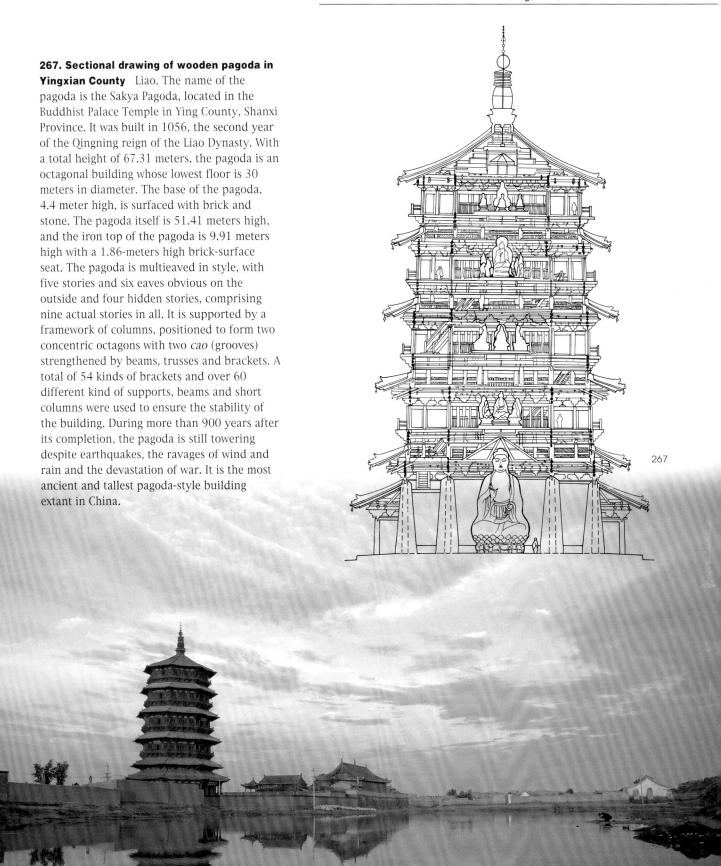

267

Western Xia

Western Xia was a regime founded by the Tuoba family of the Dangxiang ethnic group. During the last years of the Tang Dynasty, the Dangxiang formed a strong force along the middle reaches of the Yellow River. In the early years of the 11th century, the area under its control was extended to what is the northern part of present-day Shaanxi Province, the Ningxia Huizu Autonomous Region, Gansu Province, Qinghai Province and the southwestern part of the Inner Mongolia Autonomous Region. In 1038, Yuan Hao proclaimed himself emperor and the announced title of his reign, "Great Xia" (called Western Xia in historical records). He made Xingzhou (present-day Yinchuan, Ningxia) his capital. Copying the political system of the Northern Song, he organized his regime, created a written language of the Western Xia by adopting the strokes of Chinese characters, and introduced a system of imperial examinations. Border clashes frequently occurred between the Song and Western Xia, causing heavy casualties on both sides, interrupting reciprocal trade and hindering economic development. In 1044, the Song and Western Xia regimes negotiated peace and Yuan Hao declared himself a vassal of the Song. The Northern Song granted Yuan Hao the surname of Zhao (the surname of the Song imperial family) and made him the king of Xia. Both sides reopened border trade. Under the economic and cultural influence of the Han people, rapid social progress was made by the Dangxiang. The Western Xia gradually entered its heyday and began a triangular balance of power with the Song and Liao. The Western Xia existed for 189 years until it was destroyed in 1227 by the Mongol Genghis Khan.

268

in order to identify a messenger. The Dangxiang people were horsemen who lived mainly on herding and hunting. As they were at war constantly with the Song and Liao, they depended entirely on horse-riding messengers to deliver documents and pass on orders.

268. *Qianyou yuanbao* coins Western Xia currency. This coin is made of copper. Qianyou was the reign title of Zhao Renxiao, Emperor Renzong of Xia (1170–1193). The Western Xia kingdom minted more than 20 kinds of coins, including both copper and iron ones; some were inscribed in the Western Xia language and others in Chinese, all coins bearing their reign titles. The coins of Western Xia were exquisitely minted and the characters on them regular, indicating that the kingdom's economy and culture had reached a considerably high level.

269. Waist warrant in Western Xia language Western Xia pass, full length 6.8 cm. This so-called waist warrant, made of copper, was a certificate for crossing a checkpoint. It bears the name of the bearer and could be fastened to his girdle to be produced for guards at checkpoints

270-1

270. Edict plate in the Western Xia language

Western Xia document; total height 18.5 cm, diameter 14.7cm. Made of copper, the edict plate is composed of two round copper plates to be engaged by teeth with a cavity in between. There is a rectangular handle on the upper side, and the two plates combine to form a whole. On the outside of one plate is a carved spiral design of flowers and within the design a two-line Chinese character meaning "edict", inscribed in intaglio. On the other plate are carved four Western Xia characters meaning "urgent, go swiftly on horseback". Such articles served as proof of identity for a messenger who delivered documents and orders during the Western Xia Dynasty. Ancient Han books were translated into the Western Xia language, as were records and Buddhist scriptures. It was also extensively used in government documents, coins, seals and tallies.

270-2

271

271. Brown glazed porcelain flask with carved design Western Xia utensil for carrying water; height 33.3 cm, diameter 9 cm, belly diameter 32 cm; found in Haiyuan County, Ningxia Huizu Autonomous Region, in 1985. The flask has a small mouth, flared rim and is carved with prick design on one side. Its belly is flat and round; on the obverse side are two sets of brown glazed peony designs and on the back a circular ring base. The reason for making the flask flat with a small mouth and two ears was to facilitate the carrying of water on horseback; the ring foot on the back of the belly was to keep the flask stable when it was placed on the ground. This kind of porcelain flask was modelled on a leather water bag and the prick design added to the edge represented the leather straps used to sew a real leather flask. The flask embodies the distinct cultural features of the northern tribes.

272. White porcelain plate tile   Western Xia building material; 16.1 cm long, 12.3 cm wide, 0.8 cm thick; unearthed from No.8 tomb of the imperial mausoleum of Western Xia in Yinchuan, Ningxia Huizu Autonomous Region, in 1974. The tile surface is white glazed, and the glaze is bright and smooth and even in thickness with broken ice crackles-a high-grade building material. From this one can imagine the magnificence of the buildings in Western Xia imperial mausoleum. The mausoleum is located at the eastern foot of Helan Mountain, 25 kilometers to the west of Yinchuan. Its area is 4 kilometers wide from east to west and 10 kilometers long from south to north. Eight emperors were buried there in a pattern that followed the terrain; there were over 140 subordinate tombs. After Genghis Khan led the Mongolian troops in putting an end to the Kingdom of Western Xia, they totally destroyed the imperial mausoleum and nearly all the buildings above ground were demolished. More destruction was caused by the unlawful excavations of later periods. That is the reason why very few relics survived in the imperial mausoleum.

273. Green glazed semi-cylindrical tile with animal-mask design   Western Xia building material; remnant 35.5 cm long, 1.4 cm thick; unearthed at Western Xia imperial mausoleum in Yinchuan, Ningxia Huizu Autonomous Region, in 1972. The tile-end of this semi-cylindrical tile is decorated with an animal-mask design and its surface glazed in a sparkling, bright green. The application of green glaze on tiles and tile-ends began in the Northern Wei period and there were very few of them even in the Tang Dynasty. The proportion of such tiles and tile-ends increased considerably in the imperial mausoleum of the Western Xia, but they were still used mainly in building palaces and mausoleums.

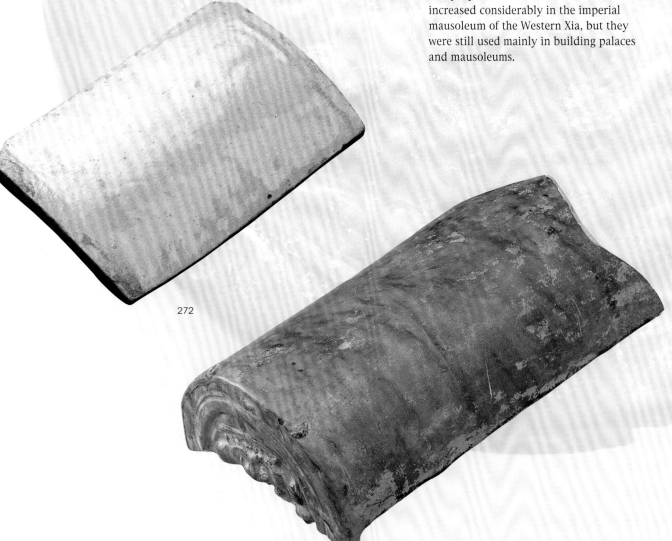

272

273

274. Green glazed ridge-end Western Xia building material; 152 cm high, 92 cm wide, 32 cm thick; unearthed from the ruins of a pavilion west of the Western Xia imperial mausoleum in Yinchuan, Ningxia Huizu Autonomous Region, in 1972. A ridge-end is the ornament at the two ends of the main ridge of the roof. This ridge-end is in the shape of dragon head and fishtail which were baked separately. Decorated all over with scale design, it is green-glazed. The glaze is bright, and the ridge-end is tall, thick, and full of power and grandeur.

274

**275. Remnant of stele inscribed in the
Western Xia language**   Western Xia relic;
21 cm high, 15.5 cm wide; unearthed from
the imperial mausoleum of Western Xia in
Yinchuan, Ningxia Huizu Autonomous Region,
in 1972. There had been steles in front of each
tomb in the Western Xia imperial mausoleum,
but all were destroyed and only broken pieces
remain. During 1972-1977, archaeologists
excavated one imperial mausoleum and four
subordinate tombs here, cleaned up two stele
pavilions attached to imperial mausoleum and
unearthed 3272 pieces of stele remnants. The
steles were inscribed in both the Western Xia
and Chinese languages. The characters on this
piece of remnant are Western Xia ones.

275

Jin

The Nuzhen were an ancient nationality in northeast China. They first lived in the Songhua (Sungari) and Heilongjiang river valleys. The Nuzhen people were good horsemen and archers, and liked farming, fishing and hunting. In the middle of the 11th century, the Wanyan tribe, a branch of the Nuzhen, gained power gradually, forming a tribal alliance which it led. In 1113, Aguda, the chieftain of the Wanyan tribe, succeeded to the leadership of the alliance; he was deeply respected and supported by the tribesmen. In 1115, Wanyan Aguda proclaimed himself emperor, the title of his reign dynasty the "Great Jin", and that of his reign "Shouguo". He made Huining Prefecture (present-day Acheng County, Heilongjiang Province) his capital. From that time on, the troops of the Jin constantly invaded Liao and destroyed that state in 1125. After Wanyan Aguda ascended the throne, he reorganized the clan formation of the Nuzhen people, making it more suitable to warfare. He developed the written Nuzhen language, based on the strokes of the Chinese characters. In 1127, the Jin extinguished the Northern Song and occupied the wide area north of the Huaihe River, then confronted the Southern Song for a long time. In 1234, the Jin Dynasty itself was ended by the Mongol invasion.

276-1

277-1

278

276-2

277-2

277. Copper seal of the "military governor of the Hedongnan Area Command" Jin article; 7 cm both in length and in width. The knob of the seal is rectangular with a character meaning "up" carved on its top. On the right side are carved in intaglio Chinese characters meaning "the 10th month of 12th year of Dading reign" and on the left side are carved in intaglio Chinese

276. Copper seal of the "Prefect of Hanzhou" Jin relic; 6.3 cm both in length and width; unearthed in Haibu, Jiutai County, Jilin Province. The inscription on this seal includes six Chinese characters meaning "the seal of the Prefect of Hanzhou" in seal character in relief; four characters meaning "2nd year of the Dading reign" (1162) are in intaglio on the back of the seal. Jin established 5 capitals, 14 governors, 19 area commands and a total of 197 prefectures and 683 counties. The design of the official seals used in the Jin Dynasty more or less followed that of the Song and Liao. Seals were made of gold, jade, silver or copper. The seals of emperor were mostly made of gold or jade while ordinary official seals made of copper, carved in seal character and in red color, all with rectangular knobs. Hanzhou was a prefecture in the Shangjing Area Command, and the copper seal of the prefect of Hanzhou was the seal of the senior officer of the prefecture.

279

characters meaning" made under supervision of *shaofu*". The inscription on the obverse side are Chinese characters of seal style in relief meaning "seal of the military governor of Hedongnan Area Command". This was the official seal of the military governor so mentioned. The 12th year of Dading reign was the year 1172, the time of casting. "Made under supervision of *shaofu*" means the seal was cast by the government.

278. *Zhenglong yuanbao* coins   Jin currency. The inscription on the copper coins of the Jin Dynasty mostly used regular Chinese characters. The absolute majority of Jin coins bear reign titles. Prince Hailing moved the capital to the Middle Capital (present-day Beijing) and the minting of coins was begun in 1158. Zhenglong coins were the earliest copper coins minted in the Jin Dynasty.

279. Iron plough mirror   Jin farm implement; 32 cm long, 29 cm wide, 2 cm thick; unearthed in Jiaozhuang Village, Fangshan District, Beijing, in 1960. The plough mirror was also known as a "mouldboard". Installed above the shovel of a plough, it was of a composite iron plough. The Nuzhen people originally lived on herding and hunting. After the Jin occupied the vast area north of the Huaihe River, where the Han and the people of other nationalities were still engaged in agriculture, the people of various nationalities in the area of the Upper Capital of Jin gradually changed from a nomadic life to farming.

280. Gilded silver casket with pendants Jin waist pendant; full length 37.7 cm; unearthed from a Jin tomb in Zhongxing, Suibin County, Heilongjiang Province, in 1973. It was a luxurious ornament worn by Nuzhen nobility as a waist ornament, and was wrapped in several layers of silk when unearthed. The upper part of it is a gilded silver casket with snap fasteners. Below the casket is a multi-facet crystal ball sewn with yellow silk thread. The lowest part is formed by 15 red agate beads. Under the casket there is also a rectangular gold ornament flanked by rectangular interlocking floral designs, inlaid with two pieces of red agate. The casket and its pendants are made of choice material and its craftsmanship is superb. It is a fine example of handicrafts in the mid and late period of the Jin Dynasty.

280

281

281. Bronze mirror depicting Liu Yi transmitting a letter   Jin cosmetic article; diameter 10 cm, thickness of rim 0.2 cm, weight 100 grams; unearthed in Acheng County, Heilongjiang Province, in 1964. In the design on the back of the mirror there is a big tree with its branches extending towards both sides. A young man and young woman are standing under the tree, cupping their hands before their chests as if communicating something. There are grass and flowers around their feet and a surging river. A servant leading a horse is standing by the riverside. The picture shows the youngest daughter of the dragon king of Dongting Lake tending sheep by the roadside and complaining to Liu Yi about her unfortunate marriage to the small dragon of the Jinghe River. Liu Yi has promised to deliver a letter for her. The scene was inspired by the tale written by Li Chaowei of the Tang Dynasty, entitled *The Story of Liu Yi.*

282. Big bronze mirror with twin-fish design   Jin cosmetic article; diameter 36.7 cm, weight 4, 300 grams; unearthed in Acheng County, Heilongjiang Province, in 1964. Shiny and smooth, the surface of the mirror can still reflect an image even now. There is a knob in the center of the mirror's back, along with a vivid design of two carps swimming around the knob. The mirror is the biggest, heaviest and most exquisite bronze mirror extant of the Jin Dynasty.

282-1

283

283. Black glazed porcelain vases   Jin vessels; the right one 14.5 cm high, 4.5 cm in diameter, 4.8 cm in foot diameter; the left one 14.8 cm high, 4.4 cm in diameter, 4.8 cm in base diameters; unearthed in Shilipu Village in the southern suburbs of Datong, Shanxi Province. The shape, quality and the color of the glaze of these two porcelain vases are entirely the same, leaving one to assume that they were baked in the same place at the same time. On the belly of each vase there are three iron openwork patterns, similar to the black glazed porcelain baked in the Dingyao Kiln on the central plains, namely, the so-called "black Ding". After the Jin state exterminated the Northern Song and occupied the wide area north of the Huaihe River, the Dingyao Kiln fell within the area ruled by Jin. The white glazed, black glazed, green glazed and caramel glazed utensils baked in the Dingyao Kiln at that time naturally became the porcelain produced by the Jin Dynasty.

284. White glazed porcelain pillow with carved acanthus pattern   Jin daily-use utensil; 23.3 cm long, 20 cm wide, 12.8 cm high. The pillow has an oval surface and is slanted, hollowed-out and glazed in white. On the surface and walls of the pillow is carved red acanthus design, reflecting the art traditions of the Han.

284

285-2

285-1

all over, very neat and attractive. It is a fine example of the Dingyao white porcelain produced during the Jin Dynasty.

286. White glazed porcelain bowl with incised fish design Jin vessel; 11 cm high, 26.2 cm in diameter, with a 12 cm base diameter; unearthed from a cellar of the Jin Dynasty north of the city of Nong'an, Jilin Province, in 1985.There is a concave ring on the outer wall below the rim of the bowl with a corresponding embossment on the inner wall. The outer wall is plain and the inside is carved with two fishes surrounded by the design of ripples, water and grass. The design is natural and smooth and lines forceful.

285. White glazed plate with carved dragon design Jin vessel; 6.6 cm high, diameter 29.8 cm, base diameter 9.8 cm; unearthed from a cellar of the Jin Dynasty north of the city of Nong'an, Jilin Province, in 1985. A total of four white glazed plates with a carved dragon design were unearthed from the cellar. This is one of the four. On the inner wall of the plate is carved a ring of bow-string pattern, while in the center of the plate is carved a coiled dragon with its head and tail connected; its four limbs stretched with three claws on each limb, and its body covered all over with scales and shells. The biscuit of the porcelain plate is rather thin and the plate is white glazed

286-1

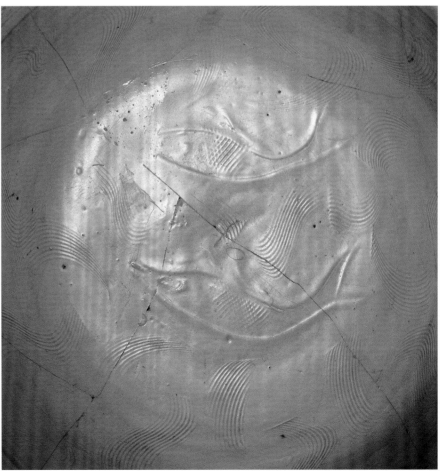

286-2

Sketch Map of Boundary Between Southern Song and Jin

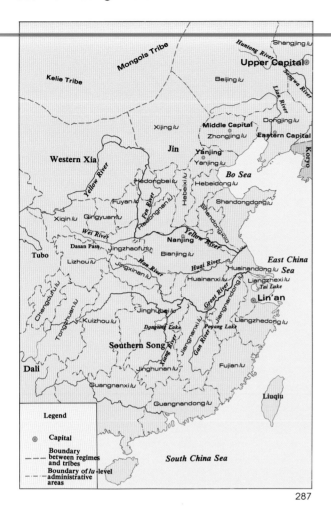

Legend

◎ Capital

— Boundary between regimes and tribes

- - Boundary of *lu*-level administrative areas

287

Founding of the Southern Song and Confrontation between Song and Jin

After the end of the Northern Song, Zhao Gou, the ninth son of the Song Emperor Huizong proclaimed himself emperor in the Southern Capital (present-day Shangqiu, Henan Province). He later moved to Lin'an (present-day Hangzhou, Zhejiang Province), and founded the Southern Song Dynasty. In the early years after the founding of Southern Song, Jin troops invaded the south repeatedly while Song troops also carried out frequent northern expeditions, recovering some lost territories. In 1141, the Song and Jin reached the "Shaoxing Peace Agreement" (Shaoxing was the reign title of the Southern Song), resulting in a long period of peace. Southern Song was eliminated by the Mongols in 1279.

287. Sketch map of boundary between Southern Song and Jin   In the first year of the Southern Song Dynasty, Jin troops invaded the south several times, attempting to occupy the area south of the Yangtze River and Sichuan. However, they met with resistance by the Song troops. In the area ruled by Jin, the Han people organized uprisings and waged different forms of struggle. In 1141, the 11th year of the Shaoxing reign of Song, the Song and Jin reached a peace agreement. The Song state declared itself a vassal of Jin, took the boundary from the Huaihe River to Dasanguan Pass (present-day southwest of Baoji, Shaanxi Province), and paid an annual tribute in the amount of 250,000 taels of silver and 250,000 rolls of silk.

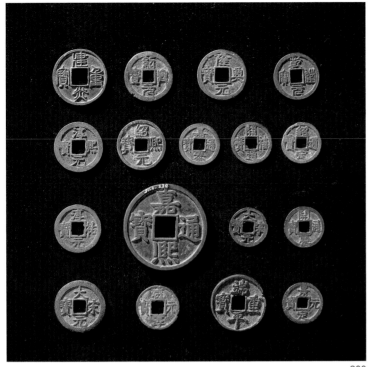

288

288. Southern Song copper coins

Southern Song currency. Following the system of the Northern Song, the Southern Song government minted coins bearing reign titles; each kind of coin used different scripts. Due to inflation, the government also issued a large amount of paper money and the amount of coins minted was not as much as those of the Northern Song.

289. Picture of Four Generals of the Restoration
Southern Song; 26 cm vertically, 90.6 cm horizontally. It was said that the portrait was drawn by Liu Songnian, a painter at the Academy of Painting during the period under the Shaoxi reign of the Southern Song (1190–1194). In order to force the Southern Song court to surrender, the Jin court repeatedly sent troops to the south but

was resolutely resisted by Southern Song military leaders. Han Shizhong, one of the military leaders, led 8,000 soldiers to intercept 200,000 Jin troops at Zhenjiang and encircled them at Huangtiandang for 48 days. Another military leader, Yue Fei, led an army composed of his family members and friends to inflict heavy losses to the main force of the Jin troops. The historians of the Southern Song Dynasty called this part of history, which covered the rebuilding of Song Dynasty by Zhao Gou, Emperor Gaozhong of Song, and the resistance put up by Song troops against the Jin invasion in the early years of the Southern Song, a "restoration" of power. Liu Guangshi, Han Shizhong, Zhang Jun and Yue Fei depicted in the Picture of Four Generals of the Restoration were all noted military leaders who resisted the Jin aggression during this period.

Economy

With a tenancy system popularized in the country, the peasants in the Song Dynasty became less dependent on the landlords and showed an increased enthusiasm for farming. During its long period of peace and stability, the dynasty saw developments in agriculture and the handicraft industry, with both agricultural and artisan output raised by a big margin. Improved transportation and overpopulation in the countryside led to a wholesale migration of people from rural areas to the cities and the emergence of many new large and medium-sized towns. The mercantile economy developed as never before, with fairs held in almost all villages and small towns. Whether in busy metropolises or newly emerging towns, independent industrialists and businessmen were grouped into *hang* or *tuan* according to their trade and, with a fine division of labor, entered into increasingly strong competition. A form of paper money, the earliest in the world, was issued in the Sichuan area in the middle of the Northern Song and was widely used in the country by the Southern Song. Foreign trade flourished, too. The Song Dynasty far surpassed its predecessors in the number of countries that had trade relations with China and in the amounts of imports and exports exchanged.

Agriculture

In the Song Dynasty many new irrigation works were built, resulting in a further expansion of cultivated areas. Cultivators were in widespread use in north China and the Central Plains; steady improvements were made in farm tools such as plows, rakes, hoes and sickles. The peasants attached great importance to intensive and meticulous farming, bringing about a sustained increase in grain yield. Unification of the country made possible exchanges of crop species and farming technique between the north and south. One result was that the planting of rice expanded northward.

290. "Weeding" and "Harvesting" Rubbings of Qing stone engravings, 54.5 cm long, 36 cm wide. The Song Dynasty called on the people to reclaim land and build irrigation works. Pictures of plowing, harvesting, weaving and silkworm breeding were painted and displayed in the imperial palace. Early in the Southern Song Dynasty, Lou Shu, magistrate of Yuqian, did a series of 45 paintings titled "Farming and Weaving." Later, during the reign of the Qing emperor Qianlong, stone engravings based on the series of Song paintings were made and placed in the imperial garden, the Yuanmingyuan. In 1860 the English and French armies set the garden on fire, seriously damaging the stone engravings. Twenty-three of the engravings survived and were later appropriated by Xu Shichang, a northern warlord. In 1960 the National Museum of Chinese History took possession of the engravings.

291. Transplanting of Cereals During the Song Dynasty The Northern and Southern Song witnessed a wider exchange of crop varieties between the north and the south. To prevent losses caused by floods and droughts, Zhancheng rice, a strain native to Fujian, was transplanted to Liangzhe and the Jianghuai Plain on a large scale. Early rice of Jiangdong was transplanted to Hebei, while wheat, millet, broomcorn millet, peas and beans were introduced from north of the Huai River to southern areas. Many places in the south and southeast such as Jiangnan, Liangzhe, Jinghu, Fujian and Guangdong began to cultivate food grains other than rice and wheat.

Transplanting of Cereals During the Song Dynasty

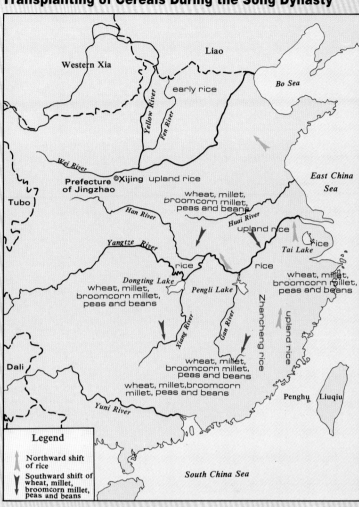

291

290-2

292

293

292. Iron moldboard Farm tool, 30.6 cm long, 24.5 cm wide, Northern Song; unearthed in 1952 at Baisha Reservoir, Yuxian, Henan Province. The plow of the Song Dynasty was composed of three main parts:the sole, the moldboard, and the share. The sole was made of wood. Joined to the handle, it moved parallel to the ground when plowing. The moldboard and the share were made of iron. Placed in front of the sole, they broke up and turned the earth. The moldboard was in the shape of a peach. Because it looked something like an ancient bronze mirror, it was also called *lijing* in Chinese, meaning literally "plow mirror."

293. Iron plowshare Farm tool, 26 cm long, 20.8 cm wide, Northern Song; unearthed in Luoyang, Henan Province. The plowshare of the Song Dynasty had a pointed or round head, designed for turning over different kinds of soil. The edge of the blade was usually made of wrought iron or steel so that it did not break easily and could be used for deep plowing.

294. Four-toothed iron rake Farm tool, 18 cm long, 17.5 cm wide, Northern Song; unearthed in 1955 in Fenghuanghe, Yangzhou, Jiangsu Province. The rake was an important tool for loosening the soil. The ancient Chinese made a point of loosening the soil after plowing and of removing

weeds and gathering them for compost. Because a toothed rake performed many functions and was indispensable to meticulous farming, it was widely used in the Song Dynasty countryside.

295. Iron *juetou* Farm tool, 37.5 cm long, 13.7 cm wide, Northern Song; unearthed in 1952 at Baisha Reservoir, Yuxian, Henan Province. The population of China had reached 100 million by the end of the Northern

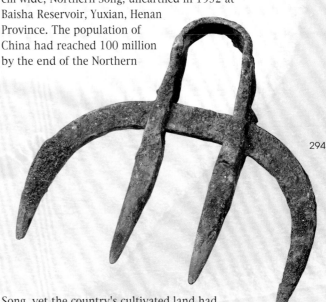

294

Song, yet the country's cultivated land had increased very little. Techniques of intensive farming received ever closer attention in the most populous areas. "Better reap good harvests over small areas than poor harvests over large ones,"says an agricultural book written early in the Southern Song. The importance of sowing in good time, rational manuring and field management was well-understood by rural folk. When it came to farm implements, tools such as the iron *juetou* and curved iron hoes were in common use.

296. Curved iron hoe Farm tool, 63.7 cm long, blade 22.1 cm wide, Northern Song; unearthed in 1952 at Baisha Reservoir, Yuxian, Henan Province. With a flat, straight blade and a handle that is curved at the front and hollowed for fixing a wooden shaft, this hoe of the Song Dynasty resembles the kind of iron hoe that is still used today in some of China's rural areas.

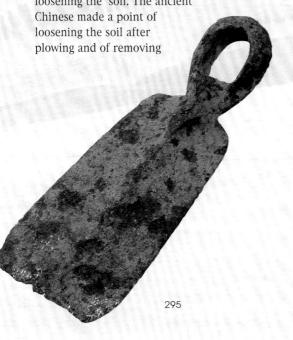

295

296

Handicrafts

The development of the Song Dynasty handicraft industry was characterized by a broader scope of business of the handicraft workshops in cities and towns, an ever greater commercialization of household handicraft production, and increasing specialization. In mining, metallurgy, shipbuilding, paper making, the making of porcelain, and spinning and weaving, the Song Dynasty surpassed all previous periods in terms of both technology and output.

298

297. Two-eared vase of the Guan Kiln
Ornament, 22.8 cm high, rim 8.3 cm in diameter, base 9.6 cm in diameter, Southern Song. The porcelain of the Song Dynasty far surpassed the levels of previous periods in shape, glaze color, quality of the body, and output. The five most famous Song kilns were the Jun, Ru, Ge, Guan and Ding. The Guan Kiln, run by the central government in Kaifeng, was used to produce porcelain articles for the emperor. Many of its products were ornaments modeled on antiques. The vase in the picture, an imitation of an ancient bronze item, features a straight neck, a bulging belly, and two tube-shaped lugs that correspond to two rectangular holes in the base. These were used for fixing the cord. A gem of Song porcelain, it has a rich glaze and looks elegant and dignified.

298. Three-legged grayish-green burner with bow-string design, fired in the Guan Kiln Ornament, 8.6 cm high, 15.8 cm in diameter at the top and 14.3 at the bottom, Southern Song. Most of the porcelain articles produced in the Guan Kiln during the Southern Song Dynasty featured a grayish-green glaze with yellowish-brown cracks known as "gold and iron wire." Modeled on an ancient wine vessel, the burner in the picture has a straight mouth and a flat bottom. It is a typical example of imitating the ancient style.

299. Burner with fish-shaped handles of the Ge Kiln Ornament, 8.8 cm high, 11.9 cm in diameter at the top and 9.2 at the bottom, Song Dynasty. It is said that two brothers surnamed Zhang each set up a kiln for making porcelain in Longquan (now Longquan County, Zhejiang Province). One of the kilns was known as Ge Kiln and the other as the Di Kiln (*ge* and *di* mean elder and younger brother in Chinese). The Ge Kiln was one of the five most famous kilns of the Song Dynasty. Though no record of the kiln exists in Song books and its location has never been found, some of its products have been handed down from generation to generation. There are similarities between the wares of the Ge and the Guan Kiln. For instance, the roughcasts of the porcelains from the two kilns are usually grayish black. The color can be seen at the bottom or base of the pieces. The glaze is mostly a grayish-green color or light yellow and contains large and small cracks described as "gold and iron wire." Products of the kilns included basins, bowls, dishes and many imitations of antiques. The burner in the picture is a fine ornament made in the ancient style. It has a slightly flared mouth, a bulging belly, and two symmetric fish-shaped handles. With smooth, harmonious lines, it looks simple and elegant.

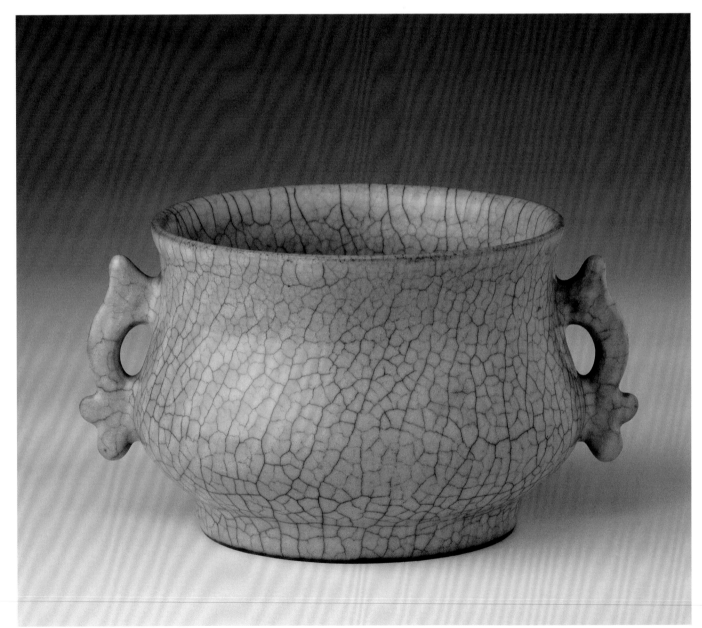

300-1

300. Basin of the Ru Kiln Ornament, 3.5 cm high, 13.6 cm in diameter at the top and 9.3 at the bottom, Northern Song. The Ru Kiln was located in Ruzhou (now Baofeng County, Henan Province), hence the name of the kiln. It was set up in the late Northern Song to produce porcelain especially for the use of the imperial court. As the kiln was operated for only a little more than 20 years, its wares are rare today. Classified with the northern celadon, the Ru kiln porcelain pieces feature fine-textured bodies with the color of incense ash, and glazes that are mostly sky blue but sometimes grayish green or white, with fine cracks on the surface. According to records found in Southern Song books, the kiln added agate to the glazing substance when making the porcelain. A modern test confirms that bits of agate exist in the glaze, which is why it sparkles like emeralds.

300-2

301. Begonia-shaped rose-red flowerpot of the Jun Kiln   Ornament, 14.5 cm high, rim 19.5-24.5 cm in diameter, Song Dynasty. The Jun Kiln was actually an extensive network of kilns in what is now Yuxian, Henan Province. Over 100 sites of the kilns have been found there. One of the kilns was set up by the government to produce flowerpots, basins and wine vessels specially for display in the imperial court. With greenish blue as its key color, the porcelain of the Jun Kiln is classified as northern celadon. Through "kiln transmutation," a technique used in the Jun Kiln, the greenish-blue wares of the kiln are tinged with a rose-red hue. Analysis shows that this red tinge was produced by reducing the copper in the firing. Another feature of the Jun Kiln porcelain is what is called its "earthworm burrowing into soil" pattern, formed at a high firing temperature when glaze with low viscosity flowed into cracks on the surface. Coated with a sky blue glaze, set off by a rose-red one, the flowerpot in the picture is beautiful yet dignified.

301

302

**302. Large rose-red flowerpot of the Jun
Kiln** Ornament, 22.7 cm high, rim 23.4
cm in diameter, Song Dynasty. The Jun
Kiln wares we see today are mostly
ornaments made for display in the
imperial court. The majority of them are
flowerpots in various shapes. Some are
square, rectangular, hexagonal or flared-
mouthed, while others are shaped like a
sunflower, lotus or begonia. The flowerpot
in the picture looks like an ancient
Chinese spittoon.

303-1

303-2

303. Mallow-petal bowl with incised day lily design of the Ding Kiln

Container, 6.1 cm high, rim 21.4 cm in diameter, base 6.6 cm in diameter, Northern Song. The Ding Kiln was located in Dingzhou (now Quyang, Hebei Province), hence its name. Set up in the Tang Dynasty, the kiln reached its zenith during the Song Dynasty. Its products were mainly articles for everyday use, such as bowls, dishes, pots, bottles, flasks, burners and pillows. The kiln was famous for its white porcelain, featuring fine-textured

bodies and a white glaze suffused with yellow. In the mid Northern Song it adopted a technique to produce bowls and dishes that are not glazed on the rim. The incised or impressed decoration done on both the inside and outside of its wares is very beautiful. Its incising technique matured in the mid and late Northern Song. The bowl in the picture, a gem of late Northern Song porcelain, shows high skill in the carving of the day lily design. The carving has a three-dimensional effect, created by matching the outline of the day lily with thin lines on the other side.

304. Turnip-shaped vase of the Yaozhou Kiln with incised floral design
Ornament, 24.2 cm high, rim 5 cm in diameter, base 6.5 cm in diameter, Song Dynasty. The Yaozhou Kiln was located in Yaozhou (now Tongchuan, Shaanxi Province), hence its name. The products of the kiln were mainly articles for daily use. For a time in the mid and late Northern Song it produced porcelain especially for the use of the imperial court. While the kiln was noted for its celadon, it also produced black and white porcelain in small quantities. Its celadon is covered with a glaze that is rather green, close to olive, and decorated mostly with incised or stamped floral design. By the mid Northern Song its technique of incising floral designs became increasingly mature. The knife-cut on the celadon was so deep that thick glaze accumulated where it left a mark, creating a three-dimensional effect. The wares of the Yaozhou Kiln vary in shape; vases alone come in a dozen or so shapes. The turnip-shaped vase in the picture, modeled after an ancient wine vessel, is a typical Yaozhou ware, featuring a short neck and a tall, thin body.

304

305

305. Two-eared bottle with bow-string design of the Longquan Kiln
Water container, 33.3 cm high, rim 11.1 cm in diameter, base 12.7 cm in diameter, Song Dynasty. The Longquan Kiln was located in what is now Longquan County, Zhejiang Province, an important district for making porcelain during the Song Dynasty. While the kiln's chief products were vessels for daily use and writing articles, it also made statues and incense burners. Classified as southern celadon, the Longquan porcelain featured a light grayish green glaze and incised decoration in the Northern Song and a grayish green glaze and embossed or underglaze relief decoration in the mid Southern Song. After the Nuzhens and Mongols occupied most of north China, famous northern kilns, such as the Ding, Ru, Jun and Yaozhou kilns, declined one after another, while in the south the Longquan Kiln, with its celadon selling to an ever wider area, rose to eminence. Under its influence, kilns in Zhejiang, Fujian and Jiangxi turned out wares similar to the Longquan celadon, forming a celadon family with its own characteristics. Via the "Silk Road of the Sea," the Longquan celadon found a market in the East Asian, East African and Arab countries.

306. Gourd-shaped bottle of the Longquan Kiln with embossed floral design Ornament, 26.9 cm high, rim 4.7 cm in diameter, base 9.2 cm in diameter, Southern Song. By the late Southern Song, the Longquan celadon had become more exquisite in both shape and decoration. This gourd-shaped bottle, coated entirely with grayish green glaze, is decorated with an interlocking branch and flower design in relief. Where the clay was exposed, white lines known as *chujin* can be observed.

306

307. Bottle with painted wave design of the Jizhou Kiln   Water container, 13.6 cm high, rim 2.8 cm in diameter, base 5.3 cm in diameter, Song Dynasty; unearthed in 1967 in Nanchang, Jiangxi Province. The Jizhou Kiln was located in Jizhou (now Ji'an, Jiangxi Province), hence its name. Built during the late Tang, the kiln saw its best days in the Southern Song period. It produced mainly black porcelain, but also white porcelain and celadon. Its wares were coated with a rich glaze and decorated with a variety of designs, which were painted on, stamped or appliqued. The bottle in the picture is exquisite in both shape and decoration. Except for the base, which is left unglazed, the entire vessel is coated with a thin white glaze and decorated underglaze with a wave pattern in purplish brown.

308. Bowl coated with a "hawksbill turtle mottle" glaze of the Jizhou Kiln   Food container, 5.3 cm high, rim 10.6 cm in diameter, base 3.4 cm in diameter, Song Dynasty. The "hawksbill turtle mottle" glaze, developed by the Jizhou Kiln, was applied mostly on round articles such as bowls and dishes. The Jizhou Kiln mainly produced black porcelain. As it was very difficult to apply decoration on black porcelain, craftsmen of the kiln added a light yellow glaze to black one. Fired at a high temperature, the black and light yellow glaze soaked into each other, producing light yellow spots on a black background that look like the mottle pattern of a hawksbill turtle.

307

308

309

309. *Yingqing* porcelain flagon and warming bowl Wine vessel, overall height 23.9 cm, rim of flagon 4.1 cm in diameter, Southern Song; unearthed in 1983 from a Southern Song tomb in Dengyunshan, Zhenjiang, Jiangsu Province. *Yingqing* porcelain, also known as bluish green-and-white porcelain, features a white glaze suffused with bluish green that is simple and tasteful. In the Song Dynasty *yingqing* porcelain was mainly produced in what is now Jingdezhen, Jiangxi Province, but also in other parts of Jiangxi and in Anhui, Fujian and Guangdong provinces. The items produced at Jingdezhen at the time were mainly articles for daily use, mostly food and wine vessels. The flagon and bowl in the picture, modeled after metal vessels, form a set of articles for warming wine. The flagon features a melon-like body and a high lid and handle, while the bowl has a flared mouth and a deep belly with a petal design that looks like a flowering lotus.

310. Lacquered toilet case   Toilet article, case 17.3 cm high and 16.4 cm in diameter, small box 3.6 cm high and 5.5 cm in diameter, Song Dynasty. In ancient China toilet cases containing combs and cosmetics for the use of women were usually made of wood and lacquered. The Song Dynasty toilet cases we see today were mostly designed for keeping articles in several layers. The case in the picture, shaped like a water chestnut flower, is a three-layer container. In the first layer are four small lacquered boxes of the same size for keeping various dressing articles. Ingeniously designed, it is a specimen of the Song Dynasty's high level of craftsmanship.

311. Zhang Si Lang silver dishes with cherry and hydrangea designs Food vessel, 1.2 cm high, rim 8.4 cm in diameter, base 6 cm in diameter, weight 27.8 g, Song Dynasty; unearthed in 1982 in Pingqiao, Liyang, Jiangsu Province. Most gold and silver items of the Song Dynasty were ingeniously designed and decorated with gorgeous patterns. Sets of such articles usually consisted of vessels that are similar in style but varied in shape and decoration. The two dishes in the picture, together with seven other similar dishes, were found in an unearthed Song Dynasty jar containing a total of 27 silver articles. The nine dishes are of the same size and shape and each bear a seal with the three characters Zhang Si Lang at the bottom. They are decorated variously with nine motifs, namely peony, cherry, hydrangea, palm leaf, plum and bamboo, gardenia, camellia, hibiscus, and lotus. Zhang Si Lang was the name of the manufacturer, and the seal can be regarded as China's earliest trademark.

311-1

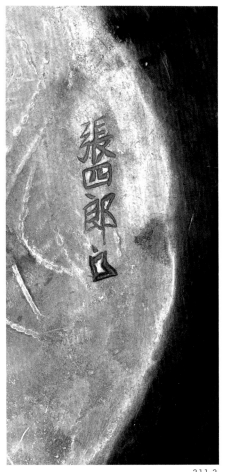

311-3

311-2

312-1

312. Shijia bronze mirror Toilet article, 16.9 cm in diameter, 0.4 cm thick, Southern Song. With the development of a mercantile economy, the Song Dynasty witnessed increasingly keen competition in industry and commerce. A reflection of this was the inscription of the name of the manufacturer and the place of production on a large number of bronze mirrors. Cast on the back of some bronze mirrors are the characters "zhen zheng yi se,"or just "zhen," meaning that they are genuine mirrors made in such and such a place. Bronze mirrors were made mostly in Huzhou, Jiankang, Raozhou and Chengdu, during this period. The Huzhou mirrors were the most numerous. Huzhou was a manufacturing center for bronze mirrors in south China; its products were sold all over the country. Among the Huzhou mirrors, those made in Shijia were the most famous. With workshops that covered an extensive area, Shijia produced a large quantity of bronze mirrors each year. The inscription on a Shijia mirror sometimes tell the seniority of the Shijia workshop in question, the address of the workshop that made the mirror, and the price. The mirror in the picture was made in Shijia, Yifengqiao, Huzhou.

312-2

313. Sunflower-shaped mirror from Jizhou Toilet article, 17.4 cm in diameter, 0.4 cm thick, Southern Song. Prior to the Tang Dynasty, Chinese bronze mirrors were mostly round. By the Song Dynasty they came in a variety of shapes. Apart from the usual round, square, sunflower-shaped and water chestnut flower-shaped mirrors, there were mirrors shaped like a shield, a bell, a heart, a *ding* (ancient Chinese cooking vessel), the Chinese character 亞, or ones with long handles. The mirror in the picture bears a six-character inscription meaning "Exquisitely made by Li Dao in Jizhou."

314. The making of well salt in Sichuan Illustration from the book *Exploiting the Works of Nature.* In the Song Dynasty various types of salt were used:sea salt, well salt and soil salt, named according to the different methods of production. Sea salt was made by boiling seawater in the coastal areas of Jingdong, Hebei, Liangzhe, Huainan, Fujian and Guangnan. Soil salt was made by poor peasants in some parts of Shaanxi and Hebei, who obtained the salt by boiling saline soil. The picture here shows how Sichuanese people made well salt by digging wells to obtain brine and boiling it.

313

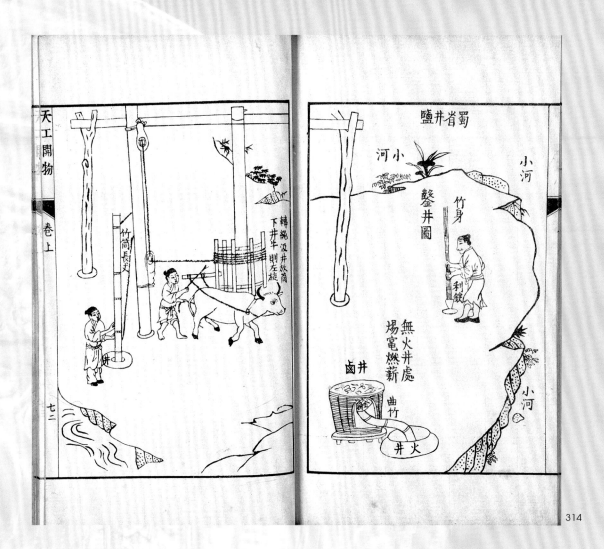

314

315. Hydraulic bellows Illustration from the book *on Agriculture*. The Song Dynasty developed a flourishing iron-smelting sector. During the Huangyou reign (1049-1053) of Emperor Renzong the country's iron output reached 3.62 million kg a year. At the time, coal was generally used as the fuel in the north, and leather bags were replaced by wind-operated bellows or even by hydraulic bellows as shown in the picture. Through axles and levers, the horizontal-wheel of the hydraulic bellows changed the circular motion into a linear back-and-forth motion to produce the blast.

Bustling Cities

In the Song Dynasty mercantile economy, urban culture flourished as never before. Cities were no longer divided into *fang* (residential districts) and *shi* (commercial districts) as previously, and there were shops, large and small, lining any street. Places of entertainment also appeared in the cities. Dongjing (now Kaifeng, Henan Province) and Lin'an (now Hangzhou, Zhejiang Province), each with a population of one million, became the political, economic and cultural centers of the Northern and Southern Song respectively.

316. Downtown streets of Dongjing

Section of the Northern Song scroll *Riverside Scene on Qingming Festival*. During the Tang Dynasty, the capital, Chang'an, was divided into *fang* (residential districts) and *shi* (commercial districts). All the *fang* gates were closed at night, and trade activities were allowed only in the *shi* during the day. All such restrictions on trade disappeared in the Song Dynasty. Both Dongjing and Lin'an, capitals of the Northern and Southern Song respectively, were famous for their brisk night markets. As a hub of land and water communications, Dongjing was an economic center where cereals, livestock products, vegetables, fruits, tea, medicines, textiles and various kinds of handicrafts, shipped from all parts of the country, were sold. The streets were lined with restaurants (which alone numbered 72), shops for provisions, gold and silver exchanges, and many other kinds, catering to the imperial family, feudal nobles, officials, landlords and merchants who lived there. Scattered in the city were dozens of *wazi*, where theatrical and other performances were given. *Riverside Scene on Qingming Festival*, a scroll painting by the Northern Song artist Zhang Zeduan, captures the hustle and bustle of Dongjing. From the picture we see row upon row of shops, jostling crowds, and an endless stream of horses and carriages.

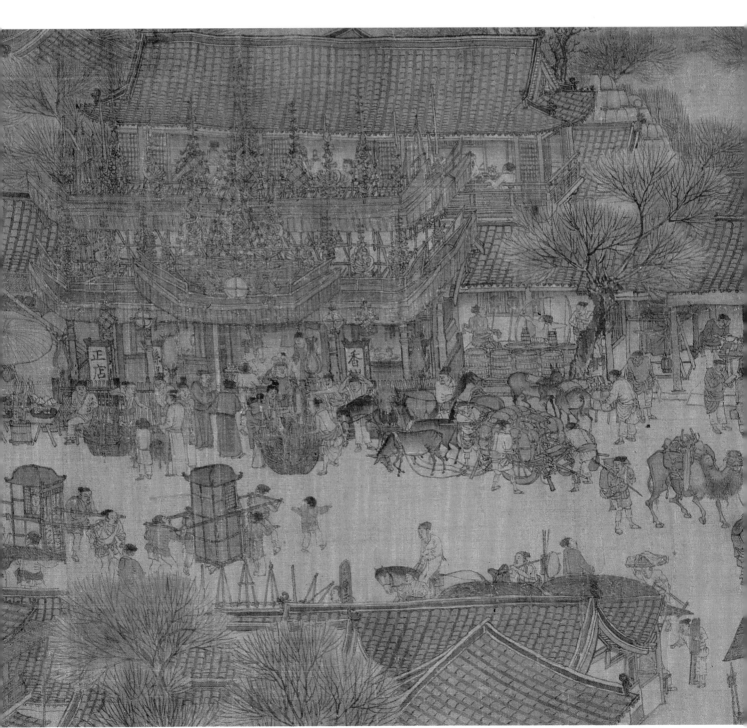

317. Transportation on the Bian River
Section of *Riverside Scene on Qingming Festival*. The Bian River, which flowed through Dongjing, was the main waterway that connected the capital to the grain growing areas in the southeast. Several million piculs of rice were shipped to the capital by boat each year. Passenger and cargo boats busily plied the Bian River. *Riverside Scene on Qingming Festival* vividly depicts such a scene.

318-1

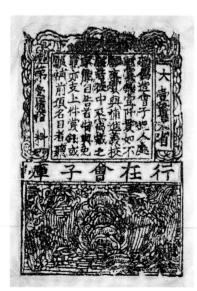

318-2

318. Copperplate for printing *huizi* paper money   18.4 cm long, 12.4 cm wide, Southern Song. In the mid Northern Song the world's earliest form of paper money, known as *jiaozi*, appeared in the Sichuan area, where iron cash had previously circulated as the chief form of money. In 1160, the 30th year of the Shaoxing reign of Emperor Gaozong, the Southern Song government issued another form of paper money, called *huizi*, and set up an office in charge of it in Lin'an. The face value of a *huizi* was first one *guan*, then 200 *wen*, 300 *wen* and 500 *wen*. As a means of meeting military spending and solving financial difficulties, the Southern Song government issued large amounts of *huizi* many times, leading to market chaos and devaluation of the currency.

319. Copperplate for printing an advertisement of Liu's Needle Shop 12.4 cm long, 13.2 cm wide, Song Dynasty. With the abolition of the *fang-shi* system, stores and handicraftsmen's workshops appeared in almost all the streets and lanes of the Song Dynasty cities. As competition became increasingly acute, many stores promoted the sale of their goods through advertisements or window displays. The copperplate in the picture was used to print an advertisement, probably the world's earliest. It told potential customers that Liu's Needle Shop in Jinan, whose trademark was a white rabbit pounding medicine in a mortar, specialized in making first-rate needles. This also indicates that producers generally marketed their own products at the time.

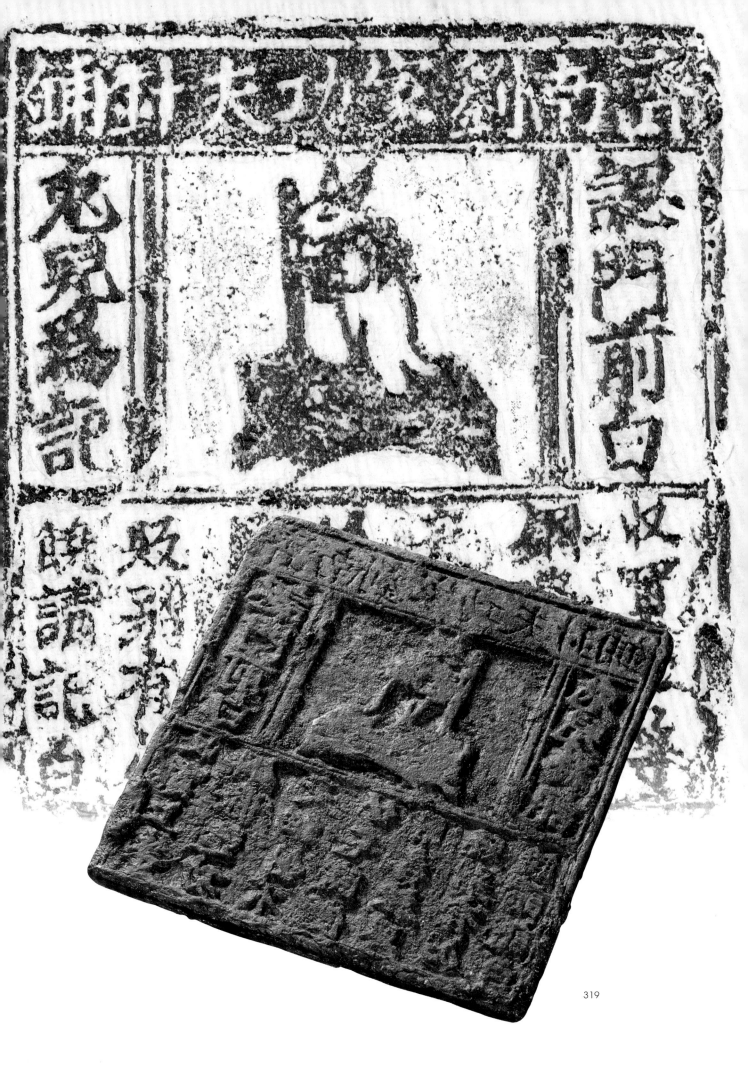

319

320

320. Bronze mirror depicting a game of cuju   Toilet article, 10.6 cm in diameter, 0.6 cm thick, Song Dynasty. *Cuju*, a type of ancient Chinese football, was first played only by the imperial family and the nobility, but later became popular among the people. In the Song Dynasty both men and women played *cuju*. On the back of this bronze mirror is a picture of a man and a woman playing ball and several others watching. The woman, with her hair worn in a topknot, is kicking a football, while the man, wearing a scarf and leaning forward, seems to be playing defense.

321

321. Bronze mirror with picture of a puppet show Toilet article, 11 cm long on each side, 0.2 cm thick, Song Dynasty. Recreational activities in the cities of the Song Dynasty were varied and colorful. On important festivals the government organized actors and acrobats to perform in the streets, while at ordinary times performances were given in the *wazi*, also known as *washe*, where plays and acrobatics were staged. In both Dongjing and Lin'an, capitals of the Northern and Southern Song respectively, there were dozens of *wazi*, with several *goulan* (open-air theaters) in each. The largest *goulan* in Dongjing had a seating capacity of several thousand. Puppet shows were a favorite art form with *wazi* audiences. In the Song Dynasty, puppet plays of various styles were performed. The picture here shows the performance of a puppet play in the *zhangtou* style. A boy manipulates the puppets with a wooden rod behind the screen. Sitting behind him is a man who seems to be narrating the play. In front of the screen are young men and women watching the play.

322. Woman Binding Up Her Hair (brick engraving) 37.3 cm long, 11.3 cm wide

323. Woman Washing Dishes (brick engraving) 39 cm long, 16 cm wide

324. Woman Cleaning Fish (brick engraving) 34.2 cm long, 24 cm wide

Relief figures, Northern Song; allegedly unearthed in Yanshi, Henan Province. With the development of the mercantile economy and the urban population increase in the Song Dynasty, a large number of literary and artistic works reflecting the life of the urban class appeared. The brick reliefs pictured here are examples of these works. With vivid imagery and smooth, flowing lines, they depict the daily life of a woman in the city.

323

324

325-1

325-2

325. Ding Dusai Acting in a Play (brick engraving) Figure, 28.4 cm long, 9.3 cm wide, Song Dynasty. According to historical records, Ding Dusai was a famous variety entertainer in Kaifeng in the late Northern Song. In normal times, he performed in the *wazi*, but during the Lantern Festival he would act on a makeshift stage put up in front of the imperial palace. This brick engraving shows Ding Dusai during a performance.

326. Map of Pingjiang (rubbing from a stone tablet) Stone tablet 284 cm high and 140 cm wide, Southern Song. Pingjiang (now Suzhou, Jiangsu Province) was a thriving city during the Southern Song Dynasty. As the map shows, the city had a network of rivers and canals, with streets running parallel to the waterway. Nine main streets (five running north to south and four running east to west) and their branches crisscrossed to form many neighborhoods, large and small. Scattered around the city were government offices, mansions, temples, gardens, bridges, markets, academics, warehouses and historical sites. The map of Pingjiang, the earliest of its kind in China, was engraved on this stone tablet in 1229, the second year of the Shaoding reign of Emperor Lizong. The tablet is now kept in Wenmiao, Suzhou.

326-1

326-2

Development of Foreign Trade

The Song Dynasty saw an unprecedented development of China's trade with foreign countries. A government department called Shibosi was established to take charge of foreign trade. Guangzhou, Quanzhou and Mingzhou (now Ningbo, Zhejiang Province) became the country's three largest ports, from which Chinese exports, mainly silks and porcelain, went in large quantities to Korea and Japan in the east, as well as to Western Asia and Africa.

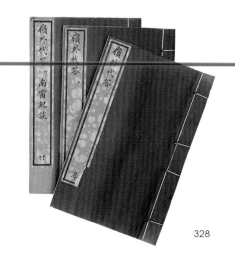

328

327. China's Communications with Foreign Countries During the Song Dynasty In the Song Dynasty China's foreign trade was carried on by both state and private enterprises, with the latter as the main force. Chinese merchant ships carried large quantities of porcelain, silks, gold and silver ware across the oceans to sell in foreign markets, while foreign merchant ships brought spices, medicine and the specialities of Western countries to China. Development of the country's shipbuilding and navigation facilitated the economic and cultural ties between China and the countries of Asia and Africa.

328. *Beyond the Five Ridges* by Zhou Qufei (Qing edition) In the 1170's, the first years of the Chunxi reign of the Southern Song emperor Xiaozong, Zhou Qufei held a government post in what is now Guilin, Guangxi Zhuang Autonomous

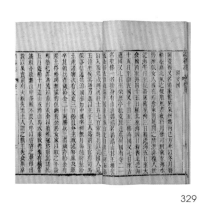

329

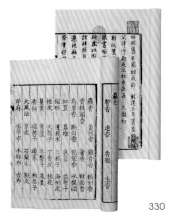

330

China's Communications with Foreign Countries During the Song Dynasty

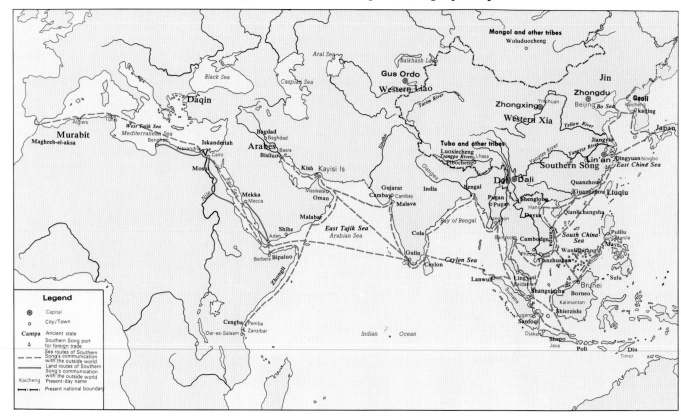

Region, and became familiar with the trade and communications south of the Five Ridges (the area covering Guangdong and Guangxi). *Beyond the Five Ridges* records the tradition and local customs of Guangdong and Guangxi and beyond the seas.

329. *Accounts of Foreign Lands* by Zhao Rushi (Qing edition) In the mid Southern Song, Zhao Rushi served as an official in charge of foreign trade in Quanzhou. *Accounts of Foreign Lands* provides information on the countries with which the Song had trade relations and on the commodities each of the countries had for sale. In the course of writing the book, Zhao Rushi consulted *Beyond the Five Ridges* and other books by Song writers and Chinese and foreign merchants who frequently traveled by sea.

330. *Annals of Siming During the Baoqing Reign* (photo-offset copy of a Song edition) Siming, also known as Mingzhou, located in what is now Ningbo, Zhejiang Province, was already an important port for foreign trade in the Tang Dynasty. It was the port of departure for most Chinese merchant ships bound for Japan and the port of arrival for most Japanese who came to the Tang empire to study Buddhism, philosophy and literature. By the Song Dynasty, the port had become even busier. From here, Chinese merchant ships sailed not only for Japan and Korea but also countries of Southeast Asia and the Arab world. As an increasing number of Arab merchants came to stay in Siming, a Persian Mansion and a mosque were built specially for them. In 1227, the third year of the Baoqing reign of the Southern Song emperor Lizong, the city's foreign trade office and warehouse were rebuilt with funds donated by Hu Ju, a prefect. *Annals of Siming During the Baoqing Reign*, completed in 1227, records in detail the commodities that went into and out of Siming at the time.

331. Bronze mirror decorated with a seagoing vessel Toilet article, 17.3 cm in diameter, 0.6 cm thick, Song Dynasty. The picture on the back of the mirror depicts a seagoing vessel sailing over the waves, with people in the bow, stern and cabin. Inscribed at the top of the picture are four characters in the seal style. In the Song Dynasty, bronze mirrors with such decorations were not unusual. That reflects the importance the Song people attached to foreign trade and

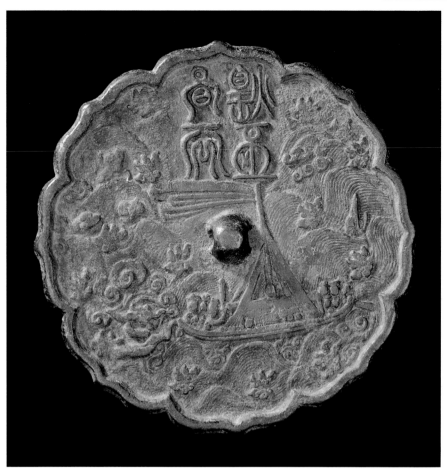
331

332

communications with the outside world.

332. Fragments of celadon Southern Song relic unearthed in Singapore. Porcelain was one of the chief exports of the Song Dynasty. According to Song records, the cabins of large Song ships

sailing abroad were sometimes crowded with merchants'goods, mostly porcelain, and the merchants had to sleep on top of their wares. Fragments of Song porcelain have been discovered in large numbers in the countries of Southeast Asia.

Science and Culture

Brilliant achievements were made in science and technology during the Song Dynasty. New discoveries and inventions were recorded in numerous spheres of human knowledge: astronomy, mathematics, mechanics, medicine, type printing, shipbuilding, gunpowder, the compass. In some areas China was far ahead of the rest of the world and made great contributions to the advancement of world science and technology. Chinese literature, history, philosophy and art also reached new heights. Many eminent scientists, inventors, historians, philosophers, men of letters, artists and poets appeared and many famous products of the time have become prized gems in the treasury of world culture.

Science and Technology

Song astronomers invented many new astronomical instruments. They carried out five large-scale celestial observations and discovered four supernovas, of which stellar maps were made. In mathematics, Song scientists made discoveries that outstripped those of their Western counterparts by many centuries. They solved the numerical values of equations of higher degrees 800 years before Western mathematicians did, and they solved simultaneous linear equations with identical remainders 500 years ahead of Western mathematicians. In architecture, the techniques of building traditional Chinese wooden houses were continually improved and perfected, and Song architects compiled and published the most complete book of architecture of their time. Notable progress was also made in the medical field. In addition to monographs on gynecology, pediatrics and forensic medicine, medical technicians of the Northern Song designed and built bronze models of the human body showing the passages for vital energy and acupoints, which further promoted the development of acupuncture and moxibustion. Gunpowder was already extensively used in war and the compass in navigation during the Song, and printing from movable type opened a new era in the history of printing. These three great inventions of China were gradually introduced into other countries in Asia and Europe, where they had an enormous impact on the development of world science and culture.

333. *Pen Notes of Dream Brook*, by Shen Kuo Shen Kuo (1031-1095), a native of Qiantang, Hangzhou (in Zhejiang Province), was a famous scientist of the Northern Song. While serving on the Board of Astronomy, he made suggestions to the emperor on how to improve various existing astronomical instruments, including the armillary sphere, clepsydra and sun dial and recommended the adoption of the solar calendar in place of the traditional Chinese calendar. In mathematics, he was the first to discover how to find the summation in arithmetic progression and how to determine the lengths of the chord and arc of a segment when the height of the segment and length of the diameter are known. In physics, he discovered the angular deviation of the geomagnetic field, elucidated scientifically the principles of imagery in concave mirrors, and studied the laws of resonance. He also made many contributions to geology, medicine, temperament and the study of ancient implements. In his late years he settled in Dream Brook Garden in Runzhou (now Zhenjiang, Jiangsu Province) and compiled all that he had seen, heard and learnt in a lifetime of study and observation into a book titled *Pen Notes of Dream Brook*. The book devoted about 40% of its pages to scientific subjects. It summarized the achievements in the natural sciences in ancient China, in particular during the Northern Song, and recounted the contributions made by what the author called "the nobodies," including his own original ideas.

334. Rubbing from tablet with celestial map Relic of Southern Song, original tablet 216 cm high, 108 cm wide. Five large-scale observations of celestial bodies were made during the Northern Song. Of these, the fourth observation undertaken during the Yuanfeng years (1078-1085) achieved the best results. With the data garnered, Huang Chang, the minister of rites, drew a

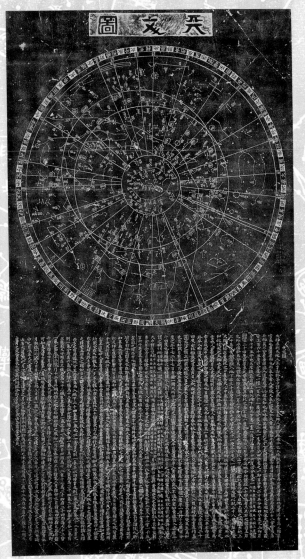

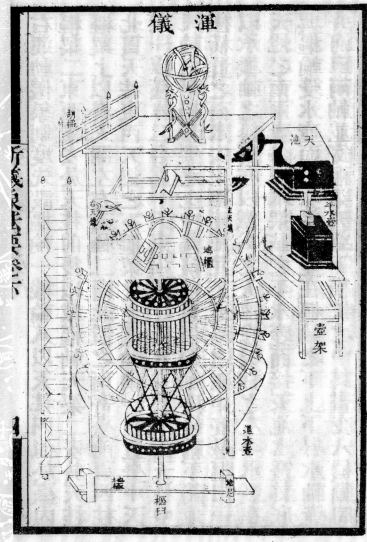

334

335

map of the constellations and stars and wrote a commentary. In 1247, Wang Zhiyuan and others reproduced the map and commentary on a stone tablet, the map on the upper half of the tablet and the commentary on the lower half. The map consisted of three concentric circles. The inner circle was 19.9 cm in diameter and showed the stars near the North Pole of the celestial sphere that could be seen the year round from latitude 35°N, on which the Eastern Capital of the Northern Song was located. This circle was called the Constantly Seen Circle. The middle circle was 52.5 cm in diameter and represented the celestial equator. Another circle, intersecting with the equator and approximately the same in diameter, represented the zodiac. The angle between the equator and the zodiac was 24 degrees (modern scientific observations show that the angle should be 23°26'). The outer circle was 85 cm in diameter, and the stars shown in it were those to the north of latitude 55°S of the celestial sphere,

that is, the stars visible to a person looking south from 35°N. The map also included 28 rays of different widths representing the 28 constellations. The Milky Way was represented by double curves. Altogether, 1,434 stars were shown on the map (as late as the 14th century European astronomers knew of only 1,022 stars).

335. Structure with water-driven armillary sphere and celestial globe (illustration in *New Design for an Armillary Sphere and Celestial Globe*)

Relic of Northern Song, original structure about 12 meters high and 6.5 meters wide at the bottom. It was built by two astronomers, Su Song and Han Gonglian, in Bianjing (now Kaifeng, Henan Province) in 1088. The main body of the structure was composed of wooden columns and beams and planked outer walls. It was divided into three stories with wooden ladders for people to climb up and down. At the back of the lowest floor was a

waterwheel together with mechanism for controlling the different parts. At the front was a bell tower for telling the time. Tiny figures would emerge at fixed hours to strike the bell. On the second floor was a celestial globe; and on the third floor, which had no roof, was an armillary sphere. A wooden shed was built over the sphere, with a removable roof so that people could observe the celestial bodies. A person on the lowest floor turned the waterwheel, causing water to circulate. A clepsydra regulated the flow, which caused the control mechanism to operate intermittently and move the bell, armillary sphere and celestial globe. After completing this structure, Su Song compiled all relevant data and information into an illustrated book titled *New Design for an Armillary Sphere and Celestial Globe*.

右隅
左積

本積 一
商除 一 一
平方 一 二 一
立方 一 三 三 一
三乘 一 四 六 四 一
四乘 一 五 十 十 五 一
五乘 一 六 十五 二十 十五 六 一

命實而除之　以廉乘商方　中藏者皆廉　右袤乃隅算　左袤乃積數

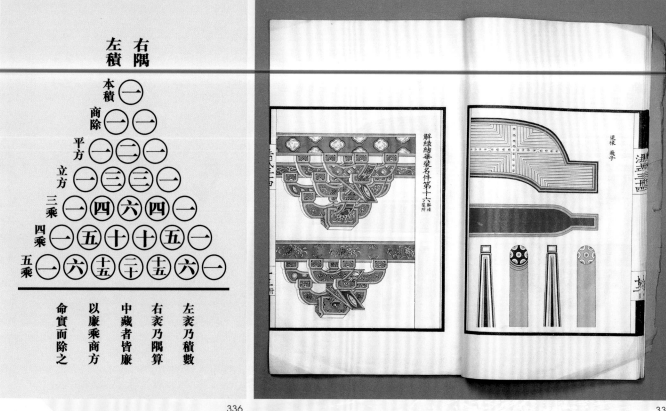

336

337

336. Table of extraction of roots This table is also called the Table of Coefficients of Terms Resulting from the Expansion of the Binomial $(a+b)^n$. It was first worked out by Jia Xian, a mathematician of the Northern Song. Later Yang Hui, a mathematician of the Southern Song, included it in his book *Xiangjie Jiuzhang Suanfa (Detailed Analysis of the Mathematical Rules in the "Nine Chapters")*, whereby it has been preserved down to the present. In the table the numbers in lines 3 to 7 represent the coefficients of terms resulting from the expansion of the binomials $(a+b)^2$, $(a+b)^3$, $(a+b)^4$, $(a+b)^5$ and $(a+b)^6$ respectively. A formula for obtaining the coefficients makes it possible to expand a binomial of any degree without multiplication. German and French mathematicians of the 1530s also worked out this table, which they called Pascal's Triangle. Chinese mathematicians call it Jia Xian's or Yang Hui's Triangle.

337. *Methods of Construction*, by Li Jie
This book was completed in 1100. Li Jie, the author, was a native of Guancheng, Zhengzhou (in Henan Province). During the 13 years that he was with the Jiangzuo Jian, a department in charge of building palaces, temples and mausoleums, he directed the construction of many large projects. On the basis of his experiences , he compiled this comprehensive work of 36 volumes, 357 chapters and 3,555 entries. 30 volumes were textual matter devoted to terminology, systems, labor and building materials. The other six contained drawings of brackets, beams, columns, doors, windows and painted designs. A summary of architectural theory and practice, the book unified architectural specifications of its time, clarified various systems of designing and construction, and formulated quotas to guide the estimation of labor and materials. It was an instructive manual of a mandatory nature, but it did not demand rigid observance of the specifications it put forward. The most complete book of architecture in the whole world during its time, it set the norms for the construction of official buildings and temples in the Central Plains, and had a far-reaching influence on architectures of later generations.

338. *Zhenghe Manual of Materia Medica, Revised Edition* The original work was written by Tang Shenwei, a famous doctor of Chengdu, Sichuan, of the Northern Song and was completed around the year 1082. It consisted of 32 volumes and was called *Manual of Materia Medica for Emergency Cases*. The draft was completed but was never published. In 1108, the second year of the Daguan reign, Lang Aicheng, a worldly-wise scholar, recommended the draft to the government and received permission to reedit the text and publish it. He changed the title to *Daguan Manual of Materia Medica for Emergency Cases*. In 1116, the sixth year of the Zhenghe reign, the emperor ordered Cao Xiaozhong to reprint the book after proofreading and revising the text. The reprint was made and was titled *Zhenghe Manual of Materia Medica, Revised Edition*. With a text of over 600,000 words, it is a collection of treatises on medicine published in Chinese classics and historic works, as well as in Buddhist writings It contains the prefaces and introductions of medical books down the ages and offers primary medical prescriptions for many kinds of diseases, with advice on what foods to be avoided when taking medicine. Altogether, 1,746 kinds of animal, herbal and mineral medicines are listed, each accompanied by illustrations. 600 of these are new entries not included in the original work by Tang Shengwei. Joseph Needham, the modern British scientist, judged it to be a far better work than European books on botany published three centuries later.

339. *Key to Therapeutics of Children's Diseases* This is a treatise in three *juan* on paediatrics, compiled by Qian Yi, a famous doctor of the Northern Song Dynasty. Qian Yi was from Yunzhou (present-day Dongping, Shandong Province). Based upon the theory of

Huang Di Nei Jing (*The Yellow Emperor's Canon of Medicine*) and taking the dialectics of the five internal organs as essentials, the treatise put forward a considerable number of new views with regard to the diagnoses of children's diseases. These prescriptions were prepared by respecting the experience of his predecessors, but without sticking entirely to convention. Quite a number of medicines for children developed by Qian Yi are still in use today.

340. *Manual of Forensic Medicine* Written by Song Ci.Song Ci (1186-1249) was from Jianyang (present-day Jianyang, Fujian Province). He served as criminal official in present-day Jiangxi, Fujian, Guangdong and Hunan, and was well-experienced in medical jurisprudence and spot inspections. In 1247, he compiled the *Manual of Forensic Medicine* on the basis of his own experience and works on medical jurisprudence of his predecessors. The book is composed of 5 *juan* and 53 entries. *Juan* I deals with regulations and an introduction, *juan* II was on autopsies, and the other three *juan* was a collection of the records of different cases of injuries and death. The book summarizes the skeleton of human body, autopsies, spot inspections, verification of death, identification of poisons, plus the methods of first-aid to be used for hanging victims, killing and wounding, drownings, frostbite, death due to thirst and abortions. In the entry under "verifying affinity by dripping blood", he put forward the relationship of the blood type of parents

and children and its importance in law. This book was 300 years earlier than the first book on medical jurisprudence published in the Western countries, written by an Italian, in 1602.

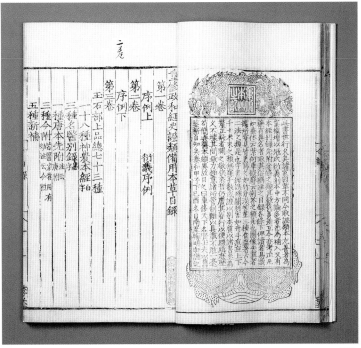

338

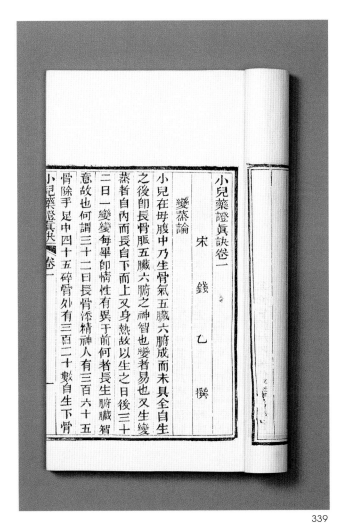

339

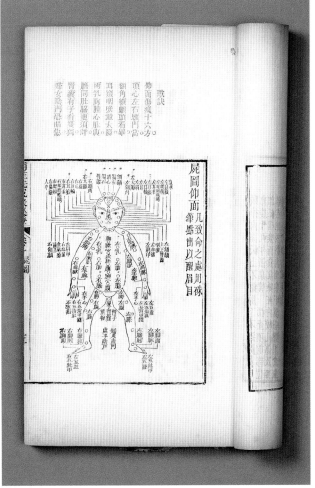

340

341. Bronze figure model for acupuncture and moxibustion

Cast in the Ming Dynasty by copying one used in the Song; full height 213 cm. New acupoints were constantly discovered in the Northern Song Dynasty, but as the points were discovered by different doctors, it was difficult to exchange views and verify information. To avoid confusion, Wang Weiyi, a medical official, cast two hollow bronze figures and marked 559 acupoints on the whole body. Of those, the names of 107 acupoints are applicable to two acupoints. Hence, altogether there were 666 acupoints on the whole body. The bronze figure was not only the model for acupuncture therapy, but also a means of teaching and examination at the medical academy. During examinations, a layer of wax would be applied to the figure, a dress put on it, and the body filled with water. The student could pierce the acupoints with a needle and would be correct if water issued from those points. The two bronze figures were placed in the academy and Xiangguo Temple respectively. When the Jin state destroyed the Northern Song, the bronze figure in the Xiangguo Temple was also destroyed , and only the one at the medical academy survived. After the Yuan put an end to the Jin, the remaining bronze figure was moved to Dadu, the Great Capital, (present-day Beijing). Due to wear and tear over a long time, it could no more be used. Then a Nepalese was ordered to make a new bronze copy. After the Ming destroyed the Yuan, the use of the bronze figure was continued. At the time of Emperor Yingzong of the Ming Dynasty, however, the bronze figure could no more be used and another new one was cast, namely, the one now extant. This copied bronze figure is true to the original of the Song Dynasty, and accurately reflects the level of the science of acupuncture and moxibustion in that era.

342. Stone carving of "Illustrated Manual on Points for Acupuncture and Moxibustion as Found on the Newly Cast Bronze Figure"

Northern Song Dynasty remnant; 99 cm high, 55 cm wide, 26 cm thick; discovered in the Ming Dynasty city wall of Beijing, in 1971. Altogether 5 pieces of carved stone were unearthed at that time. This is the No. 2 remnant stone. Three columns of characters are left on the surface. Only around a dozen small characters are left in the upper column. In the middle column there are 11 acupoints from Zhiyin to Chengshan in Points of the Bladder *Meridian of the foot Taiyang.* In the lower column there are still 7 acupoints from Yinjiao to Huiyin; and in the same column are also 12 Chinese characters meaning*"First Part of the Illustrated Manual on Points for Acupuncture and Moxibustion as Found on the Newly Cast Bronze Figure".* In the beginning, when Wang Weiyi, a medical official of the Northern Song Dynasty cast a bronze figure model for acupuncture and moxibustion, he also compiled the *Illustrated Manual on Points for Acupuncture and Moxibustion as Found on the Newly Cast Bronze Figure.* Before long, he had the complete text of the *Illustrated Manual* carved on stone. In the early Yuan era, the bronze figure and the

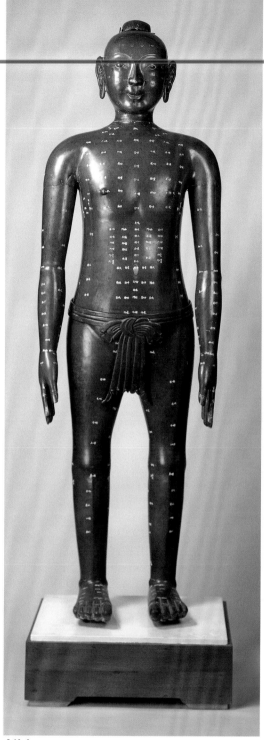

341-1

carved stone were all taken to Dadu (present-day Beijing). The stone carving of the *Illustrated Manual* were destroyed in a war at the end of the Yuan Dynasty. In the early years of the Ming Dynasty, when the city wall of Beijing was repaired, the remnant stone carvings of the *Illustrated Manual* were used as filling. The remnant discovered is believed to be a part of the Song Dynasty original.

342

341-2 ▷

343. Sketch of powder arrow Northern Song Dynasty. It was by late in 904-905, the first year of the Tianyou reign of the Tang Dynasty, that China already used a kind of incendiary weapon called "flying fire". In the Song Dynasty there were such incendiary firearms as powder arrows, fire balls and fire caltrops. Powder arrows were made by binding a powder ball on an arrow shaft, igniting the fuse and shooting it on a bow. It was also called a "bow fire arrow". If a crossbow was used for shooting, the arrow was called the "crossbow fire arrow". The production of powder arrows in the Song Dynasty was done on a large scale. In 1083, the 6th year of the Yuanfeng reign, a total of 250,000 powder arrows was distributed in one lot to the garrison troops of the Lanhui Area Command. In 1221, the 14th year of the Jiading reign of the Southern Song Dynasty, when the Jin troops besieged Qizhou Prefecture (present-day northeast of Qichun, Hubei Province), the Song troops defending the city stepped up the production of powder weapons. Within days, a total of 7,000 crossbow fire arrows and 10,000 bow fire arrows were made. In the later stage of the Southern Song Dynasty, in the sea battle of Shijiu Island, Shandong Province, the Song general Li Bao ordered his soldiers to shoot powder arrows at the Jin vessels and several hundred enemy vessels immediately caught fire. The Jin troops were defeated. This was evidence of the large number of powder arrows possessed by the Song troops.

344. Sketch of pear-blossom spear In 1132, the 2nd year of the Shaoxing reign of the Song Dynasty, Chen Gui, a Song general, garrisoned De'an (present-day De'an County, Jiangxi Province). He invented a kind of tubular firearm called a "fire spear". He bound a powder tube on the front end of a long bamboo pole to be used by two soldiers to attack the enemy as the flames spurted out. Later, someone loaded the powder tube on the front end of a long spear. As the spurt of powder looked like the dance of a pear blossom, the weapon was called the "pear-blossom spear". In this way, even if all the powder was exhausted, the spear could still be used for fighting. In the Jin Dynasty, improvements were made by the Jin troops resisting the Yuan forces. The powder tube in those days was rolled up in 16 layers of paper, and in addition to powder, iron fragments and broken porcelain pieces were also loaded in the tube, to be shot out when the powder exploded.

345. Sketch of shooting fire spear In 1259, the first year of the Kaiqing reign of the Southern Song Dynasty, the Song troops in Shouchun Prefecture (present-day Shouchun, Anhui Province) invented a new type of tubular firearm which could shoot "bullets". It was called the "shooting fire spear". A big bamboo tube was used for its body and powder and "bullets" were loaded inside. After igniting the fuse, flames burst out and bullets were shot out to a range of about 230 meters. The "shooting fire spear" was the world's first gun.

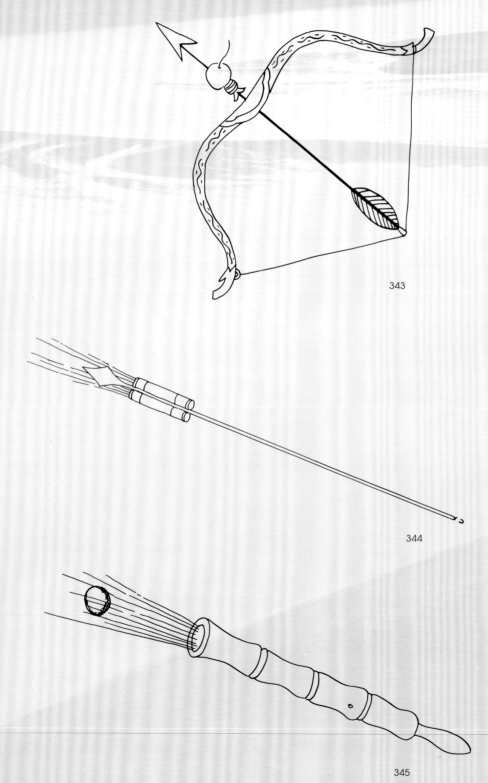

343

344

345

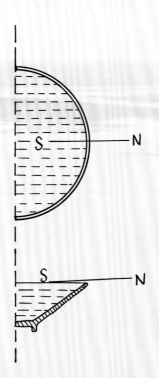

346

346. Sketch of nail-type and bowl-rim type compasses These were the two types of compass made in the Northern Song Dynasty. The principle was to place a magnetic needle on a finger-nail or on bow-rim, and with the contact point as support, the magnetic needle could swing to the left and to the right. When it was at a standstill, its two ends pointed to the south and to north.

347. Restored model of floating-type compass Northern Song Dynasty article; diameter 10 cm, height 2.3 cm. This type of compass was made by a magnetic needle used to pierce a few sections of rush and then placed into a bowl containing water. Lighter than water, the rush would float on its surface with the

magnetic needle. When at a standstill, the two ends of the needle pointed to the south and north. Of the four types of compasses, the floating compass was the most valuable in actual use. As water in a bowl maintains a level surface, so long as it is not overturned or subject to an intense shake, the magnetic needle can be used continuously. It was therefore selected for the navigation of seagoing vessels. At the time (1099-1102), Chinese seagoing vessels sailing out of Guangzhou harbor already used this type of compass. In 1123, the 5th year of the Xuanhe reign, when Xu Jing, the envoy of the Northern Song court, and his party were on a diplomatic mission to Korea, their ship was navigated by the floating-type compass. After that, the skill of navigating by compass spread to other countries in Asia and Europe, ushering in a new era in the history of navigation.

347

348. Restored model of suspension-type compass   Northern Song Dynasty article; height 38 cm, length of the sides of its base frame work 21.5 cm. The magnetic needle is attached with wax to a single thread of silk and hung in the center of the wooden framework; below the framework is placed a bearing plate on which 8 Heavenly Stems and 12 Earthly Branches as well as 4 Diagrams are used to indicate 24 bearings. The magnetic needle hangs above the center of the bearing plate. Because of the effect of terrestrial magnetism, the needle points to the south and north when it is at a standstill. This type of compass is very sensitive. Its shortcoming is that it can only be used in a quiet or windless place. Otherwise, the needle swings constantly and it is impossible to get a bearing.

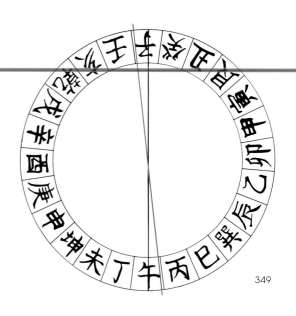

349

349. Sketch of terrestrial magnetism deflection   In testing the suspension-type compass, Shen Kuo of the Northern Song Dynasty observed that the actual direction of the magnetic needle was not due south or due north, but slanted slightly to the east at its southern end. Thus he discovered terrestrial magnetism deflection. The discovery was of great significance. Because the earth is an enormous magnetic field, the line linking the south and north magnetic poles is called the magnetic meridian. The earth also has a South Pole and North Pole, and the line linking the two is called the terrestrial meridian. The magnetic pole and the terrestrial pole do not coincide. Therefore, the magnetic meridian and the terrestrial meridian intersect to form an angle, namely, the terrestrial magnetism deflection. The magnetic pole is not fixed, but drifts within certain limits, resulting in different terrestrial magnetism deflections in different places; the terrestrial magnetism deflection in the same place also changes with the lapse of time. The scientific application of southward pointing implements can only be achieved by mastering the law of changes of terrestrial magnetism deflection.

350. Schematic model of movable clay type Northern Song Dynasty; vertical 37.5 cm, horizontal 43 cm. During 1041-1048, the Qingli reign of the Song Dynasty, Bi Sheng invented typography. He made a small rectangular piece of clay, carved inverted characters in relief on one end, then hardened it by firing, forming a piece of movable clay type for use in printing. The printing was done by spreading mixture of rosin, wax and paper ash on a heated iron plate and arranging the type on the plate. When a plate was fully arranged with the type, the bottom of the iron plate was warmed over fire and the mixture would smelt with the heat. A plate was then used to press the types flat. When the type cooled and solidified, printing could be carried out. After the printing of the first plate was over, the iron plate was heated again to soften the mixture, and the pieces of type could be taken off and used again. The invention opened up a new era in printing.

350

Culture and Art

The poetry, *ci* (special poetic form using sentence patterns based on song melodies) and prose of the Song Dynasty occupy an important position in the history of Chinese literature. Unlike the ornate style of the late Tang Dynasty and the Five Dynasties, the Song style of poetry, *ci* and prose tended to be easy, pure and fresh. During the Southern Song Dynasty, when resistance against the Jin and the restoration of the Central Plains were key social issues, solemn, stirring and lofty sentiments were more often expressed in literary works. In the field of history, a large number of writings and collections of material were completed; new forms of history were presented in separate accounts of important events and narration according to categories appeared. The philosophical thinking of the Confucianists of the Song Dynasty was called *li xue* (Neo-Confucianism). The concepts of both idealism and a naive materialism existed in Neo-Confucianism with the former occupying a dominant position and its theory having great influence on later ages. Moreover, considerable achievements were attained during the Song Dynasty in the fields of painting, calligraphy, sculpture and traditional opera.

351. *Collected Works of Ouyang Wenzhong Gong* Published during the Wanli reign of the Ming Dynasty, this is a collection of the poetic writings of Ouyang Xiu of the Northern Song Dynasty. Ouyang Xiu (1007-1072), styled Liu Yi Jushi, from Luling, Jizhou (present-day Yongfeng County, Jiangxi Province), was a famous man of letters and historian of the Northern Song. As an important official of the imperial government, he supported the reforms of Fan Zhongyan in his early years; in his old age he tended to be conservative, opposed the reforms of Wang Anshi and tried all he could to depreciate the reforms of Wang in agriculture. In literature he was the leader of prose reform in the Song Dynasty. He inherited the literary tradition of Han Yu and Liu Zongyuan of the Tang Dynasty, opposed the stringing together of ornate phrases and the pursuit of resplendent style in writing, and energetically stood for putting literature into practice. His writings were smooth and simple-deeply influenced such men of letters as Zeng Gong, Wang Anshi, Su Xun, Su Shi and Su Zhe. The poetry of Ouyang Xiu was pure, fresh and natural. The collection of his *ci* is called *The Ci of Liu Yi*. His achievements in history were also outstanding. He worked alone to compile the *Records of the Five Dynasties* also called *History of the Five Dynasties* and compiled jointly with Song Qi and others the *Book of Tang* (or *New Book of Tang*).

352. Portrait of Su Shi Original stone kept in the Liurong Pagoda in Guangzhou, Guangdong Province. Su Shi (1037-1101), styled Dong Po Jushi, from Meishan, Meizhou (present-day Meishan County, Sichuan Province), was a celebrated man of letters of the Northern Song Dynasty, who made very high attainments in poetry, *ci*, prose, calligraphy and painting. He was bold and unconstrained, cherished both conservative and reformist thoughts, and rose and fell several times during his official career. Su Shi was one of the "eight great masters of the Tang and Song Dynasties" in the movement of prose reform and his writings were easy, graceful, smooth and superior in reasoning. His poetry was pure, easy, natural, extensive in subject matter, rich in exaggerated analogy, and vigorous in style. In contrast to the graceful, restrained and flowery diction of the late Tang and the Five Dynasties, he enlarged the scope of the subject matter of his *ci*, heightened its artistic conception and opened up a bold and unrestrained school in the field of *ci*. Su Shi was good at running hand and regular calligraphic scripts incorporated the strong points of various schools and created a new concept. He is considered the leader of four master calligraphers of the Song Dynasty. In painting, he liked to draw withered trees and queer-looking rocks and was also good at sketching bamboo. Su Shi had very great influence

352

in the literary world and gathered around him Huang Tingjian, Qin Guan, Cao Wujiu and Chen Shidao, known as the "four scholars of the Su school". In addition Zhang Lei and Li Zhi, known as the "six gentlemen of the Su school".

353. *Melodies of Bai Shi Daoren* Block-printed edition of the Qing Dynasty. This is a collection of the *ci* and *qu* (a type of verse for singing) of Jiang Kui of the Southern Song Dynasty. Jiang Kui (1155-1221), styled Bai Shi Daoren (White Rock Taoist Priest), from Poyang, Raozhou

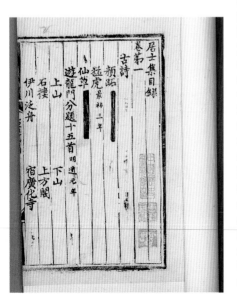

351

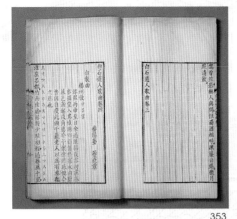

353

(present-day Poyang, Jiangxi Province), was good at both poetry and *ci*, and proficient in the rise and fall of tones in writing. After the signing of the "Shaoxing Peace Agreement" between Song and Jin, both sides accepted the Huaihe River as the boundary. That permitted the Southern Song court to establish temporary stability over a part of the country. This gave rise to a general interest in leading a life of pleasure and unbridled licence. That mood influenced the poetry style and the *ci* of some writers. In the works of Jiang Kui, one seldom finds heroic and mournful tones but stress, instead, on the harmony between rules, forms and syllable, along with a concentration on pure artistry and devotion to sentimental verses or accounts of travels. Some of his works dealt with current events but were low-spirited. He had a good knowledge of music theory and once presented a memorial on music to the emperor. This is one of the collections of the works of Jiang Kui, composed of four *juan*. In the book, verses are sidenoted with music scores; some are even noted with the fingering to be used when playing. This is the only extant collection of *ci* sidenoted with music scores from the Song Dynasty.

354. *Capital Edition of Popular Fictions*
Photolithographic edition of the Ming Dynasty. In the Song Dynasty a form of story-telling was in vogue, popularly known as *shuohua* (talking). The manuscript used by shuohua was called *huaben*. *Shuohua* was divided into two categories: "history" and "fiction". "History" was mostly based on historical records. Certain historical incidents were

chosen and their plots slightly exaggerated to create easy-to-understand stories. "Fiction" originated in everyday or oral legends. It involved extensive subject matter, focusing on things like retribution of good and evil, love affairs, spirits and gods, as well as the activities of robbers, swordmen, courtesans, etc.. The stories reflected the pleasure, anger, sorrow and joy of people and were more attractive to audiences than "history". This book was the manuscript of "fiction" revised and polished by scholars, so it is also a collection of folk literature. It includes 7 short stories such as *Nian Yu Guanyin* and *Pu Sa Man*. Later, it was rewritten by Feng Menglong of the Ming Dynasty to include the *Stories to Warn the World* and the *Stories to Awaken the World*.

355. *Western Chamber in Various Modes of Ancient Music*
Ming-dynasty edition. This is a literary work used for story-telling to the accompaniment of stringed instruments. It was written by a man by the surname of Dong who won first place in a provincial imperial examination. The material used for it was drawn from *The Story of Yingying* written by Yuan Zhen of the Tang Dynasty, but important changes were made to the plot. It stresses the contradictions between Hongniang (a maid), Yingying (a young lady) and a scholar named Zhang, on one hand, and an old lady (Yingying's mother) on the other. The conclusion was that scholar Zhang and Yingying married. The text was

sung in 14 modes of ancient Chinese music. In performing, a performer would have three functions concurrently: playing the *biba* (a plucked string instrument) with his hand, singing and doing the spoken part. The form was rather similar to present-day story-telling to the accompaniment of stringed instruments in Suzhou. As it was accompanied by a *biba*, the book was also called *Western Chamber Played by Stringed Instrument* or *Western Chamber Story-telling to the Accompaniment of Stringed Instrument*. In later generations it was generally called *Western Chamber of Dong*. The celebrated work *Western Chamber* of Wang Shipu of the Yuan Dynasty was a revised version of this book.

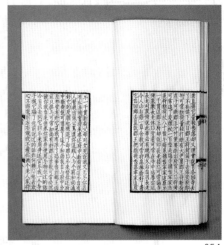

354

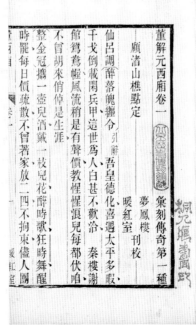

355-1

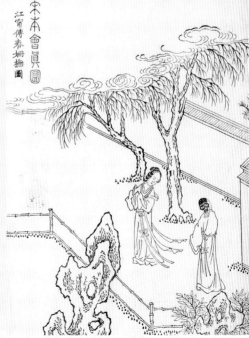

355-2

356

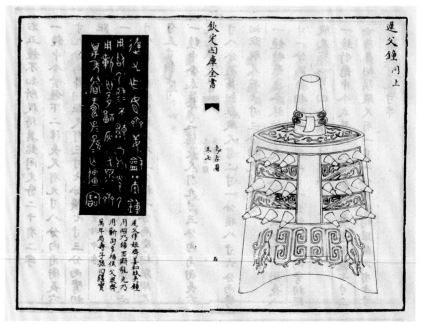

357

extant. They are in regular script, with some small characters written in between. Many parts of the script are covered with changes in ink. The complete *History as a Mirror* comprises 294 volumes and covers the period from 403 BC to AD 959. It is an important chronological history, with Sima Guang, the great historian of Northern Song, as the chief editor. But the extant contents of the manuscript are not continuous; each historical event is often introduced in just a few words serving as the beginning, followed by "and so on" in small characters, and then another story begins. It shows that the manuscript provided only a detailed outline of the book. At the end of the historical events are five lines of acknowledgement of help received, which are also in Sima Guang's

356. Portrait of Sima Guang   Sima Guang (1019-1086), from Xia County, Shanzhou (present-day Xia County, Shanxi Province), was a noted politician and historian of the Northern Song Dynasty. In the time of Emperor Shenzong of the Song Dynasty, Sima Guang was appointed an academician of the Imperial Academy and Grand Censor. He actively opposed the reforms of Wang Anshi and became the leader of the conservatives. After Emperor Zhezong ascended the throne, Sima Guang was the prime minister and energetically stood for the abolition of Wang Anshi's reforms. For the purpose of summarizing the experience and lessons of the success and failure and rise and fall of the dynasties in past ages for the reference of the court, Sima Guang compiled 8 *juan* of *General Records*, a history covering the period from the Warring States to the Second Emperor of the Qin Dynasty, and presented it to the Song Emperor Yingzong in 1066, the third year of the Zhiping reign. Emperor Yingzong ordered Sima Guang to continue the compilation which Sima Guang accomplished, together with Liu Shu and others, in 1084, the 7th year

of the Yuanfeng reign. Emperor Shenzong conferred on the works the title of *Zi Zhi Tong Jian* (History as a Mirror).

357. Manuscript of *History as a Mirror*   Relic of Northern Song, 29 lines totaling 460 characters of the manuscript are

358

359

handwriting. The final part is a postscript. The manuscript bears over 100 seals of collectors of the royal families and others.

358. A page from the *Illustrations of Archaeological Collections* This book, compiled by Lu Dalin of Northern Song, was published in 1092. It is in 10 volumes. The contents cover bronzewares of the Shang and Zhou dynasties and musical instruments, jade articles and other relics of the Qin and Han. For each relic, an exact drawing was made, showing not only its shape but the inscription on it. Also given are details such as size, capacity and weight, the results of research on the object, and the place where it was unearthed or preserved. The book, in a well-knit style, is the earliest work extant on the study of China's bronze and stone inscriptions.

359. Portrait of Zhu Xi An eminent physicist and educator of the Southern Song Dynasty, Zhu Xi (1130-1200) was a native of Wuyuan, Huizhou (present-day Wuyuan County, Jiangxi Province). He served in various local and central institutions. During his lifetime he was mostly engaged in writing books and giving lectures on Confucian classics, history, literature, temperament and the natural sciences. His most important works concerned the exposition of philosophical ideas. He developed the theory of relationship between *li* (reason) and *qi* (vigor) put forward by Cheng Hao and Cheng Yi of the Northern Song asserting that *li* and *qi* were present everywhere in the universe, but *li* was first and *qi* second, and *li* was the essence of *qi*. The origin of *li* was "heavenly reason,"

which was the feudal ethical code that consisted of the three cardinal guides (ruler guides subject, father guides son, and husband guides wife) and five constant virtues (benevolence, righteousness, propriety, wisdom and fidelity). He regarded heavenly reason and human desires as opposites, and asked people to preserve heavenly reason but eliminate human desires. Based on the great achievements of the rational school of the Northern Song, Zhu Xi set up an ideological system of objective idealism. His theory was not predominant at the time; it was even belittled as a "false philosophy." Later on, however, it was regarded as orthodox Confucianism and had a great impact on the philosophies of the Ming and Qing dynasties.

360. Mingzan's poem inscribed on a scroll (section) with postscript by Huang Tingjian   Scroll height 25 cm, length 1004 cm, diameter of each character about 20 cm. Huang Tingjian (1045-1105), who had the sobriquets Shangu Daoren (Taoist of a Mountain Valley) and Fuweng (Old Man Fu), was a native of Fenning, Hongzhou (present-day Xiushui County, Jiangxi Province). He was an accomplished poet but is best known for his fine handwriting, being one of the four greatest calligraphers of the Northern Song. His forte was the "semi-cursive

script" and "grass script." This scroll with a poem by Mingzan (Monk Lancan of Tang), in Huang Tingjian's handwriting and with his postscript, was cut into two sections by people of later generations. Only the section shown here bearing Huang's postscript is extant. The postscript says: "In the seventh month of the third year (1100) of the Yuanfu reign of Song emperor Zhezong, Old Man Fu sailed upriver to Qingyi from Rong Prefecture. On the 24th he reached Liao Ziping's house at Niukou Village and stayed there overnight. Liao entertained

him with wine in an elegant pavilion in a lotus pond, and host and guest drank and played chess under candlelight." Seals of the collectors Jia Sidao of Southern Song, Zhao Mengfu of Yuan, Xiang Yuanbian of Ming and others appear at the beginning and end of the scroll. Between 1094 and 1098, Huang Tingjian was the prefect of Ezhou (present-day Wuhan, Hubei Province), but later he was demoted to a minor post at Fuzhou (present-day Fuling County, Sichuan Province). Subsequently, he moved to Rong Prefecture (present-day Yibin, Sichuan Province). In 1100, Emperor Zhezong died and Emperor Huizong succeeded to the throne. The new emperor appointed Huang Tingjian the chief of Taiping Prefecture (present-day Dangtu, Anhui Province). Before he took office, Huang paid a visit to his aunt in Qingshen (present-day Qingshen County, Sichuan Province). He took a boat trip upriver on the 21st day of the seventh month, reached Niukou Village on the 24th and stayed at Liao Zhiping's house. That night he drank in buoyant spirits at Liao's house, and it was probably then that he copied Mingzan's poem on a scroll and recorded his trip from Rong Prefecture to Niukou Village.

360-1

360-2

360-3

361. Reading by the window on a snowy day   Painting on thin silk, Song Dynasty, height 49.2 cm, length 31 cm. On the left is a high and steep cliff, on which grow trees with luxuriant foliage. In the distance are mountains resembling a hazy belt. At the foot of the cliff is a courtyard, its gate tightly closed. Groves of green bamboos grow at the side of the cottage, in which a man is reading by the window. On the lower left are the signatures of Li Song and Li Zongcheng, which are imitations added by others later. The painting has a close-knit composition. The mountain rocks are done with *cun* strokes, which cause the rock surface to split and roughen like chapped skin. Epochally, it is a painting of the late Northern Song or early Southern Song. In terms of personal style, it followed the techniques of Li Tang. But the "chaps" are disorderly; they lack refinement. So the painting must have been done by someone who followed Li Tang's rules but was not Li Tang himself. Li Tang was a *daizhao*, meaning "waiting to be summoned," the highest rank of the Royal Academy of Painting during the reign of Emperor Huizong of Song. His paintings had a great influence on the Royal Academy of Painting of Southern Song; they were the forerunners of the Academy's ink-and-wash school.

A Chronological Table

581	Yang Jian proclaims himself emperor, and changes the dynastic name to Sui.
582	Sui establishes its new capital at Daxing (Chang'an).
589	Sui conquers Chen, unifying the whole of China.
605—610	Construction of the Grand Canal.
618	Sui is overthrown. Li Yuan proclaims himself emperor and changes the dynastic name to Tang.
624	The equal land system and the *zu-yong-diao* system of taxation are set up.
629—645	Xuan Zang is in Tianzhu (India) to study Buddhism.
630	The Eastern Turks Khanate is conquered.
641	Tang princess Wencheng enters Tibet.
657	The Western Turks Khanate is conquered.
698	Dazuorong, chief of Sumo section, Mohe tribe, establishes his regime.
709	Tang princess Jincheng enters Tibet.
712	Tang government confers on Dazuorong the title of Prince of Bohai Prefecture and renames his regime Bohai.
724	Monk Yi Xing's first survey of the meridian.
738	Tang government titles Piluoge King of Yunnan.

753	Jian Zhen undertakes a trip to Japan.
755—763	An-Shi Rebellion.
823	Erection of the "Tablet of Tang-Bo Alliance" in Lhasa.
840	Huihu Khanate is conquered by Xiajiasi tribe.
869	The Tubo Dynasty is overthrown.
904	Gunpowder is used for the first time in war.
907	Zhu Wen usurps the state power of Tang and changes the dynastic name to Liang. Tang is overthrown.
916	Yelu Abaoji establishes the Qidan (Khitan) regime.
960	Zhao Kuangyin establishes the Northern Song Dynasty.
979	Northern Song conquers Northern Han, unifying the areas from the Yellow River valley to Lingnan.
1004	"Chanyuan Alliance" pact is concluded between the Song and Liao.
1038	Yuan Hao, chief of the Dangxiang tribe, establishes a new regime named Daxia, or Great Xia, known to historians as Xi Xia or Western Xia.
1041—1048	Bi Sheng invents movable-type printing.
1069	Wang Anshi carries out reforms.
1115	Akutta, chief of the Nuzhen tribe, establishes the Jin Dynasty.
1125	Jin conquers Liao.
1127	Jin conquers Northern Song; Zhao Gou establishes Southern Song at Shangqiu.
1141	Song and Jin enter into a "Shaoxing Peace Agreement."
1153	Jin moves its capital to Yanjing and renames it Zhongdu, or Middle Capital.
1206	Genghis Khan unifies all Mongol tribes and establishes a state with a slave system.
1214	Jin moves its capital to Kaifeng.
1227	The Mongols conquer Xi Xia.
1234	The Jin Dynasty is overthrown.
1271	Kublai, the Great Khan of Mongols, changes his dynastic name to Yuan and in the following year moves his capital to Dadu.
1279	Yuan conquers the Southern Song, unifying the whole of China.

图书在版编目（CIP）数据

华夏之路（三）：英文版／俞伟超主编；
中国历史博物馆编.
北京：朝华出版社，1997.12

ISBN 7-5054-0507-1

Ⅰ.华…

Ⅱ.① 俞… ② 中…
Ⅲ.中国－历史－画册－英文
Ⅳ.K209-64

中国版本图书馆CIP数据核字（97）第07050号

华夏之路

（英文版）

第三册

中国历史博物馆编

朝华出版社出版

中国北京车公庄西路35号　邮政编码 100044

深圳雅昌彩色印刷有限公司制版印刷

中国国际图书贸易总公司发行

中国北京车公庄西路35号

北京邮政信箱399号　邮政编码 100044

1997年第1版　第1次印刷

ISBN 7-5054-0507-1/J·0246

38600

84-E-792D

中华人民共和国印制